Josie – you write
so well – thought
you might like to
try this. Notice the
author – Love,
Virginia
Xmas 2006

Writing from Life

Writing from Life

Telling Your Soul's Story

Susan Wittig Albert, Ph.D.

A Jeremy P. Tarcher/Putnam Book
published by G. P. Putnam's Sons
New York

Most Tarcher/Putnam books are available at special quantity discounts for bulk purchases for sales promotions, premiums, fund-raising, and educational needs. Special books or book excerpts also can be created to fit special needs. For details, write or telephone Special Markets, The Putnam Publishing Group, 200 Madison Ave., New York, NY 10016; (212) 951-8891.

A Jeremy P. Tarcher/Putnam Book
Published by G. P. Putnam's Sons
Publishers Since 1838
200 Madison Avenue
New York, NY 10016
http://www.putnam.com/putnam

Library of Congress Cataloging-in-Publication Data

Albert, Susan Wittig.
    Writing from life : telling your soul's story / Susan Wittig Albert.
      p.   cm.
    "A Jeremy P. Tarcher/Putnam book."
    ISBN 0-87477-848-4 (alk. paper)
    1. Autobiographical memory.   2. Diaries—Therapeutic use.   3. Diaries—
Authorship.   I. Title.
    BF378.A87A53   1997
    808'.06692—dc20   96-20142 CIP

Book design by Chris Welch
Cover design by Susan Shankin
Front cover photograph © 1994 by Elizabeth Simpson/FPG International Corp.

Printed in the United States of America
10 9 8 7 6 5 4 3 2 1

This book is printed on acid-free paper. ∞

*This book is dedicated to
the women who have shared
their stories with me.*

Contents

Preface

Our lives are made of story: stories handed down from our parents, stories we have created out of our experience, stories about our loves, our work, our explorations, our joys, our disappointments, our learnings—the soul's story. Creating story, we create and re-create ourselves, finding our sacred place in the world of human dreams and achievements on the green earth we inhabit with our fellow human beings.

Since the late 1980s, I have been teaching classes and workshops that encourage women to tell, and record in writing, the stories of their lives: joyful, painful, wondering, *necessary* stories, stories drawn deep out of the soul. In these writing-from-life classes, as in a life-drawing class, we study ourselves: how it feels to be woman, what it is like to be spirit in a human body, what it means to be spirit *and* human in a world that is being rapidly overtaken by man-made machines. We explore ourselves in personal memoirs, autobiographical sketches, and journal entries, and we share our explorations with others on this journey—this woman's journey, this human journey, the soul's journey. I have taught dozens of classes, have worked with hundreds of students, and have been riveted by thousands of stories, all written and read by women in their own voices, speaking their own speech.

This book is a guide to creating your life story, a manual drawn from my courses on life-writing. It is designed exclusively for women, because our stories must be told, must be heard. It is organized thematically, because I believe that our lives are built around certain important, certain vital themes. It invites you to write *your* life, because I believe that writing is a lifesaving act. If you despair of living as you want to live, this guide can help you to see that the way lies open before you, full of power and potential. If you feel uncertain and unsure of your direction, it can tune your ear to the voice of the inner journeyer who knows which way to go. If you feel joyful, it can help you open your heart and sing. And all along the way, you will read the stories of other women, stories that are there to guide you in celebrating your *own* story.

My Story

I began teaching writing in the late 1960s. I loved seeing the excitement and delight of my college students as they began to express themselves more fully, more precisely, more persuasively in writing. Those were also the years when my three children were growing up, so my life was full of family as well as work. Halfway through the 1980s, though, with my children grown and gone, a new chapter opened in my life story, and new themes began to emerge. I had climbed the academic career ladder, moving from classroom teaching to a deanship to a university vice presidency. But the work that once brought me pleasure now almost consumed me. I had achieved the recognition many women dream of, but it didn't satisfy me. I felt lost and empty, soulless. My creativity had been ambushed by my career success. My soul was buried under an avalanche of work compulsions.

In 1985, the uneasy situation became a crisis, and I decided to leave my position. In an attempt to sort out my thoughts and feelings, I embarked on an intensive course in self-understanding. I read feminist works, Jungian and transpersonal psychology, sociology, poetry—any writer, *every* writer who might have something to teach me about myself. I underlined the pages of my books with yellow markers, wrote notes in the margins, engaged in spirited mental arguments with the writers. But most especially, I wrote in my journal, trying to look as deeply as possible into myself, hoping to find a new direction for the future by unraveling the twists and turns of the past. My journal, as it took shape in that year, became more of a recollection of who I had been than who I was at that point. Writing those accounts of my life was my most important therapy.

This is the background against which my writing-from-life classes began to take shape. In 1987, full of excitement about Jungian and transpersonal psychology, I taught my first personal-writing course for the Jung Society in Austin, Texas. Over the years since, I have taught many more classes, workshops, seminars, and retreats, all focusing on autobiographical writing. Most of the participants are women, for it is women who seem most compelled to find their real voices, to tell the stories of their lives. At the end of each course, I hear them say something like this: "Telling my soul's story, writing it down, listening to other women's soul stories—it's the most important thing that's ever happened to me. I can see my life more clearly, feel it more deeply. I can even see through the stories other people have told me about my life. What a liberation!" And with each course—for I am still teaching, trying out new material, new organizations—I feel more strongly our urgent need to give voice to our stories—our *sacred* stories, drawn from the dailiness of our ordinary lives, drawn from the depths of our souls.

Welcome to the circle of women who know they must speak their stories.

Welcome to your own true voice.

Writing from Life

Introduction

The Power of Story

Storytelling is at the heart of life. As a child, I was never bored because I could always get on with my story. I still love to walk by the water or in the woods listening to the story that never ends. Always my imagination is creating a form that gives shape to otherwise sporadic events in everyday life. . . .

Gradually I am recognizing the meaning of my existence through my own myth.

—Marion Woodman

Why We Must Tell Our Stories

As women, we have always found ourselves in story. From the beginning of human existence, while we planted and harvested and prepared food, spun thread and wove cloth, tended our babies and cared for our elderly parents, we told one another the stories of our lives, and the lives of our grandmothers and mothers and daughters and granddaughters. Our shared stories became a many-voiced chorus singing the same song: the story-song of women at work and women at play, women loving and living, women birthing, women dying. Those stories were full of pain because human lives have always been like that. They were full of joy because lives are like that, too. Pain and joy were woven like golden threads through the full, rich, round stories of women's lives, passed from mother to daughter to granddaughter through the generations, so that the experiences of women would not be forgotten.

Of course, the urge to shape our lives in story is not just a woman's urge. As women remembered themselves in story, so did men, telling

Telling a "true story" about personal experience is not just a matter of being oneself, or even of finding oneself. It is also a matter of choosing oneself.

—Harriet Goldhor Lerner

tales in which men worked and played and fought and died, honorably and dishonorably; tales in which men governed, wisely and unwisely; tales in which men loved women, fathered children, revered parents. Then men learned to write and wrote these stories down so that they could share their experiences with other men and pass their knowledge of themselves from generation to generation. When writing became printing, these stories, oral and written, were gathered into books, so that men's triumphs and tragedies would be remembered.

But what happened to women's stories when men learned to write? In one sense, nothing happened. Women still remembered themselves in story as they worked, played, and rested, and those stories still echoed through the generations, from heart to heart. But through the centuries of recorded history, far fewer women than men were initiated into the mysteries of writing, and those who did learn to write did not often write about the lives of women. Because ordinary women couldn't write, their stories of ordinary life were lost or misremembered or changed. It was the same cycle of decay we find elsewhere in the oral tradition, in primitive tribes, among enslaved peoples, in assimilated societies, overwhelmed by the rush to technology. Because the stories weren't valued, they weren't written. And because they weren't written, they weren't valued. They were just . . . well, women's stories. Tittle-tattle. Old wives' tales. Idle gossip, told to pass the empty hours when men weren't around. Not worth writing down. Not worth much in the coin of the realm.

This is not to say, of course, that women's stories vanished. Women appeared (often in starring roles) as characters in men's stories, first orally, then in writing, then in print, and much later in movies and television. But these were (and are) women's lives seen through the eyes of the male storyteller. Men told what they knew about women, what they had been taught, what other men expected to hear. That Adam was evicted from Paradise because he listened to Eve. That women are unclean (and dangerously mad) during their menstrual periods. That women can't participate in business or government because they have inferior intellects. And until women began to have unmediated access to the printed page, we had no way of crying out, "Wait! These are not our bodies, or our minds, or our lives! They are only men's imaginings of us!"

So men's stories about women were accepted, uncorrected and unchallenged, as true stories, and everybody was fooled. Including women.

For writing is such a persuasive medium that most of us believed that we were (or ought to be) like the women in men's stories. We should wait patiently at home, while men discover new continents. We should love men, while men love ideas. We should give birth to children (preferably male children) while men give birth to writing and the electric lightbulb and the airplane and the bomb. Of course, there were many women who did not want to wait for men, or love men, or give birth to men's children, but their refusals were scarcely heard and rarely heeded. Theirs were the deviant voices, singular, sinister, frightening. For many women, it was necessary (and easier) to be agreeable, to be what they were expected to be—at least on the surface.

But underneath the facade of conformable docility, beneath the appearance of a life shaped by men's stories of how women ought to think and act, there has always echoed a different story, a true story. My story. Your story. Our stories, our real, true, different lives. Our stories must be told, so that the women who come after us will know how it really was, so that they know that their mothers and grandmothers and great-grandmothers are more than just the characters in men's tales, that we are dimensional, intentional beings with minds of our own, wills of our own, and dreams of our own.

Our stories *must* be told. My story, your story, women's stories. And you and I are the only ones who can tell them, because we are the only ones who have lived them. Our stories are important. By telling them, by telling our real, true woman's story, we will challenge and correct all the myths and made-up stories about women's lives. We will help to show that women's lives aren't lived as men have taught us to imagine them. Our stories are more than idle gossip, family chitchat, more than old wives' tales—although they are these things, too, and isn't that wonderful?

We must, yes, we *must*, tell the truth.

Memory is the crux of our humanity. Without memory we have no identities. That is really why I am committing an autobiography.

—Erica Jong

Very few women yet have written truthful autobiographies.

—Virginia Woolf

I am an old person who has experienced many things and I have much to talk about. I will tell my talk, of the things I have done and the things that my parents and others have done. But don't let the people I live with hear what I say.

—Nisa, a woman of the Kalahari Desert

Story as a Healing Art

If we feel an urgent social and political need to tell our true stories, we also feel, often unconsciously, an even more urgent psychological need. Every day, all over the United States, women sit together in kitchens and classrooms, on park benches and at office desks, around tables in

A woman's tongue is a candlewick. Always burning.

—Carolina María de Jesus

Stories are medicine.

—Clarissa Pinkola Estés

Each time I write, each time the authentic words break through, I am changed. The older order that I was collapses and dies. I do not know what words will appear on the page. I follow language. I follow the sound of the words, and I am surprised and transformed by what I record.

—Susan Griffin

cafes, around living rooms, telling their true stories. "I have to do this," a woman in one of my classes said. "I'm afraid that if I don't tell my story, I won't be *real!*"

This storytelling work—and it is difficult, demanding work—is remarkably, rewardingly healthy. As we reveal ourselves in story, we become aware of the continuing core of our lives under the fragmented surface of our experience. As we become conscious of the mutifaceted, multichaptered "I" who is the storyteller, we can trace out the paradoxical and even contradictory versions of ourselves that we create for different occasions, different audiences—and the threads that weave all these chapters, all these versions into one whole. Most important, as we become aware of ourselves as storytellers, we realize that what we understand and imagine about ourselves *is* a story. It is only one way of representing our experiences, of composing and recomposing our lives. Our stories are *not* the experiences themselves. This realization is deeply healing. How?

Psychologists tell us that in order to make sense of what's happening in the chaotic and often threatening external world, we create internal frames of reference, narrative structures, stories. Sometimes our stories are affirmative and constructive, opening us to a generous and loving universe. Sometimes they are negative, limiting our choices, our actions, our dreams, reflecting a universe that is more malignant than benign. Sometimes we actively define our stories: we portray ourselves as resourceful, hopeful persons capable of creating our own futures. Sometimes we passively allow our stories to define us: we see ourselves as persons with a confining past, persons without resources, without hope, victims of outside forces over which we have no control. Understanding that our stories *are* stories—and hence open to radical revision—can help us begin to heal from the wounds that experience necessarily inflicts upon us as we grow and change through our interaction with an endlessly changing world of people and things and ideas.

This makes a good deal of sense, don't you think? When I can see the difference between story and event, between my interpretation of experience and experience itself, I can begin to glimpse the many creative means by which I author my own life. I become aware that my experiences, like stories, have a beginning, a middle, and an end. That my life, like all narrative, consists of plot, character, setting, theme—the fundamental constituents of story. When I have a feeling for the various plots and subplots of my life, the actions of the characters (including the main character, me!) begin to make psychological sense. When I understand how my actions lead from one result to another and another and another, I can see myself acting purposefully, the creator of my experience, my life's plot. I can respect and admire my ability to compose an orderly existence out of the disorder and apparent randomness of events and influences that are a mystery to me when I am in their midst.

Our personal narratives, thoughtfully constructed, can have an enormously significant therapeutic potential. By reminding ourselves where we have been and what we have thought and what we have done, we can develop a clearer sense of what we might think and do in the future. The world seems rich with options and alternatives, and we have power and purpose. We can choose which potentials to realize—to make real—in our lives. And more: As we remind ourselves of our stories, as we remember our pasts, however painful, we also re-mind and re-member ourselves. We soften the old scar tissue, solace aching miseries, soothe bitter hurts. In telling the truth about our lives, we can cleanse the infection and close the open, painful wounds that have distorted us, have kept us from realizing all that is possible for ourselves. And in sharing the truths, in opening our secrets together, our common wounds—women's wounds—may be healed.

The healing that can grow out of the simple act of telling our stories is often quite remarkable. Even more remarkably, this healing is not just our own healing: it is the healing of all women. That's why, as we tell our stories to ourselves, it is also important to share them with others. This sharing brings a sense of kinship, of sisterhood. We understand that we are not alone in our efforts to become conscious, whole, healthy persons. The more we learn about ourselves and our own lives, the more we want to know about the lives of other women—women of our own time and place, women of other times, other places.

Stories have such enormous potential. When I tell you the story of my life, I don't have to do anything special—just tell the truth of it as I lived it, with all its ragged edges and loose ends, all the hurtful and the healing bits. When you tell me your story, I don't have to do anything special, either: just listen and accept and reflect and be amazed. Together, telling and listening, accepting and reflecting, we are changed. Together, we reclaim the dynamic energy, the psychic power that is our inheritance. We can use that energy to compose ourselves in new ways,

It's never too late—in fiction or in life—to revise.

—Nancy Thayer

We can learn to work and speak when we are afraid in the same way we have learned to work and speak when we are tired. For . . . while we wait in silence for that final luxury of fearlessness, the weight of that silence will choke us.

—Audre Lorde

in astonishing new forms. We can empower ourselves and others to revise the script we were handed when we were born—the cultural script that tells women how to walk and talk and think and believe. If enough of us do this work now, our daughters and granddaughters will have less of it to do in the future.

Clippings: "I don't strip in public!"

As you begin to give voice to your own story, you'll run across stories that intersect your own. For years, I have kept a clipping file in which I've collected pieces that interest me, written by women in my classes and by published authors. Throughout this book, I'll be sharing items from my clipping file. This one was written by Rita Greer Allen, one of the three women who helped Marion Woodman, a Jungian analyst, create *Leaving My Father's House*. When Woodman asked her to write her experiences, she said yes, then had second thoughts:

> Why did I do that? I don't strip in public. I definitely don't strip down to my soul for everyone to see. For *anyone* to see. But "yes" I said, before fear grabbed me . . . And a kind of trembling joy entered the fear. Opportunity. The opportunity to make the journey once more, to bring more treasure from the unconscious into consciousness.
>
> But more than that. I believe that if my telling of this tale is what I leave behind me when I die, it is the most important thing I will have done with my life.

I value this clipping because it reminds me that we all share a certain reticence—natural? cultural?—about stripping ourselves naked before others' eyes, about telling the truth to others' ears. Telling our stories can be frightening. What it requires from us is trust, trust in ourselves and in those who listen.

Here is another clipping, this one written by a participant in one of my writing classes:

> I search through my notebook and I think: when will I ever be able to get all of this writing together? And what if I did? Would it matter to anyone? Perhaps just getting it down on paper for me is enough, per-

haps I am the solitary reader and hearer of these thoughts. Maybe that is enough. And then again, maybe it is not.

—Vanessa K.*

I value Vanessa's remark because it reminds me that the idea that there's nobody to hear us may be even more frightening than the thought of stripping in public.

I hope you will find the clippings in this book as valuable as I have. As you read this book, as you begin to write your *own* story, you will want to create your own clipping file. As you do, please identify each clipping with the name of the author and the name and date of the publication. Speaking as a habitual clipper, there's nothing more frustrating than not being able to remember whose story I'm reading.

Story as a Sacred Act

The story of a life works on many different levels, in many different dimensions. I can tell you about the things that have happened to me, or the people I have known and loved, or the work I have done, or the ways in which I have contributed to my community. As I tell you these personal, concrete facts of my life, deeply rooted in the realities of my time and place, I am showing you my *heart:* that part of me that has depth and substance, that values certain experiences, that connects intimately with other people. I am also opening my *soul:* that part of me that belongs to dimensions beyond the personal and the concrete, that transcends the boundaries of our space and time.

Heart and *soul.* Words so easily trivialized, but so powerfully, so spiritually, significant. Words that burn like steady fires, that glow like rubies in the depths of women's stories. Dimensions of being for which we long, and which, when we experience them, charge us with deep ener-

What would happen if one woman told the truth about her life? The world would split open.

—Muriel Rukeyser

---

* Throughout this book, pieces by student writers are indicated by the use of a given name and initial. The excerpts are used with permission, and names have been changed to protect identities.

gies, calm us with sweet peace, draw us toward far horizons of consciousness.

Our stories arise from our hearts and our souls. In this sense, telling our stories becomes a sacred gesture, opening a clear way to that deep, ecstatic center where we are most uniquely our selves, individual and unique, and yet are ourselves, joined together at the heart. Once we understand this, we see that the stories of our daily lives, so rich with the experiences of trial and error, so deeply rooted in the here-and-now, so embodied and real and various—our ordinary stories are extraordinarily spirit filled. The routine exchanges, the daily duties, the everyday work: these become the heart-rich, soul-full liturgies that sustain us, reminding us over and over that we are spiritual beings temporarily at home in human bodies, students working through a lifelong curriculum that teaches us to be human, each assigned her own daily lessons. These ordinary activities mark our sacred Book of Hours, dividing the periods of our days into times of cooking breakfast, diapering babies, calling on clients, attending meetings, writing reports, picking up kids, wiping noses, exchanging recipes, folding laundry, chopping onions, balancing the checkbook, kissing good night. Sacred moments, if we can pause long enough to see how they nurture and express and expand the soul's experience of its human being-ness. When we frame these small moments in our stories, we can begin to see and feel their larger significance—part of the soul work that is given us to do.

Sometimes sacred moments emerge out of a great darkness. Ellen, a participant in one of my writing-from-life classes, was recently divorced from her husband of fifteen years and was buying her first house—*her* first house, a symbol of newfound, hard-won independence. But there was a glitch in the process. Hours before the closing, the bank refused to approve her loan. It was a terrible rejection, another in what seemed to Ellen like an endless string of denials, rebuffs, and losses: failing her doctoral orals, watching her marriage disintegrate, not getting the teaching position she had hoped to be offered. But the next morning just at dawn, she stepped outside to put down a saucer of milk for her cat. She looked up and saw a doe and her newborn fawn grazing peacefully in the pale light.

"It was one of those moments," she told us, "when everything that's wrong suddenly seemed—not right, exactly, but okay. I don't exactly know how to say this, but whether I get the house or whether I don't, it's all right, as long as there are such beautifully ordinary things in the

*Y*our goal is to find out who you are.

—*Course in Miracles*

world, and I'm awake to see them." That realization, captured in her journal, buoyed her through the next difficult days and months.

No, Ellen didn't get the house. "But that's not the end of the story," she wrote to me several years later, from the vantage point of a new life. "If I'd gotten the house, I'd still be there. Being turned down for the mortgage was the last chapter in my old story, and the first chapter in my new one, and I'm alive to live it. That's what I realized that morning when I saw the doe and her fawn—a realization that has its own deep being, that gives birth to itself (and to me) over and over again. I will never be able to exhaust all its meaning."

Our lives are filled with such extraordinarily ordinary moments. Our souls are illuminated by them. Sharing them around the hearths of our hearts, we become tellers of sacred tales, artists of our lives.

Time is static, timeless is creative. The no may be a huge yes to the buried parts of ourselves. The yes may be more terrifying than the no. To move with the moment, to surrender to the unknown is to flow with feminine consciousness.

—Marion Woodman

From Telling to Writing

Telling our stories to one another is a powerful act—an empowering act. Even more empowering, however, is the act of *writing* our stories. Speech is temporary, transient. Spoken words rise like mist on a still pond, then evaporate, the idea often lost in the very instant of utterance and misunderstood even when we think we are being most clear.

Written words are stronger, surer. They have a longer lease-hold, a greater half-life. Because they are more substantial, they demand more in the making and offer more potential for the long term. When I capture a thought or a memory or a hope in writing, I can let it stand, with all the force and energy that it brought when it was born out of the womb of my heart. Or I can revisit it: I can revise it, sharpen it, make it more precise. With thought and reflection, I can layer it, add to it, even subtract from it. When I share this layered thought with someone else—sister, mother, friend, editor—I can add her thoughts to mine. With each revision, each sharing, my spontaneous thought becomes clearer, sharper, more detailed, more powerful. If our told stories can sweep across our souls like a strong wind, our written stories have hurricane potential!

As I thought about this book—and it's been in my head for over five years now—I knew I wanted it to be a book about writing, a book that would lead *you* to write. To write at length and with purpose, not just in

So long as a scrap of paper remains, I shall keep scribbling.

—Abby May, June 1800

fits and starts. To trace out your thoughts and dreams, to follow your memories over time and space, discovering their roots in your soul. To pick up your pen or your pencil or turn on your computer and write *your* life. To produce a book.

"A book!" you exclaim. "Oh, but I— I mean, I just couldn't— Well, of course, journal writing is one thing. I have pages and pages, and I love writing letters and maybe an essay from time to time and even a few poems and . . . And yes, I write reports for my work, and last year I did a sales brochure that everybody raved about. But a book about myself? Oh, no, I really don't think—"

Perhaps writing about your life does seem like an ambitious project. Immodest, too, when you get down to it. Egotistical, certainly. Brazen and shameless, even! If you feel that way, you've got plenty of company. Until very recently, women were taught that only famous men—and a few extraordinary women who happened to be wealthy, talented, or the lovers of famous men—have stories valuable and interesting enough to be worth the ink it takes to write them down. Ordinary women lack the eloquence to tell their tales. What's more, they don't live lives worth the trouble of recording.

But you can see, can't you, how this idea of "worthiness" imprisons us? Who sets the standard of worth? Who has the right to say, "His life experiences are worth writing down, but you over there, you woman-person, don't you bother"? It's this unspoken, invisible, but powerful standard of human worth, set down by the ruling gender, class, and race, that impounds our stories. Isn't it time we challenged this standard, broke out of the prison it imposes? Isn't it time we stiffened our spines and took up our pens? Don't we owe it to ourselves and to the future to speak the truth about our lives?

"Oh, absolutely," you say hastily. "But you're talking about women who can actually *write*. I mean, my grammar and spelling—well, they've never been that good. I got C's in English, and I had a teacher once who told me I'd never be able to—"

Ah, yes. The English Teacher from Hell, enshrined forever behind a desk in the darkest corner of the mind, dictionary at her elbow, red pencil in her hand, furiously checking our spelling and subject-verb agreement and scratching frequent *Awk!*s in the margin: "Such awkward sentences, you unlettered, ungraceful, unacceptable, awkward child, you!" The Eternal Inner Editor, a hireling of the School Board, certified to stifle the creativity of all of us ungraceful, unacceptable, awkward children. A dry sponge who soaks up the spontaneity of our writing, stems its momentum, saps its life and vigor. She can make us so miserably self-conscious of her rules and regulations and expectations that we don't have an ounce of confidence left!

But we're big girls now, and we can put this goblin in her proper place. I can lock her dictionary in her drawer, snatch her red pencil, and tear up her teaching certificate. It's my life I'm writing, not yours, I say to her (angrily, because that's how I feel). It's my voice that's talking, my speech I'm speaking, and if I choose to break your rules—well, tough shit, baby.

Of course, once I've simmered down a little I may decide not to banish this Inner Editor completely or forever. If I want to polish my writing for a larger audience, I might retrieve her dictionary and give back her red pencil. But that comes later in the process. For now, all I care about is telling my story, writing my life, and I'm not going to let her stand in my way.

There. That's how it's done. You can do that, can't you?

"Well, sure," you say. "But that isn't all that's bothering me. The thing is, I don't have trouble writing short stuff, a couple of paragraphs at a time, maybe, a page or two. But when it comes to anything longer, well . . . I don't think I've got what it takes to write a book. I mean, a *whole* book? I don't think I have the discipline to do it. In fact, I'm sure I don't."

Discipline. A word we don't like, a word that makes us cringe. I'll have more to say about this subject in a minute, but let me give you a piece of an answer now. Nobody ever writes a book all at once. As I write this, I'm writing a sentence, a word at a time. I collect sentences—three or four or seven or eight of them—into paragraphs, and two or three of those are enough to fill a page. A dozen or two dozen pages make a chapter. A covey of chapters is a book.

But right now, I'm not worried about writing a book. Right now, I simply have faith in this true word, and this one, and the next. I have faith in this honest sentence, this paragraph, this page. That's all I need. Faith. Word by word, sentence by sentence. If I care enough about telling the truth, *my* truth, my book will speak for itself.

Discipline is a bad word in our culture. People associate it with having to do what they're told. But discipline is quite a lovely word. It comes from the same root as disciple, and it means seeing yourself through the eyes of the teacher who loves you. We have that teacher within ourselves; we also have the wild animal that needs to be disciplined with love. We need all its instinctual energy and wisdom.

—Marion Woodman

Clippings: "Just get to work"

Natalie Goldberg is a novelist and teacher. In this excerpt from *Writing Down the Bones*, she tells us what she noticed about her first attempts to write. Here, she's preoccupied (as we all are) with the physical task of getting it down on the page. The physical act of writing is a good place to start.

> In developing writing practice—and remember that at the time I didn't know I was developing anything, I was just trying to figure out how to write—I looked to the most elemental things: pen and paper. I knew writers used paper. Computers weren't around much then, and I wasn't a good typist. What kind of pen? What kind of paper? . . . Spiral notebooks suited me fine. For a while, I searched out unlined ones, but they were harder to find. I wanted no excuse, "Well, I couldn't write this week because I filled my last blank notebook and Woolworth's doesn't have any." Well, Nat, then get a lined one; just get to work.

The next time you write, notice the physical act itself. What does it feel like for you to write? What kind of writing implement do you like? What kind of paper? And then just get to work.

Alice Koller's *An Unknown Woman* is a brutally honest look inside the soul. Here, Koller tells about how she began to write:

> Now I have to begin. I sit in front of my typewriter, aware of this moment as the center around which all of my preparations have swirled. I'm here to understand myself, deliberately to turn myself open to my own view. I know, as I sit here, what I must have known for many years: that I can recognize what's true about myself when I see it. It's whatever I find myself refusing to admit, whatever I say no to very fast. That blanket admission right at the start may save me a lot of time. May save me, period. I'm using that "no" to protect myself from something. What? I'll find out. I'll write down everything I can remember, so that I can see the full extent of it, pick out some patterns in what I've been denying for so long. So that's first: to get it all written. . . .

Much that you need has been lost. . . . We must use what we have to invent what we desire.

—Adrienne Rich

Koller is interested in the psychological act of putting words on the page. "I'm here to understand myself," she says, "to recognize what's true about myself." At bottom, that's why I write, too. But I also know that sometimes I'm here to celebrate myself, sometimes complain, grieve, rage. It helps to know why I'm writing, even when I don't much like my motive. And what was first for Koller is also first for us: to get it all written.

Writing Your Life

So you're writing your life. (Yes, you are. Say it a time or two, out loud, to make it real: *I am writing my life. I am telling my true story.* To make it even more real, write these words on a piece of paper and tape it on your bathroom mirror or your desk at the office, where you'll see it every day, and think of it, even say it, when you see it.)

So you're writing your life. What kind of book are you writing? What form do you want your book to take?

It's your choice. Your book can be a book to keep to yourself or share with family and friends. It can be written down in a notebook or made up of handwritten or typed pages that you insert into a three-ring binder with divisions to separate one chapter from another and containing photographs, drawings, memorabilia—illustrations of your life. More formally, you can produce your book on a word processor (maybe on a desktop publishing program with graphics and fancy borders), print it on a laser printer, and have it bound between leather covers. Whether it's long or short, private or public, handwritten or typed or printed, your book will lead you deeper into the mystery that is your life. And whatever its form and its length, you can enlarge it and expand it into several volumes, as your journey continues, as your mysteries unclose, as your search for meaning takes you deeper and further into your self. Where is it written that an entire life can be explored in a single volume?

So you're writing your life. Where will you begin? How will you organize your memories, recollections, reflections? What will come first, second, third? How many chapters will you have?

Personally, I have always felt there to be a fundamental problem with the organization of most biographies and autobiographies. That problem is time. The calendar. The ticking clock of our lives.

Autobiographies seem to be ruled by chronology, chrono-logic, tick-tock logic. "I was born in 1954. I went to grade school, high school, college. I got a job, got married in 1981, had a baby in 1985, got divorced in 1990, moved to Vermont in 1994." And so on. We live by the rhythms of days and months and years, so when we imagine ourselves writing our lives, we think of starting at the beginning and going on, decade by decade, until we get to the end.

What's the problem? The problem is that chronology confines us. It forces us to see events in tick-tock, step-wise, serial fashion: first school, then work, love, partnering, perhaps children, more work, retirement. Childhood, adolescence, young adulthood, middle age, old age.

But lived experience strikes us less like a flowchart and more like a piece of music. Pachelbel's *Canon*, for instance, has a melodic line that moves through time, marking time, measure by measure, linearly. But the *Canon* is also composed of chords—several notes sounding at one time, on several instruments. It is built around repeated themes in different keys, major and minor, each theme recalling earlier themes and fore-shadowing later ones. Music keeps time and defies time, simultaneously.

The perception of experience, its recollection, is like music. I may ex-perience an event today that resonates in the same key as an event of fif-teen years ago, and with the experience comes a gathering of familiar feeling. You may feel a difficult passage in your present life as a reverber-ating echo of a painful passage in your childhood, inviting you to return, relive, remember. To order these events chronologically can obscure their haunting thematic echoes, the chords they strike in your being.

I have observed that the best and most satisfying personal writing happens when we organize our explorations around the echoing chords, the themes of our lives. The eight thematic clusters we use in my classes are simple, timely, timeless:

> our beginnings and birthings
> our achievements, gifts, and glories
> our female bodies
> our loves, lovers, lovings
> our journeys and journeyings
> our homes and homings
> our visits to the Valley of Shadows
> our experiences of community.

Sometimes we use other groupings of experience, several of which I have suggested in Appendix 2. But these eight seem to me to have cen-tral significance. They are commonly shared and clearly defined, yet suf-ficiently open and evocative to invite many explorations, many angles of vision. I have used them to structure the chapters of this book; I hope you will use them to organize the chapters of yours.

In my classes, I ask participants to devote sixty to ninety minutes a day, reading and writing, to one after another of the eight chapters of this book. If they follow this schedule, they usually come to class with ten to twelve pages, often a great deal more. By the end of eight weeks, they have written eight chapters. Over a hundred pages—a full life, fully witnessed, seen through eight different thematic lessons.

If you want to write your life, I suggest that you follow the same schedule that we follow in our classes, spending seven to ten hours on each chapter of this book and each chapter of *your* book, for eight weeks. At the end of this time, you will have written a book in eight chapters: a story of your life.

"Okay," you may say. "I like the idea of organizing my life-stuff around topics. I see some exciting possibilities there. I might be able to do a chapter or two. But I doubt that I will have the discipline to stay with it for *eight*."

Ah yes. Discipline. How shall we stay with our stories long enough to tell the whole truth, hear ourselves out, see ourselves whole?

Writing as Practice

Natalie Goldberg insists on the value of discipline, of daily writing work. "If writing is important to you," she says, "you'll come to it every day, just as you come to the table to eat or the bed to sleep or the meditation hall to sit." A Buddhist, she asks her students to write with total attention, with focus and concentration, in the same way that they practice yoga or meditate or play tennis or make love. Above all, she asks them to write regularly, to see writing as a discipline, as a practice.

In my writing life, it's the discipline of writing practice that has made the difference. The coming back to the page, the addressing of the urgent issue, the softening of the resistant heart, the unmasking of the prospective "no"—it's the daily doing of these demanding tasks that opens my vision. But I can't do it unless I *do* it. As a Zen teacher once said, there's only one fundamental practice: tushie to cushie, every day, enlightenment. Writing practice requires the same thing: pen to paper, every day, enlightenment.

How can I say this in a way that will move you? I could state it as a

I hope I may Live to Spend my time better And have Beter Imployment for my Pen . . . Sometimes after our people is gone to Bed I get my Pen for I Dont know how to Content myself without writing Something.

—Jemima Condict, 1774

I feel that strong emotion must leave its trace; and it is only a question of discovering how we can get ourselves again attached to it, so that we shall be able to live our lives through from the start.

—Virginia Woolf

For me, writing something down is the only road out.

—Anne Tyler

rule. Every woman who hopes to tell her true story should designate a regular time every day when she ignores all other demands on her attention and simply writes.

That doesn't quite do it? Let me ask you this, then. Do you want to climb the mountain of each experience to the very top? Do you want to dive to the depths of your deepest being? Do you want to dance the lovely, graceful movements of your mind? No mountain climber or deep-sea diver or dancer will achieve her personal best by climbing or diving or dancing once a week or once a month. What she dreams of doing demands so much from her that she must focus all her energy on it for part of *every* day. She trains regularly and rigorously, even when she doesn't have time, even when she has a headache or a hot date. She submits to a daily discipline of body, mind, and spirit because it is commitment and discipline that ultimately make the difference between hitting the mark and missing it. She makes her climbing or her diving or her dancing her highest mental priority, her greatest physical challenge, her deepest spiritual practice.

And so it is for you, writing from life, writing *your* life. For some time every day—as much time as you can spare, but no less than an hour, please—let writing your life be your highest priority, your greatest challenge, your deepest practice. Climb the mountain of your hopes, dive the depths of your shadow, dance the beauty of your spirit. Do it every day. And as you do, watch yourself growing stronger and more skillful, more willing to risk, better able to climb, dive, dance. These are the qualities that writing practice demands of us. And these are the qualities that regular writing practice returns to us, multiplied a hundred times, a thousand times, more times than we can count.

Sharing Our Stories

We need to tell our stories. We need to hear other women's stories. Who else might want to hear your story? Whose stories might you want to hear?

Some women's stories have been shared in print—not only the stories of famous women, but those whose lives illustrate the challenges, hopes, and experiences that many of us share. I am thinking, for instance, of Alice Koller. Two years after she earned her doctorate in phi-

Life will go on as long as there is someone to sing, to dance, to tell stories, to listen.
—Oren Lyons

losophy, Koller still didn't have the ghost of an idea about what sort of life she wanted to claim for herself. She fled to Nantucket, where she spent three winter months looking back at her history, forward at her hopes, and inward, deep into herself. In *An Unknown Woman*, she gave us a firsthand report of the courage and persistence that is required to make this interior journey. Or there is Juliet Wittman's *Breast Cancer Journal: A Century of Petals*, which chronicles the challenge of mindfully and courageously facing a deadly disease, reminding us that at the center of our pain, we are all human, all sisters. Or Florida Scott-Maxwell's *The Measure of My Days*, written in the late years of her life, when the inward journey was the only journey left to take.

Koller's and Wittman's and Scott-Maxwell's stories weren't published because they were written by famous women. They were published because each tells the truth about one woman's experience, because each was written with energy and insight and compassion, because each speaks to the reader's own experience.

But most of us aren't interested in sharing our stories in such a broad way. What we hope for, what we want, is an intimate, face-to-face audience of like-minded women who are engaged in the regular practice of telling their stories. What we need is a weekly story circle whose members will help us stay with our writing practice and deepen and enlarge it, in the same way that the other members of our exercise class help us to stay faithful to our intention to exercise. Appendix One (pages 213–19) offers suggestions for establishing a Story Circle where you can share your work and explore the writing and reading exercises in this book. Please, read those pages thoughtfully, imagining how much benefit you might derive, how much you could learn about yourself and others, by sharing your stories with such a group—a spiritual community, no less, of women whose souls yearn for boon companions with whom to share the way.

Toward a Book of Your Own

So where are you now?

At the beginning, don't you think?

That's where we all start. With "Beginnings and Birthings." All you have to do is turn the page and pick up your pen.

Chapter One

Beginnings and Birthings

I have written my life in small sketches, a little today, a little yesterday, as I have thought of it, as I remember all the things from childhood on through the years, good ones and unpleasant ones, that is how they come out and that is how we have to take them.

—*Anna Mary Moses (Grandma Moses)*

Beginnings

I was born in a busy Chicago hospital, just at noon on the second day of the brand-new year 1940, with the world peering anxiously over the precipice of war. President Roosevelt had submitted a record-breaking $14-million defense budget while proclaiming U.S. neutrality, the New York World's Fair had opened to a goggle-eyed public, *Gone with the Wind* was the year's leading movie, the average cost of a new car was $766, and bread cost eight cents a loaf. The sun was in Capricorn, the moon was in Libra, and Aries was rising over the eastern horizon.

But my mother was not concerned with such social or celestial events. She was doing the belly-work of birthing: pushing, panting, waiting, pushing again. Breathing with the pain, staying with the rhythms of breath and body, past caring whether her first child was boy or girl, so long as it was healthy.

Then the miraculous moment: "You came out kicking," she says now, retelling with pride a story she has told me so often that both of us know it by heart. "And the nurse held you up, red as a raspberry, and you squalled, and she said 'Listen to that voice! This one's going to tell the world all about it!'"

My birth, according to my mother, author and narrator, the world's first and foremost expert on the subject of me. I become I by being born into her personal narrative, which is already in progress when I make my first appearance. I emerge out of her life-narrative and am shaped by it. To fully understand my own story, I might begin with hers, and her mother's, and her mother's: stories in the motherline into which I am born. Or I might try to understand my father's story, and his father's. Or I might take a different tack and reconstruct the life my mother and father had together before I was born: the story of their meeting and falling in love, and the interesting obstacles that stood in the path of their marriage. The narrative possibilities are almost infinite.

But while beginnings can be traced backward and still further backward into the dimmest reaches of recollection, a story has to begin somewhere. I choose to open my story on the day that I was born.

At what moment do you choose to open yours?

Investigating Your Beginnings

To answer that question, and to go on from there, you'll need to turn archivist, archaeologist, and amateur detective, unearth old memories, excavate old facts, dust off old documents. Here are a few ideas for investigating the circumstances surrounding your birth.

Find out as much as you can about the time, day, year, and place of your birth. If your birth mother is still alive, ask her to tell you everything she remembers, and write it down or tape it. If not, ask an elderly relative, search out your baby book, or hunt through family documents. If you are one of the five to six million adoptees in the United States and you grew up knowing little or nothing about your birth parents, you will have to decide to what extent you want to fill in the gaps in your knowledge. (Currently, there are around 400 groups in the United States that assist adoptees in searching for their birth parents. Your public library may be able to help you locate search-and-support resources in your area.) Perhaps you will decide that the day of your adoption was as significant as the date

*The moment of birth,
the beginning,
requires patience, implies
progress.
You are not alone.*

—"Beginning,"
Hexagram 3, *The I Ching*

The world is round and the place which may seem like the end may also be only the beginning.

—Ivy Baker Priest

Don't be afraid your life will end; be afraid that it will never begin.

—Grace Hansen

of your actual birth: if that is the case, choose that day as your birth day, and ask your adoptive parents to tell you the story of your adoption.

When you've learned as much as you can from personal sources, go to the library and browse through magazines and newspapers published during the period you've chosen as the beginning of your story. What sort of world were you born into? What was the season, the weather? What movies were playing in the local theaters? What songs were people listening to? What cars were they driving? How long were women's skirts? How did men wear their hair? What news stories made headlines? Who was president? What challenges did our government face? What were the most significant issues confronting other countries? These facts about the world may seem remote from you, but they are a part of the larger picture, the frame that surrounds your personal story. Understanding it can help you to see yourself in the context of your times, can be an invaluable resource for placing yourself in a world that existed and thrived before you arrived in it.

Prompts

As a writer, I know how hard it is to get going, to pull ideas out of the head, the heart, the belly, to put words on the page. Sometimes it's easier with a little priming of the pump. Here are several open-ended statements that invite completion. If one appeals to you, adopt it as a starting point (change it as much as you like, of course) and see where it takes you:

   a. In the beginning, before I was, there was . . .
   b. My story begins when . . .
   c. I always celebrate my birthday by . . .
   d. In the year I was born, they were dancing the . . . , going to the movies to see . . . , listening to . . . , and wearing . . .

Clippings: The Back Seat of My Father's Chrysler

Here are a few examples of the beginnings of stories created by people who have attended my classes and workshops. Perhaps they will give you some ideas for ways to pen your own story. The first one opens with a humorous touch; the second has a touching poignancy. You might try borrowing their opening lines: *I began on a* ——— *day* (what kind of weather was it?), or *My parents always celebrated my birthday with a* ———. Notice, too, that all three are full of details and particularities.

I began on a dark and stormy night, and my mother almost didn't make it to the Frazier County Hospital, forty miles away. She said it looked like it might be a dead heat between the stork and the doctor. "I didn't want you to be born on the backseat of that old Chrysler," she told me, when I was sixteen and presumably old enough to understand why. I've always wondered, though, whether there was something about the backseat of my father's Chrysler that Mama didn't want to tell me.

　　　　　　　　　　　　　　　　　　　　—Alicia J.

My dad always celebrated my birthday with a cake and candles, but it wasn't a happy day. Mother—vivacious, very pretty, and only twenty-three years old—died giving birth to me. He brought me home from the hospital on the same day he buried her. I used to stare at her photograph and imagine that heaven must be a magnificent place, hung with crystal chandeliers and carpeted with red plush like the Palace Theater, if it could keep her from coming home for my birthday.

　　　　　　　　　　　　　　　　　　　　—Kelly O.

I was adopted when I was six, so I don't know anything about my birth. What I do remember is the day I met my mother and father—the ones who chose me out of all the other children they had to choose from. I remember that it was a spring day and rainy, and Mom came into the room wearing a drippy green raincoat and her blond bangs were damp. She had the prettiest smile I had ever seen, and Dad was the tallest man in the world, so tall I had to look up and up and up to see his face. Mom whispered, kind of marveling, "Isn't she a pretty little thing?" and Dad boomed out, "Pretty as a daisy!" in that bold voice of his, and swept me up. "Let's take our daisy home with us." And after that, I was always "my Daisy" to him.

　　　　　　　　　　　　　　　　　　　　—Molly Y.

Writer Marya Mannes, in her autobiography *Out of My Time*, describes herself as a young child seen through the lens of a camera and the affectionate eyes of her family:

The snapshots show a plump child with very light hair and very round and serious eyes. Between [the pictures] her mother wrote that she was flirtatious, curious, temperamental, greedy for food, animals, water to swim in, fields of flowers, and, of course, attention. She ran, danced, made scenes when thwarted, melted when not. It appears that she was quiet only when asleep; or on the pot, in moments of contemplation so prolonged that—on the testimony of her brother five years her senior—a new nurse finally picked her up by her hair and removed her, screaming. (The nurse was fired that night.) At the age of three, curiosity impelled her to drink a bottle of ink. Through the intervention of horrified parents and a doctor, who upended her and flushed her out, she survived. So did the legend, repeated through several decades, that the ink has been coming out of her ever since.

How would your parents or other family members have described you? Can you recall an anecdote that explains some special characteristic of yours, like the ink episode in Mannes's memoir, that seems to persist through the decades of your life?

Diane Mees wrote this reflective, retrospective opening to her autobiographical article called "Searching for My Birth Mother."

From the time I was very young I've known I was adopted. In my home adoption was talked about naturally, and we never made a big deal of it. I adored my parents, yet as far back as I can remember I felt I didn't fit in. Unlike biological children, I couldn't look in the mirror and be reminded of my mother's nose or my dad's high cheekbones.

This caused me great pain—especially at family gatherings, because then I was more conscious of how different I was from everyone else. I was tall and had curly brown hair and brown eyes, whereas my mother, aunt, and cousin were short and had green eyes and straight black hair. Whom did I look like? I wondered. Not having anyone to identify with made me feel isolated. I felt I didn't belong.

Maybe you wondered, at some point or another, whether you "belonged." Maybe you felt that there was a secret part of you that nobody truly understood. Cynthia Ozick, in her autobiographical essay, "A Drugstore in Winter," gives us a wry look into her own secret identity as a writer.

I am incognito. No one knows who I truly am. The teachers in P.S. 71 don't know. Rabbi Meskin, my *cheder* teacher, doesn't know. Tessie the lion-eyed landlady doesn't know. Even Hymie the fountain clerk can't know—though he understands other things better than anyone: how to tighten roller skates with a skate key for instance, and how to ride a horse . . . My brother is older than I am, and doesn't like me; he builds radios in his bedroom, he is already W2LOM, and operates his transmitter (*da-di-da-dit, da-da-di-da*) so penetratingly that Mrs. Eva Brady, across the way, complains. Mrs. Brady has a subscription to *The Writer;* I fill a closet with her old copies. How to Find a Plot. Narrative and Character, the Writer's Tools. Because my brother has his ham license, I say, "I have a license too." "What kind of license?" my brother asks, falling into the trap. "Poetic license," I reply. My brother hates me.

As you glance back over these last three examples, notice the difference in each writer's point of view and tone. Mannes speaks in a detached third-person voice, as if from a great distance. Mees looks from the present into the past, in her own first-person voice, with a serious tone. Ozick uses first person, present tense to situate us in her past in a style that is immediate and engaging.

The Past in Pictures

Art is born in attention. Its midwife is detail. . . . The singular image is what haunts us and becomes art. Even in the midst of pain, this singular image brings delight.

—Julia Cameron

Photographs give us a revealing glimpse into our earlier lives. Photographs of ourselves as children are especially helpful, because we have so few actual memories of those early days. They can even become a substitute for memory, and we locate the event or the people not in our past, but on the pages of the family album or in the family film archives (and, these days, in the family video collection).

If you have photographs of yourself as a baby or young child, you can include them in your book as well, on the page along with the relevant text, or in special sections. Perhaps you'd like to draw special frames around your photos, or use collage techniques (mixing photos with other mementos) to create special "memory pages."

Photographs can also help us retrieve recollections that, without the camera, might be lost forever in the vast landscape of the past. Perhaps you've had the experience of looking at a photograph and suddenly remembering the name of someone you haven't thought of in years, and along with the name comes a flood of memories of another time, another place. As you write your story book, collect the photographs and other mementos—newspaper clips, letters, notes, announcements—from the period, to help you recall the events and feelings of that day and time.

When you use a photograph in your text, you may want to write specifically about it. On a preceding page, you read Marya Mannes's description of a photograph of herself, "a plump child with very light hair and very round and serious eyes." Here's another description, this one from Olive Higgins Prouty's memoir, *Pencil Shavings*. When she was four, little Olive's beloved nurse, Nana, died and her life changed:

> There was no one who had time to wash and iron starched dresses or to roll up hair on rags, no one near at hand to straighten bows and to smooth locks. I have two photographs that tell the story. The photograph taken before Nana died is that of a round-cheeked little girl dressed in a ruffled frock and wearing a gold chain and locket. Every curl is in place, every finger, too. Her expression is serene, her smile angelic.
>
> In the photograph taken after the departure of her nurse the child is dressed in black wool. There are no curls. Her hair is an ugly length, barely covering her ears. She wears it in bangs that are clotted and tossed. There is no angelic smile. She is holding a small tiger cat in her arms and her expression is fierce as if someone had threatened to rob her of her cat. She is still suffering, no doubt, from the results of having been wrapped up too long in too much cotton wool.

Looking casually at the two photographs, you might be tempted to feel sorry for the girl with the cat, who has lost the woman who made her feel loved and cared for, made her beautiful. But Prouty's last sentence suggests that the fierce child has gained a sturdy independence that will serve her better, in the long run, than beauty. In that final sentence, Prouty *sees through* (to use Janet Frame's term) the deceptions practiced on little girls of her time and social class (and still sometimes practiced on our daughters!)—dressing them in ruffled frocks, protecting them from experience, producing fragile and helpless women.

Here's another example from a writer who has seen through her earlier memories. This passage was written by a seventy-year-old woman in a class:

Writing an autobiography, usually thought of as a looking back, can just as well be a looking across or through, with the passing of time giving an X-ray quality to the eye.

—Janet Frame

Most human beings today waste some twenty-five to thirty years of their lives before they break through the actual and conventional lies which surround them.

—Isadora Duncan

That's my mother in the photograph, in her best Sunday dress. That's me, on her lap. I'm four, and smiling. I was always smiling. "Who's that ugly little girl with the angry frown on her face?" Mother would say, looking at me. "It's not my pretty Pearl. *She* always smiles." When the frown went away, she'd say, "Oh, *there's* my pretty Pearl. I was afraid we'd lost her!" I was smiling, always smiling, no matter how angry or sad or lost I felt inside. It was a lesson in deception and self-deception. It was the first lesson I had to unlearn when I began to search for my real self. I keep this photograph on my desk to remind me to let my face tell the truth about the feelings in my heart!

—Pearl J.

As you look through your childhood photographs, perhaps you will find one that you can see through. What is the truth behind the appearances? What realities can you see now that were invisible to you and others at the time?

Firsts

The first part of your first chapter was taken up with your birth, which is only the first of many firsts that mark your life. Let's fill the second part of your chapter with other occasions that shine with a special brilliance in your memory, for they represent the beginning of something new. A moment that's full of wonder, or awe, or excitement—even though someone else might have thought it just an ordinary occasion. A time of fear, of pain, even of loss. A moment that opens a door to a new place, a different sense of self, a changed understanding of what is or what could be. This point in your chapter is a good place to capture some of these firsts.

Is this a breakthrough, or what?

—Lily Tomlin

To get started, try a *timed writing*, which is a good way to force yourself to put things down on paper. To do a timed writing, simply set a timer (five minutes is a good length) and keep on writing until it goes off. An alternative to the timer is a short piece of music that you enjoy. (I have two in very different moods that I love to write by: Pachelbel's slow, melodious *Canon* and Marais's sprightly *The Bells of St. Genevieve*.) In addition to setting a time limit and sticking to it, there are just two other hard-and-fast rules for a timed writing: 1) don't stop writing, no matter what; and 2) don't edit. Just listen to the voice inside you and write.

The following list contains some timed-writing topics. I suggest that you try one of them now, and come back later and choose others. And it's fun to experiment. For instance, do one timed writing in the present tense, another in the past. (Which one feels more immediate and direct?) Write one in the first-person "I," another in the third-person "she." (What do you see when you write about yourself as if you were another person?) Try one timed writing all in dialogue, having a conversation with somebody (your first best friend, perhaps, or your first baby). Or write one as a five-minute letter (how about the first boy you ever kissed?). A half dozen of these firsts can be combined into the middle section of your chapter:

first memory
first toy
first conscious awareness of being yourself
first day of school
first recital
first best friend
first airplane flight
first dance, first formal dress
first painting or artwork
first bikini
first kiss
first car
first sexual experience
first baby
first paycheck
first apartment
first child's wedding
first grandchild

The secret of getting ahead is getting started.

—Sally Berger

Clippings: "A Ruffled Blue Dumpling"

Here are two paragraphs that writers created from the list of timed-writing topics. Both are rich in the striking details that recreate a memorable scene. The first shows us a rebellious young girl who does what she's told, hating it; the second shows a young girl whose natural and innocent rebellion leads to tragedy.

My first piano recital, age ten. Oh, God, what a torment. How long I suffered to learn my "piece," a hideously percussive thing called "Wild Horses." If I'd had my way, wild horses could not have dragged me to that event! Or to Mrs. Hamer's third-floor rear apartment for the three or four fittings that eventually resulted in a fancy eyelet dress that made me look like a ruffled blue dumpling. Or to Kinney's Shoe Store for white sandals to go with the blue eyelet dress, where I discovered to my horror that I was to wear WHITE SOCKS!!! Or to Mr. Gruber's studio, time and again, for rehearsals. Or finally to the First Methodist Church, on the fateful night, for the recital. When it was over, Mr. Gruber patted me on the back and said I'd done a "fair job." But all I can remember is the ruffles scratching my arms as I played, and catching the heel of my white sandal in the hem of my eyelet dress and tumbling off the stage, and my mother's face, flaming red.

—Alyssa R.

She lived down the alley and across Mr. Hardison's vacant lot. Her name was Mary Ann and she was my first best friend. She showed me how to sneak out at night (easy as apple pie: out the window, feel for the porch roof with a toe, down the ladder conveniently left leaning against the east side of the house). It was Mary Ann (blond and blue-eyed to my dark hair, dark eyes) who dared me to kiss Jason Pettigrew on the lips. It was Mary Ann who flooded our bathroom when she put her very first used Kotex down the toilet, who yelled so hard at the basketball games that she peed her pants, and who cried harder than I did when Mrs. McAllister ran over my cat. And it was Mary Ann who got pregnant by Michael Murray when she was fifteen, and got shipped off to a home for unwed mothers, and finally to live with her aunt in California because her parents were ashamed to have her back. And got killed the next year hitching a ride to L.A. to listen to the Grateful Dead.

—Pamela T.

In an account of her life published in *Body & Soul: Ten American Women*, actress Geraldine Fitzgerald recalls her first conscious awareness of herself as someone with the power of choice:

I remember sitting in a tree when I was about four. I had been getting a hard time from all the other children in our gang—I was a rather small and bullied child—and I didn't see much prospect of things improving in the near future. But while I was hiding in this tree, I thought, There must be other places than this place I am in. I could go to another place so I don't have to have the others knock me around. It was the first notion of, there is an alternative. I date the beginning of my life from that moment.

The urgency of Nancy Mairs's first menstruation comes through her first-person, present-tense voice in *Remembering the Bone House*. The event she describes is one that all women share. Does it strike a chord in your memory?

Happily, my period starts fairly early, just before I turn twelve. I'm prepared. My blue box of Kotex and my white elastic belt with the metal clasps on each end are stowed in my bedroom closet. Then, of course, I'm nowhere near my bedroom closet when it starts. I'm spending a few days with Aunt Jane and Uncle Kip. I peer anxiously at a brownish spot on the crotch of my underpants. Oh no. It can't be. But the next time I go to the bathroom, a couple more spots have appeared. And a couple more the time after that. I can't ignore them. They're not going away. Composing myself, I tell Jane I'll have to borrow a belt and some Kotex. . . .

It's not much of a period. Just some rusty streaks on a pad for a couple of days. No matter. I've got it.

This passage, from *Memoirs of a Modernist's Daughter*, by Eleanor Munro, captures the fragile ironies of the first sexual desire in a time before television and the movies made vicarious sexual experience easily available even to young children.

We paired off with experimental mates. First kisses led on to a hand on a blouse; the next night, the hand within; then trembling lips would be pressed for the first time to a nipple. By the summer's end, we were lying for hours in each other's arms, but chastely, for this was still the early 1940s. In a spirit of inquiry, therefore, I lay one summer night on the swinging bench on our porch while my boyfriend of the season took a handkerchief out of his pocket and laid it over the erection he had produced out of his trousers. "So you won't have to touch it," he said. In the shadows, with one finger, gingerly I explored its length, then circled it with my hand. The next day in a swimming pool with my girlfriends, I spied an iron water spout. I swam to it and spanned it with my thumb and fingers. It was the same! Thereafter all afternoon in joy and curiosity I eyed it and from time to time swam casually over to confirm the fitting with my hand.

In *Long Quiet Highway*, Natalie Goldberg tells us that she first came to realize that the details of daily life could have enormous significance when she read Erica Jong's book of poems, *Fruits and Vegetables*:

> I read about sautéing an onion, cutting an eggplant, and a quiet gully opened between the divided rivers in my brain . . . The gully let the waters come together: A connection was made. . . . I could write about what I lived. I could make conscious, valuable, even deep, my daily life: my walks around the block, my knees, my purchase of toothpaste, the pigeons I saw every morning on the telephone wire, my teeth, my grandmother, her chicken, her challah, her face, my hands, the men I kissed and didn't kiss then, the gray sky of Michigan, the subways of New York and my knowledge of the Hudson River. I could use the material of my life for writing; I could write about Brooklyn, just as Yeats wrote about Inverness.

Births and Birthings

Do not follow where the path may lead. Go instead where there is no path and leave a trail.

—Muriel Strode

When we think of giving birth, we usually think of giving birth to a child, a momentous event in a woman's life. For many of us, it may seem to be the purpose of life, the centerpoint, the focus of energy and spirit. But in the span of a lifetime, we give birth in thousands of ways. We open ourselves to new experience, new places, new things to do, new ways to see. We create new things, activities, art, places, plans, ideas. If we limit our definition of the generative process to birthing children, we won't be able to see our creativity in its larger perspective. One woman wrote:

> I've never had children, and I always thought I missed something really vital and mysteriously necessary by not giving birth. But now I see how many times I've conceived! My catering business, for instance. That was a new idea, born out of my love affair with cooking

and the practical necessity of paying the bills after my husband's corporation downsized him out of a job. Who would have guessed how healthy that brainchild would be? Who would have guessed that three years later I'd conceive again and give birth to a restaurant?

—Jan C.

How many times in your life have you conceived and given birth to something so new and different that it took your breath away? In this part of your chapter, you will explore those birthings.

Like human births, our creative birthings require effort, work, and hope. They're often difficult because they almost always require a sacrifice: to get something radically new you often have to give up something you already have. Here is a passage from *A Dreamer's Log Cabin*, written by Laurie Shepherd, who built her own log cabin in the wilds of northern Minnesota. It describes what she was willing to sacrifice in order to give birth to her life's vision:

I realized that if what we call human nature can be changed, then absolutely anything is possible. And from that moment, my life changed.

—Shirley MacLaine

> I've been asked why I choose poverty. Not everyone understands how I could leave the security of a teaching job to live alone in a tiny cabin, in an area where jobs are scarce and often temporary.
>
> Actually, I never chose to be poor. My choice was to build a cabin in northern Minnesota. I realized that poverty would almost certainly be a consequence of that choice.
>
> There are many days when my resources dwindle to some loose change and a can or two of soup. Then I look around. I'm sitting in a comfortable home I've dreamed of all my life. It's all paid for. Just outside the door are eight acres of woods and the Mississippi River. The setting is tranquil and welcoming.
>
> I'm living just the way I've always wanted to live. This gives me a real sense of personal freedom. It required some scrimping and saving to get here, but now that I'm here, money has very little to do with my way of living.
>
> Recently I was asked what changes I would make if I was suddenly blessed with a windfall of money. I honestly don't think I would change anything. I certainly wouldn't move, install electricity and buy a television set, or put a toilet in the house.
>
> I might eat a little better.

Some birthings (like Laurie's) require physical labor, stiff muscles, sacrifice. Other birthings require a different way of seeing ourselves and our relationships; the pain of coming to terms with new realities; the emergence, out of pain, of a new sense of self. Sometimes this new self may not find easy acceptance. One woman wrote compellingly of the pain of telling her mother that she was a lesbian—and the self-recognition born out of that difficult moment:

> I'll never forget her face when I came out to her. It crumpled, as if the bones inside were cracking and her paper-skin was ripping. I wanted to cry, I wanted to scream, I wanted to hold her, hit her, all at once. She just stood there, her eyes like dark holes, her paper-face crumpling. "How *can* you?" was what finally came out of her mouth.
>
> "I can't not," I said, not pleading or begging, just telling the truth. "This is how I am. This is me, Mom. It's been me for a long time."
>
> The holes got bigger, darker. "I didn't make you this way. You're not my daughter."
>
> "You mean, I'm not the daughter you wanted."
>
> "You're . . . not . . . my . . . daughter." Each word separate, distinct, a rock.
>
> "I'm myself."
>
> And suddenly, out of her pain, her anger, her loss, I *was*, as if I had been born again. Not to her this time, but to *me*. Not her daughter, but my own. Me, born to me on this day of my coming out, my mother as angry midwife. Myself. My Self!
>
> —Hannah T.

The pain of leaving an old identity and venturing into a new one can also come when we move out of a career. Several years ago, I wrote a book about women who had left successful careers. After *Work of Her Own* was published, I received a letter from a woman I'll call Kate, who had been an attorney for fifteen years. She had a successful practice that paid her well but had begun to realize that she was no longer happy practicing law. Finally, she placed her cases with other lawyers and closed her office. This is how she described the next year.

> I had no idea what I wanted to do or who I was. All I knew was that I wasn't who I had been. The next nine months were an absolute hell, a black hole. My friends thought I was crazy to give up the money and the status. My father kept worrying about how I was going to support myself. My lover couldn't deal with my depressions. When he moved out, he took our cat, which depressed me even more.

Supposing you have tried and failed again and again. You may have a fresh start any moment you choose, for this thing that we call "failure" is not the falling down, but the staying down.

—Mary Pickford

But as time went on and I began to explore possibilities, I began to see that there was a great deal more to me than I had thought, and toward the end of that year, things changed. I got a sense that my old self had died and that something new was being born, a piece at a time. The piece that loved music. The part that was interested in psychology. The potter, the bicyclist, the vegetarian, the meditator. The part that got interested in psychology enrolled in a degree program, and in another year, I'll be able to have my own practice. When I look back on the long process of giving birth to myself, I'm amazed at the pain, the effort, the sheer *joy* of it all. What a wonderful life this is. What an incredible gift!

Which brings up another important matter. As all storytellers know, as *you* know, stories can be shaped and reshaped. No version is fixed, no edition is final. One day I'm depressed, and I emphasize the dark details in my life-story; the next day I'm able to make a joke out of yesterday's gloom. As we tell our stories to ourselves and others, we choose which elements to highlight, which to shadow, which to leave out altogether. As Kate tells the story of her year, she doesn't linger over the nine months of darkness and depression. Her focus is not the pain, but on the *birth*; not on what is past, but what is to come.

Not all births of the self, births of the soul, are as dramatic as those we've read about here. Birthing happens every day, in many ways, large and small. Once we become aware of it, we see it in our own life, in the lives of our loved ones, our friends. Old things come to an end, are outgrown, or outworn. New life emerges out of grief and loss and pain, and with it a sense of wonder, of joy. What *interesting* lives we lead!

Inspiration does not come like a bolt, nor is it kinetic, energetic striving, but it comes into us slowly and quietly and all the time, though we must regularly and every day give it a little chance to start flowing, prime it with a little solitude and idleness.

—Brenda Ueland

Clippings: "Reader, I Stared"

In this excerpt from "*One* Child of One's Own," Alice Walker writes about the "one genuine miracle" that changed her from a woman who lived in her head to one who used her womb:

> What is true about giving birth is . . . that it is miraculous. It might even be the one genuine miracle in life . . .
> For one thing, though my stomach was huge and the baby (?!) constantly causing turbulence within it, I did not believe a baby, in

person, would come out of me. I mean, look what had gone *in*. (Men have every right to be envious of the womb. I'm envious of it myself, and I have one.) But there she was, coming out, a black, curling lock of hair the first part to be seen, followed by nearly ten pounds of—a human being!

Reader, I *stared*. But this hymn of praise I, anyhow, have heard before, and will not permit myself to repeat it. . . . The point is, I was changed forever. From a woman whose "womb" had been, in a sense, in her head; that is to say, certain small seeds had gone in, rather different if not larger or better "creations" had come out, to a woman who had "conceived" books in her head, and had also engendered at least one human being in her body.

In *Leaving My Father's House*, by Marion Woodman, Rita Greer Allen reflects on procreation and purpose in a personal narrative that was written two weeks before her sixty-fifth birthday, long after she realized that she would have no children. She has not used her womb, but she knows she has given birth, over and over.

It is the creative potential itself in human beings that is the image of God.

—Mary Daly

The chief purpose of one's life on earth is to perpetuate the race. True?

If so, then I have failed. Not one child to carry my genes, or Bob's or those of our forebears into the future. But I have come to terms with that. Painfully . . .

If it has not been to create children, it has been to create film, to create sculpture. My purpose, I believe, has been to honor the powerful energy between the opposites, not only in the passion of sexual activity, nor in procreating, but in the feminine itself, the masculine itself, and the powerful creative energy that pulsates between them in all bodies, in all psyches, in all things.

Is this god? I don't know. I feel that I am coming close to *something*.

Now, think about your own life, about the effort and labor required to conceive and bring forth your dreams, about the things you gave up in order to give birth to something new—a child, a business, an idea, a house, a relationship, a new way to work. Make a list of your birthings, in chronological order, or in thematic order (family, work, relationships), or simply in the order in which they occur to you—in whatever order makes sense.

Then choose one and write about it. (Question: Is your book itself a birthing? What new self might be emerging from the womb of your intention?)

Ways to Expand Your First Chapter

If you've done the writings suggested here, you have created your own first chapter, in three sections: your beginning; important first events in your life; and things, ideas, and people you've conceived and given birth to. Now that you have this firm, strong framework for your first chapter, you can leave it and go on. Or, if you choose, you can expand it, now or later.

You don't get to choose how you're going to die. Or when. You can decide how you're going to live now.

—Joan Baez

If you choose to expand your chapter, here are five ways you can do it. Choose as many as you like, and follow the instructions for each. When you are finished, collect your writing and the other material you have created and put it in your binder or file as Chapter One. You're on your way to your book!

1. Return to your list of firsts, choose several, and write about them. Experiment with voice and tense. Cram your writing with detail, so that you taste, smell, touch, hear, *feel* the experience.

2. Return to your list of birthings, choose another, and create a twice-told tale. First, write the story with a focus on the labor and pain and effort required to give birth to whatever was emerging. Then write the story again, with a focus on the emergence itself.

3. Some painful birthings can be almost too traumatic to relive. If your story is like that, and the pain is very great, it is all the more important for you to tell it. (Storytelling is a "healing art," writes Clarissa Pinkola Estés, author of *Women Who Run with the Wolves*. "Some are called to this art, and the best, to my lights, are those who have lain with the story and found all its matching parts inside them and at depth.")

But it is important not to be overwhelmed by the pain. One way to do this is to make a fairy tale or a myth out of the story. A participant in one of my classes began her account of her painful relationship with her mother this way: "Once upon a time, there was a magical birth. A baby wolf, covered with gray fur and with needle-sharp baby wolf teeth, was born to a faithful family dog who had never been out of the back-yard." By writing your story as if it took place in an imaginary world, peopled with mythical characters, or filled with magical doings, you may be able to say what you need to say without being swept away by the pain.

4. In an essay called "Exploring Your Personal Myth," James Carse retells a story he learned from his college girlfriend Gerry, who in turn had heard it from her mother. "'According to my mother,' Carse's friend said, 'the way I was born was that she went to the A&P and when she came home I jumped out from behind the kitchen door and surprised her.'" Sometimes new births take us by surprise. They are so filled with life and energy that they jump out at us even before we know we're pregnant, when we're engaged with our everyday work, or shopping at the A&P. When this happens, we might not be ready—no diapers, no crib, not even a name! Have there been times in your life when something new and nameless jumped out from behind the door and surprised you? How did you respond? What had to be changed in your life to accommodate this demanding new enterprise? Include in your chapter a story of a birth that came upon you before you realized that you were expecting.

5. Often one birth leads to another. My decision to go to graduate school, for instance, was an acknowledgment of an emerging part of me, a part that needed to be born. The choice of graduate school led to the relocation of my entire family—husband, three children, and our belongings—from Illinois to California. This new place—Berkeley in the chaotic and clamorous days of the late '60s—gave birth to a new way of thinking and feeling about myself, a new vision of what was possible for my life. It led to a painful divorce, but also to a new and more independent self. Have you experienced a similar chain of birthings—one new thing leading to another in a kind of a sequence? How did these birthings affect the direction of your life?

Meditation

Birthing

In this meditation, we will make use of a birthing from the list you jotted down in response to the writing question on pages 34–35. Before you begin, you might want to go back to that list and reread what you wrote.

To use this meditation and others that appear throughout this book, have someone read it to you or read it yourself onto a tape. (You may also order an expanded version of this meditation, read by the author on audiotape. See the address in the back of this book for ordering information.) The meditation should be read slowly, observing the pauses that are marked with ellipses. Adopt whatever sitting posture suits you best: in a straight-backed chair with your feet flat on the floor, back straight, hands folded in your lap; or cross-legged on a 6-inch hard cushion on the floor, back erect, hands cupped. Your sitting posture should be alert and attentive, not slumped—but not so painful that you are distracted from your meditation by the stiffness in your knees. (For this reason, most Westerners find it easier to meditate sitting in a chair.)

Close your eyes and spend a few moments settling into your sitting posture, feeling in your body the electrical energy that is generated by moving around, being active. . . . Slowly scan your body from your head downward, relaxing into whatever sensations you feel, allowing the tenseness to drain downward, as if it were heavy: relaxing your forehead . . . jaws . . . neck . . . shoulders . . . right upper arm, forearm, wrist, fingers . . . left upper arm, forearm, wrist, fingers. . . . You don't have to hurry . . . take it slow. . . . Relax your abdominal muscles. . . . Let the tension drain downward as if it were a warm stream of water moving through you, through your hips . . . thighs . . . knees . . . ankles . . . toes. All the tension is gone. . . .

And now, just watch your breath for a moment, not trying to breathe in any special way . . . just watch the breath as it flows in and out . . . the inhale, the exhale . . . just watching the breath. . . . No thoughts, nothing to think of . . . just inner silence . . . inner calm. . . .

And now, in the calm quiet of your inner space, recall the birthing that you chose from your list of birthings. . . . Imagine a calendar that goes back many years. Turn through the pages of that calendar until you come to the time of that birthing, to the year, or the month, perhaps even to the day and the moment. . . . In your imagination, re-create the scene of the birthing. Notice the season of the year, the weather, the landscape, the headlines of the time—any detail that might anchor this memory in your mind. . . . In your imagination, as you contemplate this birth, you feel heavy, bulky, pregnant with something new. . . . What is it? What is this new thing that is coming forth out of your body, your heart, your mind? . . . How do you feel just now? Are you anxious? fearful? reluctant? Or are you excited, expectant, hopeful? . . . Is anyone with you to midwife your birthing? If so, who? . . . In what ways is she or he helpful? . . . How does this person feel about this new emergence? . . . Does this birthing affect other people? If so, who? . . . How do they feel? Do they help or hinder this birthing? . . .

Stay with this remembered scene for as long as you like, recalling in as much detail as possible the events, the feelings that surround it. . . .

And now, in your imagination, turn the pages of the calendar forward. Move to a time when what you gave birth to—the idea or the activity or the relationship or the thing or the person—has reached a kind of maturity. This moment may not even have happened yet. It may still be in the future. What is the year? . . . What does the idea or the activity or the relationship or the person you gave birth to look like now? . . . As its creator, its mother, what are your feelings about it? . . . Does it still require your careful attention, or does it have some independence? . . . If you're still anxious about its welfare, what exactly concerns you? . . . If you had a partner in this birthing, how has that person functioned as a co-parent? . . . If this birthing affected other people, how do they feel about it now? . . .

And now, as you sit quietly, imagine that this birthing contains a message for you concerning your own growth and development. . . . What is that message? . . . What significant thing have you learned from this birthing experience? . . . Has this learning changed the direction or the plot of your life story? . . . Does it point the way toward other new births?

When you have received this message and understood it, let it go. Return to your breath, slowly, gently, feeling your breath rise and fall, your weight heavy in your chair or on your cushion. . . . For a moment or two, just feel yourself *in* your body. . . . When you are ready, gently let your eyes open and stretch. Then take a few minutes to write down anything you'd like to add to the first chapter in your story book.

Celebrating the Completion of Chapter One

Congratulations! You've just completed the first chapter of your story book, a record of your births and birthings. To celebrate this good beginning, give yourself a Birth-Day party. This is something you can do alone, or with members of your Story Circle. Here are three ideas for your party.

1. Make or buy a cake with a special greeting: Happy Birth-Day to Me! (Or to "Us," if this is your Story Circle's party.) Be sure the cake has plenty of frosting flowers, lots of tiny silver balls, and a frilly lace doily. Add fresh flowers and ribbon if you like for a very special, celebratory cake!

2. Choose one of your births/birthings for special recognition. Create and decorate a Birth-Day table, and place on it an object that symbolizes this birth. Add a flower, ribbon, a balloon with a message—something that will mark the importance of this birth in your life. If you're celebrating with your Story Circle, each one can tell the story of this birth.

3. Take a picture of your Birth-Day table, and put it at the end of your first chapter. If you've created a communal Birth-Day table with your Story Circle, get copies of the photo for everyone. After all, this could be the beginning of a circle of lifelong friendships!

Chapter Two

Glories, Gifts, and Graces

Well into the twentieth century, it continued to be impossible for women to admit into their autobiographical narratives the claim of achievement, the admission of ambition, the recognition that accomplishment was neither luck nor the result of the efforts or generosity of others.

—*Carolyn Heilbrun*

Glories

As a mystery writer, I am frequently asked to speak to writers' groups, where someone asks the inevitable question: "How did you get your first mystery published?" Until fairly recently, I had a standard answer. "It was a matter of luck," I'd say. "It happened that Susanne Kirk, the mystery editor at Scribner, recognized Pecan Springs, the fictional Texas town that is the setting for the China Bayles books. After reading only a page or two of the manuscript of *Thyme of Death*, she knew that Pecan Springs was really San Marcos, where a member of her family had lived. She kept reading and was hooked. It was a bit of marvelous luck."

That was my story—until I read Carolyn Heilbrun's book *Writing a Woman's Life* and decided that this version didn't quite tell the truth. Yes, it was fortunate that the editor's recognition of the setting pulled her into the manuscript; yes, I am grateful for the synchronicity that brought us together. But Susanne is a deeply committed professional. If *Thyme of Death* hadn't been a strong book, she wouldn't have accepted

Women . . . internalize countless messages: we do not belong in important places; we do not really count; we do not really shape history and culture. And so, when we do achieve recognition, we tend to attribute our success to luck, or if not that, then to something, anything, other than our competent and entitled selves.

—Harriet Goldhor Lerner

it—no matter how much she likes Texas! Before I could get lucky, I had to be skilled, experienced, and disciplined in the art and craft of creating a story. Why should it be so difficult for me to say so?

I'm not the only woman who has a hard time claiming my achievements. In a workshop, I asked writers to describe a recent accomplishment. Here are two responses:

> Last year, I got a really lucky break. My graduate-school professor, Dr. Horner, asked me to coauthor a paper with him on a topic—the economics of gender—that we're both very interestd in. When the research was done and the paper was written, it was submitted under both our names. It was published three months ago, just before I started looking for my first teaching position. Last week, I was offered a job by a university in California, in a city where I've always wanted to live. I can hardly believe my good luck! It would never have happened without Dr. Horner's help.
>
> —Carla P.

> I finally have the home I've wanted my whole life. After a lot of searching, I was finally lucky enough to find the perfect house—a cottage, really, but just right for me—with two acres of meadow and trees. I made the down payment with money I saved from my night job as a waitress (days, I'm a secretary). I put on a new roof, fixed the plumbing, and did some work on the foundation. I even built a small barn and a paddock behind the house, and last week (after months of haunting the livestock auctions) I found the horse I've been searching for, a young filly I've named Lady Luck. I feel so blessed, so fortunate. Sometimes I even worry that my terrific luck won't hold. How could I possibly be worthy of all these good things?
>
> —Karen D.

I'd gone through life believing in the strength and competence of others; never in my own. Now, dazzled, I discovered that my capacities were real. It was like finding a fortune in the lining of an old coat.

—Joan Mills

Can you see the truth that lies behind each of these stories about luck and good fortune? Carla impressed her professor by her outstanding ability as a researcher and writer, and did most of the work (as she later told me) on the paper that bore his name as well as hers. She earned her job because she is qualified and competent, not because she was lucky or had help. And Karen, who feels blessed and fortunate, could also feel proud of her ability to earn the money for her home, manage the repairs, build a barn, and locate Lady Luck. Carla and Karen have taken their lives into their own hands, shaping their futures to fit their dreams. But they, like me, like many women, find it difficult to claim the credit for what they've done. When they write or talk about their successes, they use the passive voice ("When the research *was done* and the paper *was* written"). They attribute their success to luck and somebody else's help.

Even such extraordinary women as social reformer Jane Addams, Margaret Sanger (founder of the American birth control movement), and gifted athlete Babe Didrikson told "good luck" stories. In the introduction to the anthology *Written by Herself: Autobiographies of American Women*, Jill Ker Conway says:

> A close reading of their narratives will show them moving to the passive voice whenever they are really acting decisively (Jane Addams), or taking refuge in the convention of being drawn to act by forces of destiny outside their control (Margaret Sanger). The hard-driving athlete Babe Didrikson—who once won a national track meet serving as a one-woman team competing successfully in every event and who, when she took up golf, practiced her drive till her hands bled—let the reader think she was always led to a new sport or a new dream of excelling by a generous mentor, not by her own restless search for new challenges.

Why are we reluctant to claim our own hard-earned glory?

A big part of the answer, of course, lies buried in our experiences as women in a culture that refused to allow women to tell stories of their achievements in the public domain. Until the last few decades, women were not seen as capable of taking risk, daring greatness, or achieving memorable success. When a woman risked, dared, and achieved, her apparently inexplicable achievement could only be explained as an accident, or the result of some man's indispensable help, or the intervention of the deity. She couldn't possibly have been ambitious and purposeful enough to have done it herself. What else was a woman to do except account for her success in the usual passive way, identifying her accomplishment as the product of good fortune, a man's goodwill, or God's blessing?

But even now, knowing that we are capable of great achievement, we still find ourselves apologetic and modest when it comes to accepting recognition. My friend Margo has an idea about this. "I know we're entitled to the glory we earn," she says, "but it seems so phony. The media

Luck is not chance—
It's Toil—
Fortune's expensive smile
Is earned—.

—Emily Dickinson

Men are taught to apologize
for their weaknesses, women
for their strengths.

—Lois Wyse

dishes out way too much hoopla. Who needs to be one of their hyped-up superstars?" Another friend, Kim, adds, "Overvaluing success and recognition is as much a problem as undervaluing it, don't you think? When someone tells me I'm successful just because I'm a lawyer and make a lot of money, I want to snap back, 'Who says money is the best way to measure success?'" And yet another, Liz, remarks acidly, "I hope I *would* feel like a fraud if I thought a corporate title or a corner office made me a better person than somebody else! Power and glory based on status are cheap."

All things considered, the issue of taking credit is a complicated one, and we have to think carefully about the way we frame our success stories. To my mind, stories about our achievements have three different components, in differing proportions and with differing emphases:

> *our glories*: the achievements and successes that give us a sense of pride and authentic personal empowerment, which are the product of . . .
>> *our gifts*: the aptitudes and attitudes that contribute to our success and the education and training that sharpened and strengthened these gifts—which are enhanced by . . .
>>> *our graces*: the luck of the draw, including the time, place, and circumstances of our birth and upbringing as well as the assistance, happy accidents, and synchronicities that contribute to our success—including the fortuitous oppositions that strengthen our resolve.

If Karen D. were to retell her story by paying attention to the personal qualities that enabled her to create the home she wanted, she might write something like this:

> One thing that's true about me is that I have plenty of determination. I decide what I want and work until I get it. For two years, I saved every penny of my nighttime earnings as a waitress (days, I work in an office). When I had enough for a down payment on a house, I looked until I found a cottage with two acres of meadow and trees—a lucky accident, because somebody else had tried to buy it and got turned down for the loan just the day before I found it. I

Sometimes I worry about being a success in a mediocre world.

—Lily Tomlin

put on a new roof, fixed the plumbing, and repaired the foundation—myself, with the help of some good how-to books from the library! I built a small barn and a paddock behind the house, and last week (after months of haunting the livestock auctions) I found the perfect horse, a filly named Lady Luck. Yes, I feel blessed and fortunate and even awed, but when I look around my place, I also feel proud. Nobody built this place for me. I built it for myself!

In this version of her story, Karen appropriately attributes her glory (the home she has built) to her gifts—the determination and dedication that kept her working toward her goal. She also acknowledges her graces—the accidents that brought her the house and Lady Luck. She claims the credit for her hard work, while recognizing that a certain grace figured in her success.

Beginning Your Success Story

When I'm writing, I love to work with lists. It's hard to start from scratch, to begin with the blank page. So my writing notebooks are full of lists of things I want to write about, lists of words and phrases that intrigue me (especially Texas talk, which tickles my ear), memories, observations, exasperations. As a writer, having lists around is like having a supply of nifty tubes of oils or blobs of clay or pieces of fabric or squares of empty canvas. When I have plenty of lists, I know I'll never run out of things to write about.

Let's start your success story by making a list of the achievements you're proud of—your glories. These could include successes at work, in the community, in your family. It might include getting a college degree, giving birth to or adopting a child, marrying, beginning a new career, learning a skill, taking a trip, winning a contest, making a quilt. Set your timer for four minutes, then make a list of as many glories as you can think of, as far back as you can remember. You don't have to follow any order (although, if it helps, you might start with your first ten years, then the second, the third, and so on). Since nobody else will see this list, you don't have to go into detail; a word or two will be enough. The purpose here is to get down on paper as many glories as possible so you can work with them later.

A woman brought the following list of glories to one of my classes.

Making a list is good. It makes you start noticing material for writing in your daily life, and your writing comes out of a relationship with your life and its texture. In this way, the composting process is beginning. Your body is starting to digest and turn over your material, so even when you are not actually at the desk physically writing, there are parts of you raking, fertilizing, taking in the sun's heat, and making ready for the deep green plants of writing to grow.

—Natalie Goldberg

After she read it, we all felt breathless. "What remarkable achievements!" somebody said. The writer smiled modestly. "Oh, not really," she replied, and we all broke into delighted laughter. The habit of rejecting the applause of others goes along with our difficulty in recognizing our own glories—even if we've raised fifteen thousand silkworms!

> Did spinning, weaving, and dyeing demonstrations and projects in schools all over town.
> Taught people how to weave and spin yarn and dye it using natural dyes.
> Raised fifteen thousand silkworms.
> Was executive director of the Cultural Activities Center.
> President of doctors' wives group at the clinic.
> President of City Federation.
> Founded four civic organizations.
> Raised tons of money to build the Cultural Activities Center, the theater, the railroad museum, the swim center, etc.
> Had an art show on all of my weavings at the CAC.
> Took many workshops with famous people and then brought them here.
> Sang in 13 musical theater productions.
> Tried very hard to be a positive car pool mother, especially when driving adolescents.
> Was one of only two women on the community leadership council, with about 25 men.
> Held positions on numerous boards to pay back the community for being such a good place to raise my children.
>
> *Jeanne L.*

What happens if the ideas seem to dry up after a minute or two and you can't think of anything to write? Maybe you're screening your glories for size and substance. A glory is a glory, regardless of how much applause it gets. (Does any car pool mother get the credit she deserves?) To keep going, jot down any little glory. "Changing the oil in the car," for instance (one of my glories because it's a job I hate). Or "getting the sales report finished two days early" (a glory because you and everybody else expected it to be late). Or "remembering Tony's dental appointment."

Ready to catalogue your glories? Set your timer and go!

When you're done, look over your list. If you missed some important successes, add them now. Or take a break for a few minutes and then try the exercise again. (One thing I like about lists is that they are open-ended. There's always something else that can be added.)

Or perhaps you'd rather experiment with a brainstorming process that I call "seed work." Seed work shows you how one thing leads to another and may remind you of some achievements you left out of your list. Take a piece of unlined paper and in the middle of it, draw a small circle representing a seed. On the seed write one of the glories that appeared on the list. Then draw a stem and branches growing out of the seed. Label these with the achievements, large and small, that grew out of your seed success. Then draw roots that extend from the seed into the earth and label these with the sources of the seed success: the gifts that nurtured and supported the seed and gave it the strength to grow. What about the graces that contributed to your achievement? You can represent them as rain and sunshine.

What you create here—a list of your glories, some seed work—will introduce your chapter.

Only she who attempts the absurd can achieve the impossible.

—Sharon Schuster

Clippings: "You see the lion coming"

Susan Butcher was the first woman to win the Alaskan Iditarod, an annual 1,100-mile dogsled race from Anchorage to Nome. She entered her first race at the age of twenty-one; ten races later, she won, setting a new record for elapsed time. In these paragraphs from her essay in Carolyn Coman's book *Body & Soul*, we can detect the gifts—enthusiasm, resourcefulness, wilderness skills, physical strength—that empowered her:

> Alaska is a place where you are your own person. It doesn't matter who you are related to or who you know. Your base of acceptance is your own ability to excel. . . .
>
> In November [Butcher's second winter after arriving in Alaska], when I was living alone, I mushed over to a friend's cabin about forty miles away to share a ptarmigan for Thanksgiving. I had never been on a forty-mile trip, and it meant I had to mush all my twelve dogs at once to get there, which I'd never done. It was a wonderful trip. It was over a mountain pass to get to my friend's cabin. I got into some bad overflow and got soaked up to my waist. I was way up above the

tree line so there was no way to dry myself off. At dusk I found a shelter cabin, just slats, that slightly broke the wind. There was no wood to burn, so I took off all my wet clothes and brought the sled and all the dogs inside with me. I put four dogs in the sleeping bag with me—what the bush people call a four-dog night—to keep me warm and help me dry out some of the clothes I'd kept on. It was about twenty-five below. In the morning when I got up everything I'd taken off was frozen solid. I had to tear part of the cabin apart and burn that and thaw things out. I couldn't dry my clothes, but I thawed them so I could get back into them. Then I finished the trip. There was no brake to the sled, and from the top of the ridge down was just a really hairy ride. It was great. . . .

Eleanor Holmes Norton has been a civil rights worker in the 1960s, a First Amendment expert for the American Civil Liberties Union, and director of the Equal Employment Opportunity Commission in its difficult early days. She knows what it means to face the lions.

When I was sworn in as chair of the Equal Employment Opportunity Commission in 1977, President Carter didn't say, "I know Eleanor Norton is going to go in there and before we know it the EEOC is going to be in shape." He said—I'll never forget what he said—"If anybody can straighten out the EEOC, Eleanor can."

All right. When someone asks me, did I have any doubts I could change the EEOC, all I can say is that I was expected to. I had done something of the kind at the New York City Human Rights Commission and I had the confidence I could. If you go into as tough a situation as I did then you already have a healthy respect for the beast. You don't go up to a lion and say, "Look, I've dealt with lions before," and then you see the lion coming at you. You go in there, you realize he has sharp teeth, and not everybody who's gone in before has been a fool. . . .

Did I have doubts? . . . I've left out one piece of the mosaic—my grandmother. She lived in the house right in back of us. My grandmother thought I was the smartest child that was ever created. She never said to me, "You are the smartest child in the world," but I knew she thought it because the way she related to me made it clear that she expected great things of me. So in point of fact I believed I should get 100 on every spelling test and that I should be able to answer every question . . . Did I ever have any doubt that I could get the EEOC running effectively? All I could say was that my grandmother expected me to. . . .

You must do the thing you think you cannot do.

—Eleanor Roosevelt

I like the matter-of-fact tone in which both Butcher and Norton describe their challenges. They describe the obstacles so clearly that we *feel* them (I even feel cold when I read Susan Butcher's piece!) and sense the exhilaration of success.

Writing About Your Lions

When you write about your glories, you may be able to see them more clearly if you place them in the context of oppositions. What lions did you have to face? What obstacles did you have to overcome to achieve what you did? (Someday I'm going to ask Jeanne to tell me what it was like to raise fifteen thousand silkworms.)

Here's a writing task that will help you create the first part of your chapter. Choose one of the glories from your list and describe it. As you do, focus both on the obstacles you had to face (the lions!) and on the exhilaration of success. What did you accomplish? What did it cost? How did it feel to conquer the lions and win in the end?

Gifts

Earlier, I defined a gift as an aptitude or an attitude (perhaps enhanced and sharpened by education and training) that contributes to success. In this section of your chapter, you'll write about your gifts.

Choose one of the glories on your list and write a two- or three-page success story about it, focusing on the gifts that empowered your achievement. (Or, if you did the seed work I suggested, you might want to write about that glory and the gifts and graces that made it possible.) The following questions suggest the kind of approach you might take to organizing your story.

> What success am I celebrating here?
> What gifts did I bring to the task that made me successful?
> What kept me going?
> What training or education did it take? What was the personal cost to me?

"There's no use trying," Alice said: *"one can't believe impossible things."*

"I daresay you haven't had much practice," said the Queen. *"When I was your age, I always did it for half-an-hour a day. Why, sometimes I've believed as many as six impossible things before breakfast."*

—Lewis Carroll

*We never know how high we are
Till we are called to rise;
And then, if we are true to plan,
Our statures touch the skies.*

—Emily Dickinson

What obstacles did I have to overcome, both internally and in the
task itself? What kind of opposition did I face?

How did I feel when I realized that I had reached my goal? How
do I feel now?

What earlier acheivements did I build on to create this one? What
later successes grew out of this one?

Clippings: BIG Gifts!

Here are two success stories written by seminar participants, each celebrating a different kind of success:

They said it couldn't be done, but I did it! I just graduated from four
years of college—with three kids, just me, a single parent, nobody
else to fall back on or count on or come home to. I did it because I
had to, because if I didn't, I couldn't believe in myself or ask the kids
to believe in themselves.

What did it take? Well, for starters, it took a lot of faith, because
I couldn't see more than a couple of weeks ahead, not even to the end
of the semester.

It also took a lot of courage, especially in my sophomore year,
when Sammy broke his leg and I had to drop half my courses so I
could stay at the hospital with him.

It took planning, which surprises me now that I think about it, because I didn't think I was much of a planner.

And dedication, because I never, never gave up! I just kept going
to class during the day and studying at night and hanging in there.

In fact, just writing all this makes me see what a huge, important
thing it was for me to go to school and get my degree. I never
thought of myself as having faith in myself, or being courageous, or
able to plan, or being dedicated. These are BIG gifts! And now that
I've got my degree, I know I can use them to do anything I decide to
do, absolutely *anything!*

—Carmen G.

I'm not sure that a lot of people would consider divorce a success,
but it was for me. Telling Joe I wanted a divorce, standing up to him
when he tried to make me change my mind, getting a lawyer and
going through the whole process, figuring out how I was going to pay
my bills and live on just my salary, dealing with the sadness and grief

and loneliness—it was *all* hard, every inch of the way. But somehow, I gathered my courage to confront him with the truth about our marriage, that it had been over for years and we'd been pretending, fooling ourselves. Sticking with my decision took conviction, because he had all kinds of reasons (some of them pretty logical) for why we should stay together. The whole family objected, too—his dad, my mother, the children. And of course there was the money, too. Getting a divorce isn't so expensive, but starting a new life certainly is! It took ingenuity for me to figure out how to do it, and I had to be willing to let a lot of things go—nice furniture, new clothes, another car, a vacation. But now that I've started down this new path by myself, I feel like I've been reborn, or set free from prison. I'm growing wings and learning to fly. Every day I discover something new about myself, and I *love* the woman I am!

—Sylvia J.

Remember the admonition "Count your blessings"? Both Carmen and Sylvia have been counting their gifts. Each one is seeing the truth of her own abilities and feeling pride in that recognition. Each has something important to celebrate: herself, an independent, autonomous being, capable of choosing a goal and finding a way that will take her there, even through lion country.

When you have finished one success story and seen how easy and how much fun it was to write, try another. Let's do this one in a different format: as a newspaper article. Choose one of your glories and write a headline about it. Something like this:

Ginger Rogers did everything Fred Astaire did, but she did it backwards, in high heels.

—Anon.

LOCAL WOMAN EARNS IMPORTANT PROMOTION
"First Female Vice President," Says CEO
or
SALLY SMITH RAFTS DOWN COLORADO
Novice Rafter Successfully Negotiates Challenge

Then, in newspaper-article style, describe your success, being sure to include a recognition of your gifts. For instance, the writer of the second headline might write a paragraph like this:

When asked why her rafting trip was so successful, Sally Smith replied without hesitation. "Cooperation among the team members," she said. "And muscles and a willingness to get my hair wet and

In my early days I was a sepia Hedy Lamarr. Now I'm black and a woman, singing my own way.

—Lena Horne

an ability to fall asleep in a damp sleeping bag on the hard ground. Seriously," she added with a rueful grin, "I worked hard for several months planning my part of this expedition. To me, there's no such thing as instant success. After you've achieved what you set out to do, you realize that it took a long while and a lot of effort to put it all together."

Group triumphs like Sally's are as important as solo successes, because they teach us what we can do when we face the lions together. To round out this section, write at least one newspaper-style piece about something you've accomplished by yourself, and a success that you achieved as a member of a group. Do you feel different about the team achievement? Why?

Several of these article-style pieces, illustrated with photographs, drawings, or mementos of your achievement, would make important contributions to your chapter. Or perhaps you have newspaper clippings that could be included here—actual newsletter, newspaper, or magazine stories that have been written about your successes in the community, on the job, or at home. Include as much of this material as you can.

Graces

Earlier, I defined "graces" in the following way:

> our graces: the luck of the draw, including the time, place, and circumstances of our birth and upbringing as well as the assistance, happy accidents, and synchronicities that contribute to our success—including the fortuitous oppositions that strengthen our resolve.

The heavens give of their abundance. Rejoice in riches.
—"Possession in Great Measure," Hexagram 14, *The I Ching*

Not all of our successes can be explained by our competence or our commitment. When you stop to reflect on the events of your life, you may see how grace-full and grace-inspired they really are. Here are two paragraphs that Carmen wrote, exploring the question "How did grace shape your success?"

> Grace? Isn't that something spiritual? But I know I couldn't have earned my degree if things hadn't worked right. For one thing, all the

while I was in school, none of the kids got seriously sick (except for Sammy's broken leg). For another, I could count on Mom to keep the kids evenings when I had evening classes. Mom lives just about two blocks from the campus. Also, she encouraged me, and kept me believing in myself. If it hadn't been for her, I would have given up lots of times. Maybe if I'd had a different mom, I couldn't have done this!

And getting student housing the first year was pretty lucky, too, come to think of it, because that was how I met Alison, and without her I never would've gotten through calculus! And maybe calculus was a grace, too, although I hate to admit it. I hated every minute of it; it kept me from doing lots of other things I wanted to do. But nobody could have been prouder when I got an A! I'm a little surprised when I think how much I have to be grateful for—even calculus.

In my own life, I have received more graces than I can count. Yes, I have a good mind, a strong sense of curiosity, and a belief in the possible I. But looked at in a different light, these gifts are also graces. My intellect is part of the genetic package I inherited from generations of unknown ancestors. My curiosity was encouraged by my parents, who never tired of answering my questions, or of taking me to the library. My optimistic belief in an open-ended self arises in part because I was born into a century when education is available and affordable for women as well as men, and into a culture that believes that the freedom of self-definition is an inalienable right. How much would I have been able to achieve if I had been born into another time and place?

Like Carmen, I am often surprised when I think to count my graces, for the more I count, the more there seem to be. And if pride in my accomplishments is the emotion that I naturally feel when I focus on my gifts, gratitude is the emotion I feel as I become aware of the many graces that have shaped me *and* my gifts.

I was reminded of this truth just yesterday when I received a card from my daughter, who had just received a hard-earned promotion. On the front was a cartoon drawing of a woman climber planting a flag on a snowy peak with one hand, and with the other, pulling up another climber. At the top was the line "Behind Every Great Woman . . ." Inside, the line continued " . . . Is Another Great Woman." The two smiling women were sitting side by side on the peak, and on the flag were the words "Thanks, Mom." Two strong women, each one first at the top of her own mountain, each firmly behind the other, each aware of how

Trammeled as woman might have been by might and custom, there are still many shining examples, which serve as beacon lights to show what might be attained by genius, labor, energy, and perseverance combined.

—Matilda Joslyn Gage, 1852

The women of today are the thoughts of their mothers and grandmothers, embodied, and made alive. They are active, capable, determined and bound to win . . . Millions of women, dead and gone, are speaking through us today.

—Matilda Joslyn Gage, 1880

much the other has contributed to her success. What a grace to be granted such helpers!

As our hearts open to an awareness of our graces, we are filled with joy. Such a generous universe this is, so profligate with possibilities, so extravagant with potentials—and all of them free, gifts without strings, for which we can only say thanks!

And as we see how we have grown, like green plants, out of the good earth of our time and our culture, we recognize something else in ourselves: our *interdependence.* Yes, we are independent, autonomous beings, able to create our own successes. But yes! we are interdependent beings, shaped by the contexts into which we are born. Our successes are built upon the achievements of others, on their compassion, their generosity, their competencies, *their* gifts. We are woven together, shining strands in a multistranded braid. Your glories, mine, ours—how can we tell the difference? Behind all great women—are all great women!

And what of your particular graces?

When you look at your glories and the gifts that empowered you to achieve them, can you see grace threaded through like a golden thread?

So, for this section of your chapter, write about your graces. You could do this as a multipage narrative, or as one or more short anecdotes, telling about the lucky chance that enabled you to achieve a particular success. Or you could do it in a letter—always a good way to include material in your book—to someone who helped you achieve. And as you write, let yourself feel grateful. Gratitude is the richest, most joyful feeling humans are privileged to experience.

Failures and Other Fine Fiascoes

"There is not a fiercer hell than failure," the poet John Keats wrote. Indeed, failure is difficult. It is not an experience that we happily invite into our lives. But failure is far more universal than success. There is not one of us who has not lived through numerous failures, some minor, some major.

The value of a failure lies in what we do with it. If we deny it or diminish it, we can't learn from it. When I fail, I have to face it squarely, ask myself why I failed—and be willing to learn from the answer. Then I can take another try. This time, having had a dry run at it, my chances for success are much greater. From this perspective, failure is a necessary step toward achievement—a grace, in other words. In fact, it's a rare glory that isn't graced with at least one failure!

To test this out for yourself, choose one of the successes from your list. Think back over the processes that led to it: all the things you did, the things that happened, the things that didn't happen the way they were supposed to. For your chapter, write a page or two describing the failures and other fiascoes that led to your ultimate success. What did you learn? How did your learning shape your success? Would your achievement have been different if it hadn't been for that early failure?

Mama exhorted her children at every opportunity to "jump at de sun." We might not land on the sun, but at least we would get off the ground.

—Zora Neale Hurston

Clippings: Failure

In her mid-twenties, Sara Ruddick experienced what she called a "work paralysis." But as she shows in the following excerpt, her experience led her to ask how many other women had faced the same problem. Her question led to the book, *Working It Out: 23 Women Writers, Artists, Scientists, and Scholars Talk about Their Lives and Work.*

> I was twenty-six years old, and had completed four years of graduate school, when I followed my husband to his job, intending to write a dissertation. I had no children. My husband was interested in my work and supportive of any time or effort it took. He and I easily shared the few jobs involved in maintaining ourselves in our small apartment. In short, I had no excuse for a work paralysis so complete that for some months I was unable to read or talk about anything relating to my thesis, let alone to write about it. Although I recovered in some months from the worst of this paralysis and eventually wrote the thesis, I suffered for many years afterwards from serious inhibitions, halfheartedness, and vacillation in my work—the legacy, in a milder form, of paralysis . . .
>
> [Several years later] the isolation and paralysis of the thesis years returned to haunt my night thoughts. . . . I looked for books about work, work problems, the meaning of work. I was disappointed. . . . Despairing of books, I turned to people, to friends whose work—writing, teaching, thinking, making—resembled mine. I found that many people had been puzzled about their work, or, for a time, unable to work. We began to talk and out of that talk this book was born.

Success and failure are both greatly overrated. But failure gives you a whole lot more to talk about.

—Hildegard Knef

If it is important to share our success stories, it is much more important to share our stories about failure. When we tell one another how we have failed and discover that our experiences are similar, we may learn that our lack of success stems not from something within each of us alone, but from something that includes all of us together: from our shared history as women, from our culture, from our hopes and dreams.

Or perhaps we learn that what our culture defines as failure isn't really failure, but something else altogether. That was the lesson I learned when I examined my reasons for abandoning my successful academic career—an abandonment that my professional friends (female as well as male) viewed as a failure. But when I began to talk with other successful women who had left careers, I discovered that we had only redefined our ideas of achievement, building new and more creative ideas of what it means to be a successful woman. From our common understanding of the challenges of work grew the book *Work of Her Own:* a joint testimony to the importance of sharing our failures!

This is why I ask you to include your setbacks among your success stories. If we disavow our failures, we are not fully exploring all of our experience. If we acknowledge where we have fallen short as well as where we have succeeded, we will be able to respect and admire ourselves for what we aim to do as well as what we achieve.

Putting Your Second Chapter Together

So far, you've created a list (and perhaps a seed drawing) of your achievements. You've written one or more success stories, focusing on what you did and the gifts that empowered you to achieve. You've written about the help, the good fortune, or the accidents—the graces—that enabled you to use your gifts to the best advantage. And you've written about your failures and their contribution to your later successes. If you've done all the exercises suggested here, you should have a substantial body of material for your second chapter.

If you'd like to expand your chapter even further, here are some additional strategies to consider.

1. Create a "personal achievement history." Choose a glory from each of the periods of your life: childhood, adolescence, young adulthood, the middle years, the later years. How did your glories grow? What different gifts did you rely on during these different periods? What graces supported your successes? Did these change as you grew older?

2. Write about a success from each of four major areas of your life. Choose a glory from your work life, your family and personal life, your creative life, your recreative life. What different gifts have you developed in each of these areas? Do your gifts ever create conflicts between different areas of your life? In which area have you celebrated the most glories? What does that suggest about the focus of your energies? How do you feel about the distribution of glories?

3. Write about different kinds of achievements. Choose a success that seems to have come more through grace than through your gifts. Compare it to an achievement that you feel you created mostly by yourself. How are they different? Do you feel differently about them? What have you learned from each of these successes?

4. Find a success story written by a woman you particularly admire (check Appendix Three for some possible readings) and study it thoughtfully. Does the writer identify any specific gifts as important to her success? Reading between the lines, what gifts can you identify? Which of her gifts seems particularly important to her achievements? What special graces did she receive? How did this combination of gifts and graces shape her achievement? Why is this woman's story so appealing to you? Write a page in response to these questions and add it to your chapter. (You might repeat this exercise with several of your heroes.)

5. Write an introduction and/or a conclusion to your chapter, putting your achievements into the perspective of your family, your community, or your culture. Have you been particularly graced by family or fortune or good timing? Or has life challenged you to overcome many obstacles? What do these larger frameworks enable you to see about the successes you have achieved?

I have fought hard for everything I've gotten, and I'm proud of what I have done. Yes, I am a woman, and yes it is a victory for me to win the Iditarod, *but it* isn't *amazing—I did it because I am capable, and women are capable.*

—Susan Butcher

Meditation

Gifts, Graces, and Glories

Close your eyes and spend a few moments settling into your sitting posture, feeling in your body the electrical energy that is generated by moving around, being active . . . Slowly scan your body from your head downward, relaxing into whatever sensations you feel, allowing the tenseness to drain downward, as if it were a stream of warm water moving through you: relaxing your forehead . . . jaws . . . neck . . . shoulders . . . right upper arm, forearm, wrist, fingers . . . left upper arm, forearm, wrist, fingers. . . . You don't have to hurry . . . take it slow. . . . Relax your abdominal muscles. . . . Let the tension drain downward like warm water . . . hips . . . thighs . . . knees . . . ankles . . . toes. All the tension is gone. . . .

And now, just pay attention to your breath for a moment, not trying to breathe in a special way . . . just watch the breath as it flows in and out . . . the inhale, the exhale . . . just watching the breath. . . . No thoughts, nothing to think of . . . just inner silence . . . inner calm. . . .

And now, in the calm, dark quiet of your inner space, imagine a movie screen. You are about to see two short films. Take whatever comes onto the screen without attempting to change it.

The film is called *My Glory Story*—there it is, the title on the screen. And there *you* are, filling the whole picture. You have just achieved something important—one of the glories of your life. What are you doing? . . . What is your age? . . . What are your circumstances? . . . What is the nature of this success? . . . Now the film moves to a flashback, earlier in time. The camera zooms in. It's you again, working toward your success . . . What are you doing? . . . What gifts are you bringing to your task? What skills and competencies are you practicing in this picture? . . . And now the camera zooms out, showing a much larger picture, showing not just the gifts but the graces . . . What kind of support makes your success possible? What kind of accidents and synchronicities helped you to create your glory? . . . What do you know now about your gifts and graces that you wish you had known then? . . . What do you know now about your achievement that you wish you had known then?

The screen goes white, and now the second film begins. This one is called *My Next Glory Story*—there it is, the title on the screen. And there *you* are, filling the whole picture, doing something you have always wanted to do but have not yet achieved in your real life. What is it? . . . How far in the future is this scene taking place? . . . What is your age? . . . What are your circumstances? . . . What is the nature of this success? . . . Now the scene changes to a flashback. The camera zooms in for a close-up. It's you again, working toward this new success. . . . What are you doing? . . . What gifts are you bringing to your task? . . . And now the camera zooms out, showing a much larger picture, showing not just the gifts but the graces. . . . What kind of support makes your success possible? . . .

And now your achievement appears again on the screen. . . . Take a moment to bask in the glory of your success . . . feel the pride that you're entitled to feel for having used your gifts wisely . . . feel the gratitude swell up in your heart for all the graces that made your success possible. . . . Sit quietly for a moment, giving thanks to the people who helped . . . being grateful to the universe, to God, to the sacred . . . just saying thanks.

And now, as you sit quietly, review the two films in your imagination, watching yourself. Was there something that you learned from your earlier achievement that may help you with the later one—the one that is yet to come? . . . If so, what is it? . . . Does this learning change the direction or the plot of your success story? Does it point the way toward other new achievements?

When you have received this learning and understood it, let it go and return to your breath, slowly, gently, feeling your breath rise and fall, your weight heavy in your chair or on your cushion. For a moment or two, just feel yourself *in* your body. When you are ready, gently let your eyes open, and stretch. Then take a few minutes to write down anything you'd like to add to the second chapter in your story book.

Celebrating the Completion of Chapter Two

Congratulations! You have successfully finished the second chapter of your story. (Isn't that a success all by itself?) Here are four things you might do to celebrate.

1. Take your chapter to a meeting of your Story Circle and share one or two of your success stories with the others. Bask in their admiration and in the good feeling that comes with completing a difficult task. Lis-

ten to their success stories. Compare notes about the kinds of gifts and graces that participants seem to share. Which are unique? Are there any special graces?

2. Create a ritual to celebrate the successful completion of your chapter. Choose an object that symbolizes your most significant success, one that symbolizes your greatest gift, a third that symbolizes your most amazing grace, and a fourth that symbolizes your most rewarding failure. Place them on a small altar where you will be able to see them every day (a table, a windowsill, your desk at work). Choose a quiet moment, light a candle, and as it burns, read one or two of your success stories aloud—or your entire chapter, if you feel like it.

3. Find a way to express your gratitude for your graces. Send someone a card (like the one my daughter sent to me) or flowers or a small gift. Create a gratitude ritual: make an altar, say a prayer, plant a special flower in your garden. Become a grace giver for someone else: become a Big Sister, participate in the Coats for Kids drive, volunteer at the local nursing home. Share your gifts—gracefully.

4. Give yourself a special gift that will remind you that you have successfully completed this much of your book—a small piece of jewelry, a picture, a new book. When you wear it or carry it or use it or look at it, remember that you are a gifted and graced person with a life full of glories!

Chapter Three

Body Language

Like the Rosetta stone, for those who know how to read it, the body is a living record of life given, life taken, life hoped for, life healed. . . . The body remembers, the bones remember, the joints remember, even the little finger remembers. Memory is lodged in pictures and feelings in the cells themselves. Like a sponge filled with water, anywhere the flesh is pressed, wrung, even touched lightly, a memory may flow out in a stream.

—Clarissa Pinkola Estés

Mirror, Mirror on the Wall

Our lives are written in our bodies. Our bodies themselves are stories of our deepest, most meaningful experiences, often the most painful ones, told in the language of flesh and bone, of blood and sinew. My mature body is a story written in many chapters, inscribed in cell and tissue: the brief paragraphs of my childhood body, the longer chapters of the body that planted gardens and worked at a desk and bore children, the present chapter of my postmenopausal body, aging, growing old. It is a story of my body strong and fit, my body in weakness and illness, my body the sacred temple, the instrument and agent and house of my soul.

To tell my soul's true story I must also tell the true story of my body. My body, not anyone else's. But the story of my body can only be completely understood in the context of stories of other women's bodies, and in the history of women's bodies in Western society. That history

Soul-making is allowing the eternal essence to enter and experience the outer world through all the orifices of the body—seeing, smelling, hearing, tasting, touching— so that the soul grows during its time on Earth. . . . Soul-making is constantly confronting the paradox that an eternal being is dwelling in a temporal body.

—Marion Woodman

The basic Female Body comes
with the following accessories:
garter belt, panty girdle,
crinoline, camisole, bustle,
brassiere, stomacher, chemise,
virgin zone, spike heels, nose
ring, veil, kid gloves, fishnet
stockings, fichu, bandeau,
Merry Widow, weepers, chok-
ers, barrettes, bangles, beads,
lorgnette, feather boa, basic
black, compact, Lycra stretch
one-piece with modesty panel,
designer peignoir, flannel
nightie, lace teddy, bed, head.

—Margaret Atwood

Victorian women actually
died in the cause of fashion. It
was not only a matter of the
corset crushing the body while
being worn; the internal or-
gans were forced permanently
out of position. The lower
ribs, too, grew quite out of
place and stuck into the lungs.

—Alison Gernsheim

is a sad account of use and abuse and exploitation. But I must hear it before I can be free of it, before I can tell my *own* body's story.

In our culture, we are simultaneously preoccupied with the image and appearance of our woman's body and out of touch with its flesh-and-blood reality. Growing up in the 1950s, my friends and I spent a great deal of time comparing our appearance to that of the most popular females around us: Hollywood stars, school cheerleaders, the most popular girls in our class. As best we could, we mimicked the images we saw on the screen and in the magazines. We copied makeup, clothes, and body-shaping undergarments, hair, posture, gestures, facial expressions. Young as we were, we were already crippled by our culture's message that our natural female figures and faces were not good enough: they had to be redecorated, reshaped, and reconfigured before they could earn approval. Although we weren't fully conscious of what we were doing or why, we did know that we were playing in a high-stakes game, and that a great deal hung on our ability to make ourselves attractive. In an era when marriage was the chief goal of a woman's life, an unattractive woman with an unattractive body could be a big loser.

In the last few decades, we've come a long way toward understanding the effects of these cultural messages. Important books, such as *Our Bodies, Ourselves,* have shown us some home truths about our bodies. Courses in women's history, now regularly taught at many colleges and universities, have helped us to understand how our bodies, and our feelings about our bodies, have been shaped by changing cultural demands in *all* societies. The growing recognition of women athletes and the trend toward fitness are showing us the potential of our bodies. And we have embraced the idea that marriage is not the only goal, or even the chief goal, of a woman's life.

But we are still preoccupied with appearance. Many of us consult our mirrors dozens of times a day, comparing ourselves to media images of the female body beautiful. The mirror says we're too fat, so we yo-yo from one diet to another. Our breasts are too big, so we reduce them, or not big enough, so we augment them. Our thighs are like pillows, our bellies sag, our skin is coarse—and as we grow older, these painful perceptions are compounded by the mirror's revelation that our thighs, belly, and skin are inevitably, inexorably *aging*. And since the ideal female body in our culture is a *young* body, we spend billions of dollars a year attempting to turn back the biological clock, slow the aging process, and present a more youthful image.

There is another, even sadder reason why so many women are so profoundly unhappy with their bodies. Sometime in their lives—as children, teens, adults—at least one out of four of us (more, according to some researchers) experienced the trauma of physical abuse. Violence against women's bodies is an ugly part of our society, a fact of life that has long been ignored. It is part of the story, our story.

One sad result of this physical pain is disassociation from the physical body. It is hard to stay in touch with the source of suffering. But beauty creates the very same disassociation, in the very same way. When a woman bends every effort toward making her body the perfect, perfectly beautiful body her culture says it "ought" to be, she cannot feel comfortable with her body as it *is*. She loses touch with her physical being-ness. She is severed from her sensual self. She isn't able to savor the sheer *pleasure* of spending this life in the body.

To be a whole, conscious being, to enjoy her physical body to the fullest extent, a woman must free herself both from the trauma of abuse and from the sticky cobweb of cultural rules about what is and isn't beautiful. This is not an easy task. It can only begin if she listens to the language of her body, if she tells the true story of her real body.

In this chapter of your book, you will consider your body and your mental images of it. You will construct the history of your physical body, starting with your childhood body, moving to adolescence and young womanhood, and to whatever body-time you are experiencing now. The work of healing your body images is truly a journey: a journey under your skin, into your bones, and deep into body-mind. It may be one of the most important journeys you will ever take, for in your body—in its gestures, its movements, its energy—you can see the shape of your soul.

This is your expressive body, dense with dreams, hopes, fears, longings.

This is the body you are.

My desire is to save women from nature.

—Christian Dior

To write "my body" plunges me into lived experience, particularity. I see scars, disfigurements, discolorations, damages, losses, as well as what pleases me.

—Adrienne Rich

Did you know, in the entire universe, we are the only intelligent life forms thought to have a Miss Universe contest?

—Lily Tomlin

Child's Body

Open your chapter by recalling the childhood lessons you learned about your body. Here are three writing tasks that may prod your memory. You may choose one of them now and save the others until a later time when you want to expand your chapter, or you may do all of them now.

1. Start with the first line: *"My earliest awareness of having a body was—"*. What did your body feel like? What did it look like? How heavy was it? How did it move? Were the physical sensations pleasurable or painful? How did this early awareness shape your later perceptions of your body? Set the timer or turn on your favorite piece of music and write on this subject for five or six minutes, not allowing yourself to stop, putting down on the page everything that comes into your mind. (If the writing gives you pain, breathe evenly and deeply and let the pain flow through you and out through your pen. Write *with* your pain, not against it, letting your writing carry the pain out of your body, onto the page.)

2. What body messages did you get from your family? What words did your parents use for the genitals? What did they teach you about keeping your body clean? What kind of restrictions did they place on your intimate play with other children? Were there any body taboos in your family? Write a page or two of recollections about your family's attitude toward bodies, including any anecdotes you remember. If you like, illustrate your writing with drawings, cartoons, or pictures clipped from magazines.

3. Can you recall any childhood experiences that affected your body? The experience may have actually changed your physical body in some way, either positively or negatively, or it may have changed your perception of your body. How did that long-ago experience shape your present perception of your body? Has another, later experience caused you to reimagine yourself? Write a page or two about your experience, illustrated with any photos you may have of yourself at the time the change occurred.

Clippings: Learning to Be Invisible

Many of us learned to respond to our bodies in the company of our brothers and sisters. This passage records an all-too-familiar family event:

My twin brother and I sit in six inches of tepid water in the deep porcelain tub. We are four. Grandma hands me a washcloth and instructs me to wash my "not-nice." This is what she calls my genitals. My brother, always delighted to seize on some small difference between us, tells Grandma that he will wash his "nice-nice." To my great embarrassment, this story is repeated with appreciative chuckles around the family dinner table. For years, even after I learn other words to name that part of myself, I am convinced that my "not-nice" is some sort of a deficit version of my twin's "nice-nice."

—Mildred W.

This writer recounts the anguish of living in a violated body that no longer seems to belong to her:

My earliest memories of being in my body are excruciatingly painful. When I was five, I was sexually abused by a family friend. The shame, the fear, the physical pain—it encompassed me. It filled up my whole body until there was nothing left of me. The only way I could escape was to be somewhere else in my mind when it was going on—"clicking off," I called it. The episodes ended when he moved away, but I had mastered the art of clicking off. Or it had mastered me. Later, when I started having sex, there I was, clicking off even when I wanted to be turned on. It was as if my head were stuck onto a body that belonged to somebody else.

—Rachel K.

In *A Latin Deli*, novelist and poet Judith Ortiz Cofer recalls a childhood disease that altered her physical appearance and changed the way she felt about herself:

I started out life as a pretty baby and learned to be a pretty girl from a pretty mother. Then at ten years of age I suffered one of the worst cases of chicken pox I have ever heard of. My entire body, including the inside of my ears and in between my toes, was covered with pustules that, in a fit of panic at my appearance, I scratched off of my face, leaving permanent scars. A cruel school nurse told me I would always have them—tiny cuts that looked as if a mad cat had plunged its claws deep into my skin. I grew my hair long and hid behind it for the first years of my adolescence. This was when I learned to be invisible.

If you care for a son, you don't go easy on his studies; if you care for a daughter, you don't go easy on her footbindings.

—Chinese proverb

Lucy Grealy's face was dramatically deformed in childhood, when cancer cost her a section of her jaw. It was five years before she could begin reconstructive surgery. In *Autobiography of a Face*, she writes:

> Halloween came round again, and . . . I put on a plastic witch mask and went out with Teresa. I walked down the streets suddenly bold and free: no one could see my face. I peered through the oval eye slits and did not see one person staring back at me, ready to make fun of my face. I breathed in the condensing, plastic-tainted air behind the mask and thought that I was breathing in normalcy, that this freedom and ease were what the world consisted of, that other people felt it all the time. How could they not? How could they not feel the joy of walking down the street without the threat of being made fun of? Assuming this was how other people felt all the time, I again named my own face as the thing that kept me apart, as the tangible element of what was wrong with my life and me.

Those of us who have been brought up in a patriarchal world tend to stay in our heads. . . . We try to push all the parts of ourselves that we don't like into our bodies: our greed, our jealousy, our lust. All the darkness we don't want to accept, we push down into our muscles, bones, and heart.

—Marion Woodman

Each of these writers is dealing, in a very particular, detailed way, with what made her body different from other bodies. Look back over the passages and see how these writers describe their physical differences. How about you? Was there anything about your childhood body that you felt was different from the norm, or from others' expectations? How did you feel about that difference? Becoming "invisible," dissociating from that part of us that is different or feels ugly, may be one strategy for dealing with it. If that was true for you, write about it.

Adolescent Body

Unlike traditional societies, where the passage from girlhood to young womanhood is marked by ritual, our culture ignores the first menstruation. Some mothers and daughters today are inventing their own rituals to mark this memorable occasion. But most women can honor it only in memory, recalling the pride (and the pain or the embarrassment) of their early menstrual periods, the awkwardness of physical movements they had not yet learned to coordinate, the fascination and terror of the unexplored sexual selves they were becoming. Here are two questions to help you explore this time.

1. Can you recall your first menstruation? Write down whatever you can remember of the circumstances—where you were, the time of year, the smells, the clothing you were wearing, the responses of other people. How did you feel, physically and emotionally? What seemed changed after that?

2. What was your first experience of orgasm? Were you alone, or with a partner? Write down whatever you can recall of the event. What were your physical feelings? What was your emotional response? What seemed changed after that?

Clippings: The Mess and the Mystery

When Karen S. read her writing in a seminar, there was an immediate "ah" of recognition. Does her experience match yours? (You might want to look back to page 29 and reread Nancy Mairs's paragraphs on the same subject.)

> From the time I was ten, I waited impatiently for my periods to start. Over and over, I would read the little booklet called "Becoming a Woman," and fondle every item in the special box I had hidden in my closet. I was convinced I'd started every time I sweated enough to get my panties wet. I examined and reexamined my underwear for the first signs of blood, not quite knowing what I was looking for. Would it be red? Would it spurt? Would it be hot? Would it hurt? How long would it go on? I asked my mother these questions, but they embarrassed her. I learned the answers secondhand, as my friends got their periods and told me how it was. When I finally started, a whole year after my best friend, I casually announced to my mother, "Oh, by the way, I got my period today." "Be sure to wash," she said, not looking up from the potatoes she was peeling. And that was it.
>
> —Karen S.

In a collection called *Lesbian Nuns: Breaking Silence,* ex-nun Kevyn Lutton writes about her first experience of masturbation, which was darkened by her Catholic teachings about sexuality:

> I was twelve . . . It was a hot summer day and there was nobody in the house, which was rare. I had just taken a bath and was standing naked

in front of the mirror. I started feeling myself and got totally aroused and had my first orgasm. Then I was overwhelmed with the realization: "This is IT—the ultimate sin! Now I have to go to confession before I do anything else because if I die I'll burn in hell for all eternity." That confession was a nightmare. There was this long line of people down the aisle of the church waiting to be forgiven. It was hotter than hell, but every time my turn came to enter the confessional, my courage failed and I went to the back of the line. I stayed in that stuffy church for three hours. I was so ashamed.

In an article called "Sacred Blood" in the magazine *Woman of Power,* Merida Wexler writes about her feelings about menstruation. It is not until she fully understood the importance of menstruation, she tells her reader, that she understood what it meant to be a woman:

Many years ago, I began to wonder about the overwhelmingly negative response to something so integral to women's lives. What would it be like if I gave positive attention to my periods? Could I transform the experience? Might it be a blessing rather than a "curse"?

As I focused my attention I came to regret the waste of my blood. "Please dispose of properly" reads the sign in every public women's room. I began to save my blood and return it to the earth. Alone at night, I poured it on the roots of cherished trees or fed it to houseplants. Conflicting feelings overwhelmed me. I felt a connection with something ancient and sacred, but it was also weird, distasteful. Later, when I learned the word "taboo" originally meant "menstrual blood," I was not surprised.

Slowly I began to decipher the taboos which imprison menstruation. It was like breaking a code, a sort of mirror writing. I took what I read—in anthropology, religion, magazine ads—and held it in front of a mirror. Then, in the way of mirror writing, what was backwards and incomprehensible became clear in reflection. The taboos isolating and controlling the menstruating woman reveal an awareness of her unique power. Under the repression lives the memory of the goddess She-Who-Bleeds-Yet-Does-Not-Die.

In the mirror I began to decipher myself as well. I saw it was time for me to heal this "wise wound" . . . I know it is our wholeness which is our holiness. A holy wholeness which includes the mess and mystery of menstruation.

Different families, different ethnic groups, different religions respond differently to the "mess and mystery" of the female body. What were the responses of your family, your ethnic group, your religion? How did those responses shape your perception of your body?

Mature Body

Our mature, fully female bodies are a source of great delight. We work with them, play with them, birth with them, find pleasure through them. When we have freed ourselves from our culture's prescription for beauty, we can take real joy in our bodies, whatever their shape and size. But to do this, we need to use the wisdom of our bodies. We need to listen to them, pay attention to them. The wisdom of the body is old wisdom, learned through aeons of evolution. To discard this precious knowledge, to fail to heed it, is to reject part of our human inheritance, to be less than we might be.

In caring for my body, I like to follow the suggestion that Thomas Moore offers in his book *Care of the Soul.* He reminds me that it is important to *imagine* my body, as well as to use it wisely, rest it, exercise it, and make sure it gets a healthy diet. Each part of the body has its own private life, he suggests, its own personality. The various parts of my body not only work for me, they also take pleasure in what they do. "I can imagine interviewing my kidneys," Moore says with a quiet chuckle. "Are you relaxed? Are you enjoying your activity today? Or am I doing something that is making you depressed?" In this way, he suggests, we can tap the ancient knowledge of the body and allow it to shape our lives.

In this part of your chapter, I invite you to celebrate the wisdom of your female body by talking with it, first with one part, then another, and recording the conversation on paper. To do this writing, first sit quietly for a moment and allow your mind to move into the part of your body that you want to talk with. Feel all the sensations in that body part—your hands, or your breasts, or your womb, or your feet. Feel the energy of that part, feel the blood moving through it, the nerves tingling, the whole part alive with feeling. Then imagine this body part speaking for itself, describing its private life. Here are some questions that you might ask.

In so many ways I do not know my body, my incarnation, my being clothed in flesh, my dwelling. Being present to my body, to the workings of my corpus requires a shift from a ho-hum-so-what to an amazement and wonder. It requires dwelling-thinking.

—Dianne Connelly

I dote on myself . . . there is that lot of me, and all so luscious.

—Walt Whitman

A Conversation with My Hands

What are my hands proudest of doing? What would they most like to do? What do they most enjoy making? What do they love to touch? What do they love to wear? What gives them pleasure? If my hands were a person, who would they be? What name would my hands like to be called?

The sensual is a reality in itself.

—Susan Griffin

A Conversation with My Breasts

What is the most wonderful experience my breasts have ever had? How do my breasts like to be touched? What do they love to wear? What do they fear? If my breasts were to give forth a marvelous liquid, what would it taste like? If that liquid had the ability to impart a quality of character (such as courage, love, fierceness, strength) what would it be? What name would my breasts like to be called?

A Conversation with My Uterus

What is the most intense experience my uterus has ever had? How does it feel about being out of sight? When it calls attention to itself (during my periods or when I am pregnant), how does it feel? If my uterus were a building, what building would it be? If the interior of my uterus were a room, how would it be decorated? What name would my uterus like to be called?

Inside its elaborate packaging, my body is stiff, sulky, wary. When I'm with my peers, who come by crinolines, lipstick, cars, and self-confidence naturally, my gestures show that I'm here provisionally, by their grace, that I don't rightfully belong. My shoulders stoop, I nod frantically . . . I smile sweetly . . . and my chest recedes inward so that I don't take up too much space.

—Eva Hoffman

A Conversation with My Feet

Where have my feet gone that they remember most vividly? If my feet could take a vacation, where would they most like to go? What sensual experience do my feet most enjoy? What do they most enjoy wearing? What makes them feel tired? What gives them new energy? What do I do (or wear) that hurts them? If my feet were an animal, what animal would they be? What name would they like to be called?

Clippings: No Body, No Voice

The sexual experience Christine Downing describes in her book *Women's Mysteries* occurred when she was an adult. It offers a glimpse into the experience of full sexuality that we are not often allowed:

> My own first experience of intercourse has long since almost faded from memory; it was really a hardly noticeable event in a continuum of events from heavy petting to an ability to fully enjoy, initiate, ex-

periment sexually. But I vividly remember a fantasy of first inter-course, a fantasy that accompanied lovemaking with a familiar and beloved partner, a fantasy which took hold of both of us though nei-ther of us felt we were creating it. As we made love that long, lazy af-ternoon, it seemed to both of us that we were First Man and First Woman engaged in a delightful and also momentously important discovery. This was not my or our first intercourse, but *the* first inter-course. And still today when I think of sexual awakening, I think of that event which occurred when I was in my early forties, not of the one more than twenty years earlier.

Not all of our experiences of our mature body are joyful ones. In *Carnal Acts*, Nancy Mairs writes about the devastating effects of multi-ple sclerosis, which intruded into her life at the height of her physical beauty and strength:

> I cope with my disability . . . by speaking about it, and about the whole experience of being a body, specifically a female body, out loud, in a clear, level tone that drowns out the frantic whispers of my mother, my grandmothers, all the other trainers of wayward childish tongues: "Sssh! Sssh! Nice girls don't talk like that. Don't mention sweat. Don't mention menstrual blood. . . . Don't tell."
>   No one is going to take my breath away. No one is going to leave me speechless. To be silent is to comply with the standard of femi-nine grace. But my crippled body already violates all notions of fem-inine grace. What more have I got to lose? I've gone beyond shame. I'm shameless, you might say . . .
>   I've found my voice. . . . I speak as a crippled woman. At the same time in the utterance I redeem both "cripple" and "woman" from the shameful silences by which I have often felt surrounded, contained, set apart; I give myself permission to live openly among others, to reach out for them, strike them with fingers and sighs. No body, no voice; no voice, no body. That's what I know in my bones.

Mairs is writing honestly and openly about her disability—but more than that, she is writing about having a female body, which (we have been taught) is also a disability. Unless we acknowledge our female bodies, well and ill, unless we give voice to our bodies, we ourselves are voiceless. But notice Mairs's tone: not a complaint, but a "clear, level tone" aimed to outspeak those who advised silence. When you write your body's story, use a "clear, level tone" to free it and yourself from

I was advised by my father, mother, and sisters never to mention my illness (which offered only slight visible manifestations) for fear it might deter a gentleman who wished to propose marriage. I found this silence stifling, but could only do as they directed.

—Agatha Jeffers, 1853

What is always speaking silently is the body.

—Norman O. Brown

the centuries-old silence that has been imposed on women's writing about their bodies.

Aging Body

In her recent book, *The Fountain of Age*, Betty Friedan offers a gift comparable to the one she gave women over thirty years ago, in *The Feminine Mystique*. With words, facts, and images, she argues that we must accept without fear the fact that our physical bodies exist in a cycle of time:

> I think it is time that . . . we stop denying our growing older and look at the actuality of our own experience, and that of other women and men who have gone beyond denial to a new place in their sixties, seventies, eighties. It is time to look at age on its own terms, and put names on its values and strengths as they are actually experienced, breaking through the definition of age solely as deterioration or decline from youth. Only then will we see that the problem is not age itself. . . . The problem is how to break through the cocoon of our illusory youth and risk a new stage in life.

Friedan is speaking a truth that every woman must hear, if she is to tell the true story of her real body. But she will have to listen through the clamor of cultural messages, all of which tell another story. That menopause marks the end of sexuality and attractiveness. That old age can be erased if we put old people in old people's homes. That old people themselves can be erased by being altogether forgotten.

And still other stories: A young woman can stay youthful forever by buying this beauty cream, using that moisturizing soap. A mature woman can pass for "young enough" by coloring her hair, wearing youthful clothes, and denying the evidences of her age. An old woman must acquiesce by taking her place and acknowledging the dwindling of opportunity. These litanies are accompanied by a constant subliminal drumbeat: youth is wonderful, age is dreadful; youth is healthy, age is sick; powerful youth looks across a wide landscape of opportunity; age, powerless, has exhausted all possibility.

How can we unlearn these lessons, teach ourselves to appreciate the vitality and health and energies of old age, when even to speak or write these words—*old age*—is difficult? The first thing we have to do, as Friedan says, is to "break through the cocoon of illusory youth." The first thing we have to do is to see what's real.

On her seventieth birthday, Doris Grumbach looked in the mirror. She recorded exactly what she saw in her book *Coming into the End Zone:*

> I see the pull of gravity on the soft tissues of my breasts and buttocks. I see the heavy rings that encircle my neck like Ubangi jewelry. I notice bones that seem to have thinned and shrunk. Muscles appear to be watered down. The walls of my abdomen, like Jericho, have softened and now press outward. There is nothing lovely about the sight of me. I have been taught that firm and unlined is beautiful. Shall I try to learn to love what I am left with? I wonder. It would be easier to resolve never again to look into a full-length mirror.

Looking into the mirror of age, learning to be at home in our real bodies, *is* difficult, but unexpectedly and powerfully rewarding. To extend your chapter, choose the writing task that is most appropriate to you. You may choose more than one, or construct your own. You may respond in prose or in poetry, or with a drawing or a cutout.

Crone: Great Hag of History, who has Dis-covered depths of Courage, Strength, and Wisdom in her Self.

—Mary Daly

1. If you are a premenopausal woman, write down your expectations about menopause. What do you think it will be like for you? How do you feel about it? What are your fears, your regrets? Your anticipations? How do you think menopause will affect your physical appearance, your capabilities, your stamina?

2. If you are a postmenopausal woman, look into the mirror and describe precisely what you see, as Doris Grumbach has done. What do you look like? How do you feel about what you see?

3. If you have an aging mother or grandmother, look into her face and describe precisely what you see there. How does she look to you? How does she look to herself? How does she feel about her aging body? How do *you* feel, knowing that you are following her into old age?

4. If you have no older relatives, find an elderly woman. (If this is difficult, you might ask yourself why.) Describe her. What does she look like to you? How does her appearance make you feel?

Clippings: Myself as Never Before

Once we have clearly perceived the physical reality of age, felt the fact of it in our bones and flesh, we can frame that reality in many ways— see it, as it were, in many mirrors. Here is one such mirror, created by Barbara MacDonald, in *Look Me in the Eye*.

> "I like growing old," I say to myself with surprise. I had not thought that it could be like this. There are days of excitement when I feel almost a kind of high with the changes taking place in my body, even though I know the inevitable course my body is taking will lead to debilitation and death. I say to myself frequently in wonder, "This is my body doing this thing." I cannot stop it, I don't even know what it is doing. I wouldn't know how to direct it. My own body is going through a process that only my body knows about. . . . It is still taking good care of me, but it has always had two jobs: to make sure that I live and to make sure that I die. . . . With the deep knowledge with which it has always protected me—now, even against my will, it turns my sights toward an inner world.

This mirror belongs to the poet May Sarton. It is excerpted from her published journal, *At Seventy:*

> I am more myself [at seventy] than I have ever been. There is less conflict. I am happier, more balanced, and (I heard myself say rather aggressively) "more powerful." I felt it was rather an odd word, "powerful," but I think it is true. It might have been more accurate to say, "I am better able to use my powers." I am surer of what life is all about, have less self-doubt to conquer.

And this one belongs to Florida Scott-Maxwell, whose book on the experience of aging, *The Measure of My Days*, has become a classic:

> It amounts to this: that near the end of my life when I am myself as never before, I am awareness at the mercy of multiplicity. Ideas drift in like bright clouds, arresting, momentary, but they come as visitors. A shaft of insight can enter the back of my mind and when I turn to greet it, it is gone. I did not have it, it had me. My mood is light and dancing, or is leaden. It is not I who choose my moods; I accept them, but from whom?

This mirror was created by Jeanne Brooks Carritt, in an essay called "Our Bodies Are Still Ourselves as We Age."

> I am not overly fond of my aging body when it complains to me too often and I find it difficult not to dislike my appearance and that of my contemporaries as our faces and bodies respond to the accumulation of years. It would have been easier to have grown old in a culture in which wrinkles and sagging skin were an affirmation of accumulated wisdom. . . . Nevertheless, overall I am rather enjoying the aging process. This body is still me, the one I entered the world with, and the one I will take with me when I leave. In the deep lines on my face, I can now see my brother, my father, and my maternal grandmother, none of them now living. Yes, my body is myself, and related to the universe. It is indeed sacred.

As you look back over each of these writings, ask yourself how they are different, and yet the same. What is the common body-knowledge that these four aging women share? What do they have to teach us about the mystery of aging?

The Fit Body

Toward the end of the last century, the ideal middle- and upper-class woman was delicate, fragile—and sadly unfit. But times have changed. Women hike, run, swim, and cycle. We climb Mt. Everest, sail around the world, compete in the Olympics. We excel in nearly every sport, including those, like the martial arts, once thought to be the exclusive territory of men. While not all of us want to be Olympic athletes, most of us want to ensure that our bodies are as fit as possible. We know that fitness is physically, psychologically, and spiritually empowering.

On the other hand, the idea of a fit body is rapidly becoming a cultural icon. Fitness gear, clothing, equipment, lessons, audiotapes and videotapes—these are the wares of an aggressive industry that tells us (much as the fashion industry does) that a woman's body ought to meet certain standards of fitness. The idea itself is admirable, although standards of suppleness, endurance, and strength often seem to be set so high that they can be met only by those for whom fitness is a fixation.

If you want a thing well done, get a couple of old broads to do it.

—Bette Davis

The Crone is the wise old woman who watches over our dreams and visions, who whispers secrets to our inner ears. . . . Initiate, seeker, and hermit, the Crone represents a stage of life in which wisdom is sought—a time of introversion and spiritual seeking.

—Vicki Noble

Walking, running, or bicycling for 30 to 60 minutes daily will burn fat. But experts agree that training with weights three times a week for 20 to 30 minutes is necessary to build muscle.

—Prevention magazine

Along with fitness comes the issue of weight, a vexing question for many women who spend their lives switching from one diet to another in order to slim down. (While extremes of weight *do* affect our health and fitness, of course, medical research has established a wider weight/height ratio than our society would like to accept.) Here again, many of us are plagued by standards of physical perfection that we cannot and need not meet. For some, unfortunately, those standards become goals that occupy them to the exclusion of everything else. Eating disorders are among the major ailments of our time.

You may want to include a section in your book about your own efforts to achieve fitness. Here are several questions you can use to get started.

What kind of physical fitness is important to me?
What are my overall fitness goals?
What sports or fitness programs do I engage in?
What dietary guidelines do I observe?
Has weight loss or weight gain been a particular issue for me?
What physical changes have I noticed since I began to work toward fitness?
What psychological changes have I noticed?
What effect has my program had on my social life?

Clippings: Out of Habit

Novelist Pam Houston, in an essay entitled "Out of Habit, I Start Apologizing," compares her not-so-fit body to that of an athletic woman:

I'm sitting on my front porch, blank computer screen in front of me, except two words at the top: The body. I am determined to write something positive, having just turned thirty and having sworn not to spend much of the second half of my life preoccupied with my physical imperfections as I did the first. A woman walks up the street, bone thin in a running bra, Lycra shorts, and a Walkman. I look down at my shapeless flannel nightgown, my fuzzy slippers, my belly, my hips, and turn my computer off for at least another hour. The woman is striding, big, confident strides up my street, which is the steepest in our mountain town. She looks as if she will keep that pace right up and over the mountain.

In this wry, self-deprecatory piece, Houston gives testimony to our conditioned response. Where bodies are concerned, it is difficult to stop comparing ours to others'.

The following paragraphs were part of a longer piece written by a woman who had just lost seventy-two pounds and still hadn't gotten used to her new body:

> I did it. I lost it, all seventy-two pounds of it. Fat, I hope. I hope I didn't lose any muscle, but when you're dieting you really don't care. All you care about is getting rid of it, fat, muscle, whatever. Anyway, here I am, a whole new me, slim and trim and fit after all that exercise and changing my diet and saying positive affirmations like "I am slim and trim and fit."
>
> Well, not really. The thing is that when I look in the mirror I don't see the slim, trim, fit new me, what I see is fat, dumpy, out-of-shape me. I've gotten so used to comparing my body to other women's bodies and coming out a loser that I can't break the habit! I guess my next big project will be to convince my mind that my body is really different!
>
> —Brigitte P.

We don't see things as they are, we see them as we are.

—Anaïs Nin

The Body-Mind Connection

I live only part of the life I am given. Our culture roots its understanding of the body in the science of medicine, defining the body as something that can be seen, heard, weighed, and measured, with the help of such scientific extensions of our senses as the X-ray, electron microscopy, ultrasound, and CAT scan. In this cultural view, my body extends inward from the surface of my skin, upward from the soles of my feet to the top of my skull, forward from the moment of my conception to the moment of my death. I am made of matter. I am finite. I am time bound.

But other peoples, in other cultures, have had different ways of understanding their bodies. Some cultures believe that bodies are con-

The body is a natural transmuter. It is the Philosopher's Stone, capable of converting other forms of energy and matter into itself.

—Brugh Joy

structed of energy, and that energy creates the physical forms we can see, touch, weigh, measure. The energetic field extends beyond the body form, effectively enlarging the body, extending it, connecting it to the infinity of the energetic universe. Other cultures believe that certain mental and spiritual practices can essentially transform the physical body, enlarging its powers, extending its life. Still other cultures believe that this presently incarnated body is only one in a long succession of similarly incarnated bodies, manifestations, in time, of a single, timeless soul. These expansive concepts of the body make my material, finite, time-bound body seem limited indeed!

Even in our own culture, alternative paradigms of body-understanding are becoming possible. For instance, a new field of mind/body science explores the body as an information network, an intricately functioning system of biologically responsive interconnections that allow us to function as integrated, coherent, whole beings. In this view, the mind and the body are not separate entities but part of a complex, interwoven whole. Our physical bodies reflect our mental and emotional conditions. Our minds and hearts respond to the body's varying states.

Research supports this emerging paradigm. For instance, a team at the University of Pennsylvania has found that persistent patterns of pessimistic thinking can put a person at increased risk of illness, while optimistic thinking seems to protect against depression, illness, and premature death. A research group at Stanford University has shown that people who believe they can control events in their lives recover faster from sudden illness and cope more effectively with chronic pain. Dr. Bernie Siegel, author of *Love, Medicine and Miracles,* sees a vital connection between the degree to which someone can give and receive love and that person's ability to survive cancer. Even if we don't know all the answers, the trend is clear: the state of our physical bodies is intimately connected with our patterns of thinking and feeling about ourselves and the quality of our relationships with other people and with the world.

The story of your physical body is not complete until you have given some thought to the way *you* see these matters. Here are several prompts that may move you to write down some of your ideas. These statements require only short answers, but you might want to develop one or more of them into longer paragraphs.

I sing the body electric.

—Walt Whitman

First we come to know our bodies as matter; then we discover them to be fields of energy.

—William Irwin Thompson

1. When I think of my body, I imagine that it is made of
_____

2. Because it is made of _____, my body has the capacity to _____. This capacity means that _____.

3. I believe that my physical body began when _____
_____.

4. I believe that my physical body will come to an end when_____.

5. When I am very still, I am aware that my body _____
_____.

6. My most intense personal experience of the mind/body connection:_____.

Minding the Soul's Body

In one of today's most lively and liberating spiritual traditions, women have begun to reclaim their bodies as holy vessels, receptacles of the soul. This liturgy of the body, as we might call it, is a reminder that our daily lives are full of "natural sacraments," deeply attentive, mindful moments in which we embody and enact the sacred: renewing, transforming, purifying, joining, birthing, dying. When I see my physical self and all my actions in this way, it is not hard for me to see that I live in a sacred dimension, on the cusp between the ordinary and the extraordinary. Renewing myself through sleep, transforming my food into spirit, purifying myself with washing, joining the cosmic intercourse in the act of making love, caressing the earth as I walk upon it—these are the everyday rituals through which the universe manifests itself in my life.

This sacramental consciousness allows me to be mindful of the truth that my body is my *soul's* body. There is nothing particularly religious about this observation, for most of the world's modern religions actively sever the connection between body and soul, disdaining and despising the body. But there is everything deeply *spiritual* about it, for the sacred life of the spirit is nourished by—what else?—the daily life of the body.

Once in a Quaker meeting, on a beautiful spring day when the fresh air blew temptingly through the silent circle of meditators, a Friend stood up to speak her piece and changed forever how I regarded myself and everyone else there. "I am not my body," she said. "I am not my work or my role. I am not my gender. I am not my nationality. I am not a human being . . . I am a spiritual being having a human experience."

—Christina Baldwin

This conjunction between body and spirit becomes much clearer to us as we become more mindful of the body's physical sensations. Of the sensations of hunger, of thirst, of pain. Of sleepiness, of alertness. Of sitting, standing, reaching, moving. This reminds me of what dance improvisation teacher Denise Taylor says in an essay called "Coming Home to the Body," in the book *Ordinary Magic: Everyday Life as a Spiritual Path:*

> To turn our attention to the movement of our bodies is an act of love, in the sense of self-regard. When people used to say "You have to love yourself first," I was never sure what this meant. I needed a tangible method. Techniques like visualization or writing affirmations never worked for me. But feeling my feet on the ground, the heat in my chest, the constriction in my head when I'm angry, the air over my bare feet as I walk, the sensation of my body turning in water—these all give me a sense that I am here, like it or not. There's no mistaking what is happening and there's no way to do it wrong. I am moving through the world with a sense of watching sweetly over it all. I am actually with myself, like a good friend, as I walk, run, dance, or sit down.

Writing About the Soul's Body

How about you? What are the daily physical actions, the sensations, that remind you that you are living in the soul's body? Choose one of the following questions and use it to write several pages.

1. What physical exercise do you perform that is also a kind of soul-exercise—moving and stretching while paying attention to the sensations, feelings, and memories that arise? (Yoga and the martial arts represent one such group of disciplines; rolfing, and the Alexander and Feldenkrais methods are others. Swimming, jogging, or walking may also work this way for you.) How did you learn this practice? How long have you been doing it? What changes have you noticed in your body since you began? Do these changes reflect soul-change?

2. What body-things do you do (eating, bathing, preparing for bed) that turn your attention to your body and its sensations? What do you learn as you observe the body?

All the drama of our thought, feeling, and action begins with sensations. Through mindfulness we train ourselves to be in the body to receive them.

—Denise Taylor

It is the mind that makes the body.

—Sojourner Truth

3. What clothing do you wear that seems to be a kind of soul-garment? Where did it come from? What special meanings does it hold for you or for others? How does it renew or transform you as you wear it? What does it teach you about the nature of the body's clothing? What does it suggest to you about the body as a garment for the soul? (You might also explore this question by substituting the word "jewelry" for "clothing" and "garment.")

Clippings: Exercising the Soul's Body

Here is a piece of timed writing written after a group discussed exercising the soul's body. The writer has been studying tai chi, a movement meditation practiced extensively in China. The "form" she mentions is the slow, deliberate performance of a particular sequence of movements, almost like a dance.

> I've been doing tai chi for five years. I was afraid when I started, afraid of not doing it right. Now, I know the whole form, and I am no longer afraid at class, even when I haven't practiced. The form is a mystery to me. I love it, but can't say why. It has improved my balance, but so would a lot of other things. When I do the form, I feel rooted to the earth, solid, grounded. I feel my legs as a channel for the energy flowing between the earth and my soul. In the form, I love the way my legs are so solid and my hands are so light and free. I sometimes feel the energy, my energy, my chi flowing. Not always. But sometimes. I am conscious of my breathing. Doing the form creates consciousness for me. I feel so at ease with this body knowledge that doesn't include negatives like guilt and perfection. I'm pretty lazy about it these days because I've come to have a deep trust of the form that does not include guilt when I don't do it every day. The form will be there for me always, although my movement into and away from it may change with time. Whether I do the form or not, I carry it with me, and create it anew each time I practice it, just as it creates me.
>
> —Donna L.

Putting Your Third Chapter Together

So far, you've written short (or maybe not-so-short) sections on your body as it has matured through childhood, adolescence, and adulthood. You've also written about your physical fitness and about the intimate connection between body and mind and body and soul. Your third chapter—"Body Language"—has six sections, each of which may be two or more pages in length, twelve to eighteen or more pages in all.

This chapter would lend itself very well to photographs from your personal album: photographs of yourself at various stages of your life; photographs of yourself in wellness and illness; engaging in sports or exercise; working or playing; wearing the clothing or jewelry you may have written about. You might caption each of these photographs and date them.

What else might you include in your chapter "Body Language"? If you have experienced significant periods of physical injury or illness, you may want to chronicle them here, asking yourself how your illness drew you closer to an understanding of your physical and spiritual being. Or perhaps you have had other experiences you would like to explore: out-of-body experiences, ESP and telekinetic experiences, biofeedback learning, meditation, fitness challenges, and so on. This chapter offers a wonderful potential for continued self-exploration.

Meditation

Listening to the Body

For this meditation (which will take approximately fifteen minutes), you will lie flat on your back on the floor, arms straight at your sides, feet slightly apart, toes pointing up. Your purpose is very simple: to experience and observe the body, to shift attention to one part, then another, without getting entangled in any kind of judgmental thinking. You are simply going to get in touch with the sensations of your body without considering whether it is too this or too that—your precious, *wonderful* body, which can breathe and move and see and reach and judge distances and digest and eliminate and grow, all without your conscious direction! The idea of listening to your body is to actually *feel* each part as you place your attention in it, breathing into and out of it several times, then shifting your attention to the next part. As you listen to your body, part by part, you will feel the life force that surges through you. You will *hear* your body. And as you listen, as you hear and become mindful of your body, you will feel more real, more alive.

This meditation is an excellent one to use as a kind of "anchor" practice—something you do on a regular basis, and in different contexts. Once you have learned the fine art of listening to your body, you can do it anywhere. In fact, the more often you listen and the greater the variety of contexts in which you listen, the more you will learn. If you continue it over a period of several weeks or months, you will notice that your body is *different* each time you practice: that it has different messages to convey, different urgencies, different needs. If you practice body listening when you're in traffic, when you're in the middle of a tiresome meeting, when you're shopping, when you're jogging, you will become adept at discerning important body cues. You will become aware that your physical being is constantly changing, moment to moment, day to day, as the current of life flows through it. And as you become more and more mindful of your body, you will learn something about its distinctness, its special quality. But you will also learn to distinguish between your self and your body. You will see that you are *not* your body. You will experience yourself as spirit inhabiting body.

Welcome to the human experience. Welcome to the body. Enjoy it while you have it.

Close your eyes and spend a few moments feeling your weight pressing into the floor, feeling in your body the electrical energy—a kind of twitchiness—that is generated by moving around, being active. . . . Observe this energy slowly relaxing as if it were a coiled spring unwinding little by little. . . . Feel your weight, the full, heavy stillness of your body, pressing on the floor.

Now, fold your hands over your belly and bring your attention to it. If you have been holding the belly muscles tight, let them go. . . . Feel your belly gently lift your folded hands as you breathe in . . . feel it lower your hands as you breathe out. . . . Just observe for a moment the sensations of movement . . . your belly moving with your breath . . . rising, falling. No thinking, no judging, just stay with the belly . . . all the attention in the belly. . . .

And now, shift your attention from your belly to your breath. As you breathe, allow the passage of breath to make a slight noise in your throat or your nostrils. . . . Keep your attention focused on your breathing. . . . Stay with each inbreath for its full length. . . . Stay with each outbreath for its full length. . . . No thinking, no judging, simply observe the breath, watching it flow in and flow out. As you listen to your breath, you are also listening to your body, to life, moving through you . . . just listen . . . listen to your breath. . . .

And now, shift your attention from the breath to the toes of your left foot . . . feeling the sensations in your foot, any tightness, any tingling . . . if there are no sensations, be aware of that, too . . . no thinking, no judging, just listening to any messages coming from your foot . . .

Now bring your attention higher, to the calf . . . the knee . . . the thigh . . . feeling any sensations in your left leg . . . no thinking, no judging, just listening to your leg, to the whole length of it, toes to hip . . . being alert to any messages coming from your left leg. . . .

Now shift your attention to the toes of your right foot, feeling the sensations in your foot, any tightness, any tingling . . . if there are no sensations, be aware of that, too . . . no thinking, no judging, just listening to your foot. And then gradually move up your right leg . . . calf . . . knee . . . thigh . . . no thinking, no judging, just observing your right leg, toes to hip . . . being alert to any messages coming from your right leg. . . .

Now shift your attention to your left hand . . . feeling the sensations in your fingers, your wrist . . . no thinking, no judging, just listening to your hand. . . .

Now shift your attention to your left arm, your elbow, your shoulder . . . feeling the sensations of tightness, aching, heaviness . . . no thinking, no judging, just listening to your arm and shoulder. . . .

Now shift your attention to your right hand . . . feeling the sensations in your fingers, your wrist . . . no thinking, no judging, just listening to your right hand. . . .

Now shift your attention to your right arm, your elbow, your shoulder . . . feeling the sensations of tightness, aching, heaviness . . . no thinking, no judging, just listening to your arm and shoulder. . . .

Now shift your attention to your face, neck, and throat . . . feeling the sensations as the breath flows through the nostrils, past the back of the throat, into the chest . . . listening to the quiet sound of the breath . . . feeling also the face, the jaw, the cheeks, the forehead, noticing any tension, any tingling . . . just noticing, just observing, no thinking, no judging, just listening, being alert to any messages coming from the face, neck, and throat. . . .

Now turn your attention back to the breath itself for a moment . . . feeling it moving in and out, feeling it moving through every cell of your body. . . . Then open your eyes and bring your attention to yourself, lying on the floor, rested, relaxed, fully listening. When you are ready, sit up slowly, still listening to the body as it adjusts itself to the changed posture. And finally stand, still listening. For a moment or two, just feel yourself *in* your body. When you are ready, gently stretch. Then take a few minutes to write down anything you'd like to add to the third chapter of your story book.

Celebrating the Completion of Your Chapter

Congratulations! You have successfully completed the third chapter of your story: "Body Language." Here are five things you might do to celebrate.

1. Take your chapter to a meeting of your Story Circle and share parts of it with others. Perhaps you could all share the "Child's Body" section. In what ways are your body experiences the same? In what ways are they different?

2. Give a gift to a particular part of your body, being mindful of what that body part contributes to your life. You might give a ring to your willing and able finger, earrings to your alert ears, a pedicure to your dancing feet, perfume to your naturally fragrant skin (with special thanks to the nose that allows you to appreciate it!), new makeup to your already beautiful face, a special shampoo to your shining hair. Your body is a friend for life, serving you well and faithfully even under the most adverse conditions. Celebrate it!

3. Give your pleasure-loving body a sensual experience: an herbal bath, perhaps, accompanied by candlelight, music, and your favorite chocolates. Be mindful of your body's senses. Indulge them!

4. Give your athletic body a recreative experience. Take it cycling for the afternoon, or climbing, or swimming, or walking. As you cycle or

climb or swim or walk, be attentive to your lithe muscles, powerful lungs, sturdy skeleton. Appreciate your body's strength!

5. Give your soul's body a spirit-filled experience. Instead of taking your vacation as usual this year, take a retreat: spend a quiet few days, alone, in a place that encourages you to listen to your body, to be guided by your spirit. Look for a book that lists the many spiritual retreats around the country, or browse through the New Age magazines, where retreats are often advertised. (Marcia and Jack Kelly have written two books called *Sanctuaries: A Guide to Lodgings in Monasteries, Abbeys, and Retreats of the United States.* One book covers the Northeast, the other the West Coast and Southwest.) Choose two or three retreat centers that look interesting, and ask for information. Imagine yourself in the place, think what your days might be like, picture yourself spending time in quiet solitude, getting away from it all in a place that helps you return to your self. Then, if it feels right, make a reservation, and begin now to look forward to it—even if you have to schedule it a year or two in the future. Are you thinking that you have too many family or work obligations to take a solo retreat? If so, spending some quiet time alone, listening to your body, being attentive to your spirit, is probably exactly what you need!

Chapter Four

Soul Mates

The Soul selects her own Society—
Then—shuts the Door—
To her divine Majority—
Present no more . . .

I've known her—from an ample nation—

Choose One—
Then—close the Valves of her attention—
Like Stone—

　　　　　　　—Emily Dickinson

Women welcome intimacy, attachment, and involvement. We lean toward the interdependence of love and care, while men often resist it, favoring the autonomous independence of work. Is it our nature or our nurture that creates these differences? There are arguments on both sides, and several writers (such as Carol Gilligan, in *In a Different Voice*, and Jean Baker Miller, in *Toward a New Psychology of Women*) have offered helpful explanations.

How do I love thee?
Let me count the ways . . .
—Elizabeth Barrett Browning

Whatever the reason, it is clear that women weave the fabric of their lives out of complex patterns of loves and loving. Even as we seek to develop our personal authority in the public world, we define ourselves in the context of our private relationships. But we are often confused about the balance between autonomy and affiliation, and we find ourselves choosing relationships that do not nurture growth, or perhaps even stunt us. We work through the same perplexing issues over and over again, with different emphases, in each decade of our adult lives:

How can I love in a healthy way?

How can I be intimate with another and yet be my true, authentic self?

How can I be an autonomous, authoritative person—somebody who achieves on the job—and still be deeply connected to other people?

How can I honor my responsibilities to my family and find the time and the energy to honor my responsibilities to myself?

When women add achievement in the public work-world to their strengths in the private world of personal relationships, they must confront these difficult issues. No wonder so many women feel as if they're walking a tightrope in the dark—with dragons lurking beneath!

In this chapter, we'll try to untangle some of these difficult relationship issues. We will read and write about two kinds of deeply significant affiliations: kinship connections and romantic attachments. In chapter 7, we'll write about other important self/other relationships: with friends, co-workers, and communities. In both chapters we will be concerned with our soul mates.

Soul Mates

The idea of soul mates is popular these days, and often trivialized. But I think it is an important concept. For me, the words *soul mate* describe a person with whom I have formed a profound relationship—not because I deliberately chose to be in the relationship, but because in some mysterious sense, for some mysterious purpose, I was *chosen.* In my understanding, the term involves some sort of fate or destiny: I sense a special and mysterious grace, sometimes a painful grace, in the soul-relationship. This fate or destiny or grace encourages me to grow (often unwittingly or unwillingly, in ways I would not have chosen) into a radical enlargement of my vital self. A soul mate is someone whose fruitful presence in my life—a presence that may make itself felt through pain and difficulty and separation, as well as through the joy of union and reunion—is necessary to my soul's resizing: in the experience of relationship, I am required to stretch my feelings, my perceptions, my intuitions. A soul mate is someone who helps me learn some essential lesson about who I am and where I am going—a lesson that I could not have learned under other circumstances. (Please notice that I said "helps me learn," rather than "teaches." A soul mate can intend me to take one kind of meaning from our relationship, while my soul learns something quite different.)

Over the course of my relationships with parents, children, lovers, partners, this definition of soul mate has been very helpful to me. What does the term mean to you? Spend a few minutes, please, thinking about that question. Then, to begin your chapter, write down your definition.

To me, the term "soul mate" describes a person who_____

_____

_____.

The value of the personal relationship to all things is that it creates intimacy and intimacy creates understanding and understanding creates love.

—Anaïs Nin

Definitions are useful because they narrow our focus and help us decide what does and doesn't belong to the group we're defining. But a definition can be too abstract, detached from your own personal, deeply felt experience. To really understand what "soul mate" means to you, you need to have in mind all the people to whom you have been deeply connected, who have been your soul mates. And that amounts to writing . . .

The whole is the sum of its hearts.

—Seth

A Brief History of the Heart

The purpose of this two-part exercise is to take an inventory of all your *soul-relationships*—relationships with people who have been your soul mates. This exercise is less complicated than it sounds. Here is an example of the first part. The writer notes the years spanned by her significant, soul-full relationships and jots down a few words—words that occurred to her spontaneously, without a lot of thought—to describe each:

1965–now: Mom, Dad, Gran. Props, anchors, coaches, cheerleaders
1974–now: Jeanne. Friends forever, sisters under the skin
1981–1982: Tom. Sweet, soft. First love fades fast
1985–1986: Monty. Hot-wired. Blazing start, incinerating finish, ashes
1986–now: Karen. A true colleague, co-equal, in business and otherwise. Eye-to-eye on the important things
1986–1990: Jack. Dance-away lover. Out of reach, out of sight, out of heart (but it took a while)
1991–now: Nat. Paris in the springtime, walks in the rain, yellow roses on our anniversary
1993—now: Nathan. Pure joy with jelly on his chin
1995: Elizabeth. Pain, tears, loss, love always

—Jan J.

Now for some heart work.
—Rainer Maria Rilke

As you can see from Jan's inventory, her soul mates include parents, friends, lovers, a business colleague, husband, children. Each soul mate has offered her a different way to grow, in family and in work, through love, passion, loss, pain, grief. This wasn't an easy exercise for her, and it may not be for you. But encourage yourself to do it, and stay with it until it's done, whether it takes ten minutes or ten hours. Include parents, grandparents, siblings, friends, lovers, spouses, children, partners, mentors, co-workers, bosses—anybody who fits your definition of soul mate. Be as clear as possible (but brief) in your annotations. Try to capture the heart of the relationship in a few words.

When your first inventory is done, set it aside and go to the second. (It's okay to do the first inventory in one session, the second in another.) Here, you will make a list of other people who have been important in your life—you may even have had long-term intimate relationships with them—but whom you don't consider soul mates. You can follow the same format if you choose, or just list the names, with a word or two of description. The purpose here is to decide what a soul-relationship *isn't.*

When you've finished your second list, set it aside with your first and go on with your reading. We'll come back to both in a few minutes.

My Family, Myself

In my definition, family members are our first soul mates. The family offers shelter, guidance, physical and emotional security, and love. It may also be dysfunctional, teaching lessons by the distorted, distorting rules of what psychologist Alice Miller calls a "poisonous pedagogy." Whatever the nature of the family relationship, it is the first chapter in our soul's story, teaching us how and what to believe: whether the world is safe or dangerous, whether we should trust or fear, whether we should be confident or ashamed. It shapes us to be loyal, contributing members of *our* family.

In fact, family stories often seem designed, implicitly, to remind us that we belong to a family. I remember visiting my mother and my grandmother the month after I received my doctorate, when I was on my way to Texas to take a job as an assistant professor. I had barely arrived when Grandma Franklin pulled me into the kitchen and told me (as if I didn't already know it by heart) the legend of my great-great-grandmother, Sarah Coldiron, who walked hundreds of miles to be reunited with her Cherokee mother.

Was it an accident that my grandmother chose to retell that particular family legend at that particular moment? Of course not. "Sarah Coldiron's Long Walk" is a valued myth of the motherline in my family, a story of exile and return, embellished with the often-repeated details of Sarah's homespun dress and the man's boots she wore. (The part about the clothes and her Indian ancestry, anyway, is accurate: I have a faded photograph of my great-great-grandmother, her heavy leather boots evident under the hem of her ankle-length dress, her beaked nose and fierce mouth absolute testimony to her mother's Cherokee blood.) The story illustrates the Indian motherline in which the women in our family take pride and emphasizes the strong mother-bond that is supposed to connect mothers and daughters. My grandmother was using it to remind me that I was still a daughter, Ph.D. or not, and that I should visit my mother more often. She also wanted to remind me that the women in our family are strong and unswerving, and that I could thank Sarah Coldiron for the sense of purpose that had helped me make the long journey through graduate school to my first teaching appointment.

Every family has a repertory of family folktales that teach us who we

A woman writing thinks back through her mother.

—Virginia Woolf

are and where we belong. At one level, these stories exist to hold a family together, across time and space, creating what Thomas Moore calls a *soul-family*. At another level, such stories point out some important attribute of a particular family—how it is different from, or connected to, other families. As children listen to these stories, the soul-stories of their family, they learn where they came from, who they belong to, and why they're special.

In the old days, when families lived close together, telling and listening was easy. Now, they are scattered, separated. The family connection is fragile, and adults may have only dim recollections of family stories. But that very separation makes it all the more important to remember the stories, to write them down so that the children will remember them and feel that they, too, belong to a family—a soul-family.

How about you? Do you recall any favorite family stories that explain who you are, where you came from, who you belong to, or why you're special? If you do, you can begin your chapter by writing two or three of the most important ones. (Later, you may want to write down all that you can remember and add to your collection by interviewing the older members of your family. These might be organized in a separate book, illustrated with photographs from the family album.)

Here are a few folktale motifs I've collected from listening to my family. I've given each one a title that reflects both the content of the story and the lesson it's supposed to teach. Think them over and see if any remind you of stories you might write down here.

> How Aunt Pearl chased Uncle Charlie's bull out of the garden—
>   a story of courage
> Why Aunt Maude's branch of the family has never had a
>   dime—a bad-luck story
> How Cousin Jane fed and clothed three children after her
>   husband was killed in World War I—a tale of true grit
> How the Franklin women survived by selling eggs—a
>   compendium of anecdotes from the Great Depression
> Grandma Franklin's "log cabin" tales of ingenuity and
>   resourcefulness—a pioneer parable
> Lucille Franklin and the cat that ate the cream, Mildred Franklin
>   and the stolen buggy whip, Aunt Mary Franklin and the
>   wayward goose—a collection of humorous bloopers,
>   blunders, and the mischief that children get up to

Women who are out of touch with their motherlines are lost souls. They are hungry ghosts inhabiting bodies they do not own, because for them the feminine ground is a foreign place.

—Naomi Ruth Lowinsky

Shirley Abbott began writing down her family stories when her eighty-year-old Aunt Laura asked, "Who were these women we remember?" The answer eventually became a book—*Womenfolks: Growing Up Down South*—but in the beginning, Abbott just wanted to silence her aunt's persistent question.

> Hoping to make short work of it, I replied that as far as I knew, we came from a line of scrawny old dirt-dobbers, Scotch-Irish with more than one or two Indians thrown in, and that there was no way I could go to the library and read up on southern country women, let alone our own family, because they didn't make it into the history books.
>
> But that was not enough. [Aunt Laura] wanted particulars, real things to hold in her hand, real women. She wanted the names and stories. She wanted me to raise the dead. "Who was the first of us?" she asked. "You can track her down." When I protested that I had other things to do and nothing to go on, Laura answered, "Never mind, I'll send you some papers I have. I'll tell you everything I know." And so I began work as an archaeologist might, trying to imagine what a whole village was like by looking at a few pottery pieces in the kitchen midden.

We are a race of women that of old knew no fear and feared no death, and lived great lives and hoped great hopes; and if today some of us have fallen on evil and degenerate times, there moves in us yet the throb of the old blood.

—Olive Shreiner

Family Soul Mates

When you made your initial list of soul mates, perhaps you did not include the names of family members. If your family relationship involved intense pain—the pain of anger, abandonment, even abuse—it may be hard for you to think of your family as your soul-family. But if you accept the idea that soul mate involves a kind of destiny or fate, perhaps you will also agree—at least for the sake of argument—that there is a particular destiny involved in being born into a particular family. You didn't choose your mother or your father or your brothers and sisters, or your grandparents, aunts, uncles, and cousins. They were assigned to you by some fate beyond your control. Is it too hard to imagine that there may have been a mysterious purpose behind that fate? Can you imagine that you were born into your family in order to learn some important lessons from its members?

In the next writing exercise, let's explore this idea of soul-family. Turn your attention from your parents (we'll return to them in a moment) and focus instead on your larger family, including brothers and sisters, grandparents, aunts and uncles, and cousins. Here are three questions. Take three separate pages, write one question at the top of each page, and fill the page with your response.

1. What kind of family was I assigned to? Where did it come from? What tribe or clan or nationality did it belong to? According to my family, what makes us special?

2. What did members of my family want or expect or hope to teach me about who I was, where I belonged, and why *I* was special?

3. What did I actually learn from them (in contrast to what they seemed to want me to learn)? Are there any soul-lessons here?

Collect these three pages, along with the family folktales you wrote earlier, under the heading "My Family, Myself" (or under a similar heading of your own creation). These pages make up the first section of your chapter on soul mates.

Clippings: "A Heart Kind of Braille"

This short piece was written in a workshop. In it, the writer connects with her childhood resentment of the burden of her sister's illness, and with her later, more grown-up understanding of what her sister contributed to her life.

I learned my most important soul-lesson from my diabetic sister, Julie, who was four years younger than I. When we were growing up, I hated her. Not *her*, exactly, although sometimes I did. Mostly, I hated the way her diabetes affected our family. I hated giving up desserts because Julie couldn't have sweets. I hated giving her insulin injections when Mom was at work. I hated never going on vacation because Julie's medical bills took so much money. Looking back, I realize that having Julie for a sister forced me to sacrifice a lot of things, including my childhood. That was the painful part of it, and for a long time, that's all I thought there was to it. But I also learned about closeness and caring and accepting what you can't change— and eventually, when Julie died, about letting go. Some lessons are so valuable, they're worth your life to learn.

—Janet A.

This excerpt, written by journalist Sherry Von Ohlsen, appeared in Brenda Hunter's book, *In the Company of Women:*

My sister and I have been entangled from the womb, but not because we shared it at the same time. She occupied it first. Ever since, the message has been clear: first come, first served. This message was summarized well in a birthday card she recently gave me: "Happy Birthday to my Sister the Princess," it says on the outside. On the inside: "From her Sister the Queen . . ."

Once when I was about eleven years old and triumphantly mowing the half-acre front yard with a hand mower, Sandy arrived on the scene. I said rather proudly, "Look, I did this all by myself. I'm almost finished." Four years older than I, and certainly wiser, she said: "Can I just push the mower a little bit?" . . . She struggled with the twirling metal beast no more than six feet, turned to me, unclutched the handle, and slapped her hands together. Just before running off she announced, "Now you can't say you did it all by yourself . . ."

Underlying our history from the womb on, a belief in each other surfaces despite the conflicts . . . She knows who I am. She's been there since my beginning. She'll always be there. We share a language that only families understand: a heart kind of Braille.

The language of families is a "heart kind of Braille," coded into our genes, encrypted in our shared experiences, passed from one generation to another. This language takes many forms, even competition, as we see in Von Ohlsen's piece. The trick is to read between the lines and realize how important we are to one another, even in our worst moments.

Mother

Our relationships with our parents can be the most challenging of our lives. As small children, we were part of the changing dynamic of our parents' feelings for each other, as well as for us. Whether we wish to or not, we carry this dynamic into adulthood, where its energy charges most of our grown-up relationships. To understand ourselves fully, we need to understand as much as possible about our feelings toward our parents. To tell the whole truth about our lives, we need to tell the whole truth about our parents, even though that may be a difficult task.

Think for a moment about a particular moment or a series of moments when your relationship with your mother (or the woman who took the place of your biological mother) was most compelling. What was there about the time that created such strong feelings? What were those feelings? Then take several sheets of clean paper and your timer. Write as fast as you can for three or four minutes, opening your memory and capturing your remembered feelings as accurately as possible. As you write, be as honest as you know how to be, saying only the *truth*.

Clippings: "I struggle to describe . . ."

In *Of Woman Born*, Adrienne Rich writes about her mother:

> I struggle to describe what it felt like to be her daughter, but I find myself divided, slipping under her skin; a part of me identifies too much with her. I know deep reservoirs of anger toward her still exist: the anger of a four-year-old locked in the closet (my father's orders, but my mother carried them out) for childish misbehavior; the anger of a six-year-old kept too long at piano practice (again, at his insistence, but it was she who gave the lessons) till I developed a series of facial tics . . . And I still feel the anger of a daughter, pregnant, wanting my mother desperately and feeling she had gone over to the enemy.
>
> And I know there must be deep reservoirs of anger in her . . . When I think of the conditions under which my mother became a mother, the impossible expectations, my father's distaste for pregnant women, his hatred of all that he could not control, my anger at her dissolves into grief and anger *for* her, and then dissolves back again into anger at her: the ancient, unpurged anger of the child.

This is a piece written by a participant in a weekend workshop. The writer's mother had died the month before, and her feelings were especially poignant.

Honest? True? I've always struggled with truth and lies, where Mother was concerned. When I was five and she told me we were leaving my father, I couldn't tell her how much I hated her for taking me away, because nice little girls didn't hate their mother. When I was eight and she married Richard, I wanted to tell her how disappointed I was that we weren't enough, just us, she and I, and how jealous I was of him—but I couldn't spoil her happiness. It was easier to smile and lie and tell her that I was happy. When I was sixteen, I couldn't tell her about Sam because she thought it was morally wrong for me to have sex, and if she knew how immoral I was, she would think it was her fault. It was easier just to be quiet and pretend. And at forty, I couldn't tell her she was dying of cancer, because I couldn't face the idea of losing her. It was easier to tell her she was getting better, even when I knew it was a lie.

—Louise V.

Father

Now take several more sheets of paper and the timer, and write for three or four more minutes, using the following prompt. Again, write quickly and honestly, trying to capture the most fundamental truth about your relationship with your father, or with the man who took the place of your biological father.

My father was often angry when I was most like him.

—Lillian Hellman

When I was a teenager, my feelings toward my father were ____.

When you've finished the second writing, set both pieces aside while you think a little more about you and your parents.

Clippings

These two pieces were written by workshop participants as timed-writing exercises:

When I was a teenager, I thought my father was handsome and I was proud of his success at work, but I hated the way he treated my mother. She gave him everything she had, and he didn't give anything, he just got angry. I could talk back to him, but she couldn't. She'd say, "I love him," but for me that wasn't good enough, and I wanted her to divorce him. All during my teen years, my father and I fought. When we weren't fighting, we weren't talking. We wouldn't even stay in the same room together. I felt he hated everything about me, but other people would say that when I wasn't there, he would say good things about me. He would say he was proud of me. I've never understood why he couldn't say those things *to* me.

—Becky K.

When I was a teenager, I loved my father much more than my mother. I wanted to see myself through his eyes and tried to measure myself against his expectations. I did everything I could to please him, and when I succeeded and got a hug or a word of praise, I felt as if I'd gotten a gold medal at the Olympics! There weren't a lot of hugs and not much praise, but that only made me try harder, and all my good grades and my sports achievements were due to him. Later on, when I did well in college and got promotions at work, Dad was always the one I wanted to tell, because his approval meant a lot more than Mother's. I guess you'd call me a Daddy's Girl.

—Sandra E.

The point at which a woman recognizes the limitations of her mother's power and freedom in the patriarchal world is the same point at which she will turn to father or fatherly figures to find access to the power her mother lacks.

—Polly Young-Eisendrath and Florence L. Weidemann

Our relationship with our parents, natural or adoptive, is the first and most formative relationship in our lives. In many families, the daughter-parent relationship is warm and loving, and the daughter carries a strong sense of personal authority and high self-esteem into her adult life. She knows that her parents are behind her, encouraging her to do whatever she chooses.

But because of the deeply flawed gender patterns in our patriarchal society, the daughter-parent relationship is almost certain to be conflicted. Many daughters do not leave their mothers and fathers feeling confident, encouraged, loved. Some flee, as if chased by dragons. Others creep away, escapees from a prison. Still others march out in an angry storm of protest, flying flags of independence.

When you wrote honestly about your parents a moment ago, something of your true daughter-parent story should have emerged. If you described the relationship as warm and loving, particularly if you thought it was a kind of storybook relationship, the section you are about to read may not seem immediately relevant to you. I urge you to read it, however, for two reasons. First, it probably reflects the life story of many of your female friends and acquaintances, for the American family has experienced a great deal of trauma in the last fifty years. Second, we tend to idealize our parents, attributing the difficulties in the parent-child relationship to our own "badness" or "worthlessness." We love our mothers and fathers, even though they may hurt us or abandon us, sometimes through illness and death. In fact, psychologists say, children who feel hurt or abandoned may create compensating storybook fantasies about their parents. The more intense the fantasy, the harder it is to see the truth. As you read the following sections, you may find yourself reevaluating some part of your relationship with your mother or father.

If, on the other hand, you described your parental relationships as difficult or flawed, I believe the next section will help you enormously. We are healed as we open dark feelings to the light, as we uncover old wounds. It takes courage to face these buried hurts, but you are not alone in your efforts to tell the truth. Many women in our society—in some sense, all women—are wounded daughters. We can learn to live with the truth. We cannot afford to live for a lifetime with the lie.

*For when we love, we have
no other choice
but to let each other go.*
—Rainer Maria Rilke

Healing the Motherbond

Until the last few decades, most women had essentially the same limited options that their mothers had—marriage and childbearing. In the late 1960s, however, women's choices expanded remarkably. They enrolled in college and graduate and professional programs in large numbers and made their way into careers once open only to men. Women could choose to enter a world that was significantly larger than their mothers', and most of them did.

But these expanded possibilities created a new dilemma, one for which neither we nor our mothers were prepared. We were beginning to feel the heady potential of power, while in contrast, our mothers often

Our personalities seem dangerously to blur and overlap with our mother's; and, in a desperate attempt to know where mother ends and daughter begins, we perform radical surgery.

—Adrienne Rich,
Of Woman Born

seemed to have little authority of their own. Looking at them, we saw that being female meant being dependent. To explore the full range of the possibilities now open to us in a world dominated largely by men, we needed to make ourselves over to fit a masculine model. We had to reject our mothers, turn away from them, separate from them. We had to break the motherbond.

This rejection of the mother was a new thing, both psychologically and socially speaking. Because breaking the motherbond was new, we didn't know how to do it easily. Our wrenching away was traumatic. Our mothers didn't know how to loosen the motherbond, either, for most of them had remained more or less tightly bound to their mothers. So they held on, in fear, in pain, and in hope that we might relent and come home again. For many, it was a deadly tug-of-war, mothers bent on holding on, daughters desperately pulling away.

As always, the tug-of-war shows itself in the little, everyday things. Maybe you left home for school or work and wondered whether you should call every couple of days, the way your mother wanted you to, or only when you felt like it, which would be almost never. Maybe your mother wanted to do your laundry, or give you an allowance—offers that perhaps you interpreted as blackmail: "I'll do this and that and this for you if you'll promise to always be my loving daughter." Maybe your mother played the martyr, while you did your best to ignore her pleas for attention.

"Oh, I know all about my mother and me," you may say. "All that business with my mother was over years ago." You don't and it wasn't.

—Nancy Friday

In a situation like this, you might have felt trapped, resentful, resistant. Maybe you felt guilty when you didn't go home, and hated yourself when you did. Either way, you may have felt like a victim in your mother's power game. The psychological forces here would probably measure a seven on the Richter scale.

If I am a daughter struggling to free myself from my mother's expression of the feminine, it may be useful to exaggerate my negative feelings about my mother—to see her as a manifestation of what Jungian psychologists call the archetype of the Terrible Mother. Exaggeration may even be necessary, for it can generate the psychic energy that frees me from living out my life as a character in my mother's story and propels me into my own story. And my mother may actually transform herself into the Terrible Mother: acting out the blind rage she feels at her powerlessness, exhausted and embittered by her struggles to make herself known in a patriarchal world.

Vivian Gornick's memoir, *Fierce Attachments*, is a striking example of a daughter's need to be her own woman and a mother's desire to make her daughter in her own image. Born in Brooklyn to Jewish parents, Gornick has to struggle to separate herself from her mother, a struggle that is full of rage and pain:

> My relationship with my mother is not good, and as our lives accumulate it often seems to worsen. We are locked into a narrow channel of acquaintance, intense and binding. For years at a time there is an exhaustion, a kind of softening, between us. Then the rage comes up again, hot and clear, erotic in its power to compel attention. These days it is bad between us. My mother's way of "dealing" with the bad times is to accuse me loudly and publicly of the truth. Whenever she sees me she says, "You hate me. I know you hate me." I'll be visiting her and she'll say to anyone who happens to be in the room—a neighbor, a friend, my brother, one of my nieces—"She hates me. What she has against me I don't know, but she hates me." She is equally capable of stopping a stranger on the street when we're out walking and saying, "This is my daughter. She hates me." Then she'll turn to me and plead, "What did I do to you, you should hate me so?" I never answer. I know she's burning and I'm glad to let her burn. Why not? I'm burning too.

When Gornick's father died, her mother pulled the thirteen-year-old girl into the circle of her melodramatic grief:

> . . . Her pain became my element, the country in which I lived, the rule beneath which I bowed. It commanded me, made me respond against my will. I longed endlessly to get away from her, but I could not leave the room when she was in it. I dreaded her return from work, but I was never not there when she came home. . . .

This constant pulling toward and pushing away, while fiercely exaggerated by the force of the mother's personality and made vivid by the daughter's power of language, is characteristic of a motherbond that resists even the most violent efforts to break it. Gornick's memoir offers a vividly extreme example of a mother and daughter trapped in the archetype of the Terrible Mother, neither knowing how to escape.

Not all mothers and daughters struggle so intensely, of course. Some mothers understand their daughters' need to move out into the world and let them go freely; others don't know how to struggle against their

To distance herself from her mother and the mother-hold on her, a woman may go through a period of rejection of all feminine qualities distorted by the cultural lens as inferior, passive, dependent, seductive, manipulative, and powerless.

—Maureen Murdock

My mother's frustrations powered both my feminism and my writing. But much of the power came out of my anger and my competition: my desire to outdo her, my hatred of her capitulation to her femaleness, my desire to be different because I feared I was too much like her.

—Erica Jong

daughters' desires and let them go passively. Some daughters don't feel it necessary to be different from their mothers; a few daughters are so firmly connected to their mothers that they cannot imagine a separate life. Some daughters separate themselves gradually from their mothers, diminishing the struggle. (For instance, I married and had children, like my mother, before I went outside the home to work, like my father.) And some lose their mothers in childhood and search throughout their lives for a way to reestablish the motherbond.

What about you and your mother? Whether she is living or dead, it is important for you to understand the nature of your bond. To explore this vital soul-relationship, we're going to do an exercise called "filling the page." Write each of the questions listed below at the top of a sheet of paper and fill that page and one more with your response, taking as long as you want to write. If you want to continue writing on either of the questions, use additional sheets—but fill at least two for each question. The purpose of filling-the-page writing is to force yourself to say more. Like a timed writing, you set a boundary and require yourself to fill it up. The blank paper invites us to tell the whole story.

1. How easy or difficult was it for me to separate myself from my mother and begin my own separate journey? What were the circumstances of my leaving home? How did I feel about her at that point?

2. What are my feelings about my mother now? How complete is the separation between us? What are the major issues in our relationship today?

If the writing of these pages is painful, it may be that you, like many of us, are still living under the persistent shadow of the Terrible Mother, imagined or real—or both imagined *and* real. This archetype can generate so much energy that we carry it into our adult years. It can take on a permanent reality, cutting us off from our mothers, from other women, and from our own feminine soul. Under the influence of the Terrible Mother, I may find myself isolated and alone in a male-dominated world, without any intimate connection to females, to my feminine self, or to the Feminine itself. I may have survived the mother-daughter separation, may even have written myself into a starring hero's role in a male success story, but my achievement is shadowed by a guilty sense of having betrayed some essential part of me: my mother, myself, my soul.

But it doesn't have to be that way. I may not be able to heal the rift between my mother and myself, but I can heal the motherbond: I can redefine and validate feminine values and weave them into the survival skills I learned as I became independent. I can seek guidance from strong, gentle women who will teach me about genuine feminine authority and real beauty. I can share my mother-story with other women who have had the same experience. I can rediscover my female body. I can reach out for goddesses that will enlarge my experience of my feminine soul and help me see a motherline that stretches to divinity. And if I am a mother, I can honor the need of my daughters (and sons) to go away from me into the world, and find ways to make the separation less painful.

This mothering work is hard work, long work, woman-by-woman work. It isn't done according to any formula or set of rules, and it won't be accomplished overnight. But for each one of us, it begins with a single, important act: releasing any resentment we may feel toward our mothers for being what they were.

Clippings: "Letting Go, I Love You"

In the late 1930s, in her famous *Diary*, Anne Frank wrote about her mother. Her words speak for all daughters who want to strike out on their own, into a world that lies beyond their mothers' imaginations.

> We are exact opposites in everything; so naturally we are bound to run up against each other. I don't pronounce judgment on Mummy's character, for that is something I can't judge. I only look at her as a mother, and she just doesn't succeed in being that to me; I have to be my own mother. I've drawn myself apart from them all; I am my own skipper and later on I shall see where I come to land. All this comes about particularly because I have in my mind's eye an image of what a perfect mother and wife should be; and in her whom I must call "Mother" I find no trace of that image.

A mother is not a person to lean on but a person to make leaning unnecessary.
—Dorothy Canfield Fisher

A half century later, the conflict is still there, just as strong. Erica Jong, writing in her autobiography, *Fear of Fifty*, speaks for mothers who want to let their daughters go—but who realize that young women must struggle, that the struggle and conflict are necessary for the release. Her piece is a good example of the letter form you may have used earlier, in one of your own writings:

> Molly, I want to release you . . . But if I release you too much, what will you have to fight against?
>
> You need my acceptance, but you may need my resistance more. I promise to stand firm while you come and go. I promise unwavering love while you experiment with hate. Hate is energy too—sometimes brighter-burning energy than love. Hate is often the precondition for freedom.
>
> No matter how I try to disappear, I fear I cast too big a shadow. I would erase that shadow if I could. But if I erased it, how would you know your own shadow? And with no shadow, how would you ever fly?
>
> Freedom is full of fear. But fear isn't the worst thing we face. Paralysis is.
>
> Letting go, I love you. Letting go, I hold you in my arms.

Nancy Friday, whose book about mothers, *My Mother/My Self*, became an enormous best-seller in the late 1970s, writes from a daughter's point of view about a conversation she wished she could have had with her mother. Her wistful words remind us that the tasks, and joys, of mothering can be shared. In this larger sense, an adult woman may decide to seek the mothering she did not receive from her blood mother.

> Sometimes I try to imagine a little scene that could have helped us both. In her kind, warm, shy, and self-deprecating way, Mother calls me into the bedroom . . . I am perhaps six . . . "Nancy, you know I'm not really good at this mothering business," she says. "You're a lovely child; the fault is not with you. But motherhood doesn't come easily to me . . . There are some things I know about. I'll teach them to you. The other stuff—sex and all that—well, I just can't discuss them with you because I'm not sure where they fit into my own life. We'll try to find other people, other women who can talk to you and fill the gaps . . . With their help, with what I can give, we'll see that you get the whole mother package—all the love in the world. It's just that you can't expect to get it from me."

What would happen if you had a conversation with your mother? How would you feel if, in that conversation, your mother told you the truth—*her* truth—about how it felt to be your mother, and what she had most wanted from you as a daughter? How would she respond if you told her the truth about how it felt to be her daughter, and what you had most wanted from her as a mother?

Perhaps you can't have this conversation in person: it would be too difficult, or too painful. Perhaps your mother is no longer living. Or perhaps you feel that you don't know enough about your mother's deepest thoughts and needs to speak for her. But you can certainly speak for yourself. And if you give yourself to the task, putting yourself into your mother's experience as best you can, you may find that you know more about her than you think.

Such a conversation, written down, would make a revealing contribution to your autobiographical chapter on soul mates.

My mother was dead for five years before I knew that I loved her very much.

—Lillian Hellman

Let's Pretend

To bring to a close our work on the motherbond, let's play the childhood game of "let's pretend." Let's say that somewhere in this vast universe, some moments before your conception, an important council meeting is taking place. The entity that is to become you is being assigned a particular curriculum on earth, based in a certain set of life-experiences. No particular outcome is planned for you, the student, other than your soul's growth. Your goal is to learn as much as you can from these experiences and to grow as much and in as many directions as possible, using the gifts you have been given and graced with the help of teachers—soul mates—who have been assigned to you, many of whom you would not have chosen for yourself. (You might not have chosen their methods, either, but assume that they understand the curriculum and are using the methods deliberately.) The first of these teachers is your mother. Now, answer these questions in writing, taking as many pages and as long as you like:

Few women growing up in our patriarchal society have been mothered enough; the power of our mothers, whatever their love for us and their struggles on our behalf, is too restricted.

—Adrienne Rich

> What lessons are you to learn from your mother, not just in your childhood, but over the length of your life?

In what way is your relationship with your mother essential to
　　your soul's growth?
What is the curriculum?

Healing the Father-Wound

*You don't have to deserve
your mother's love. You have
to deserve your father's. He's
more particular.*

—Robert Frost

Daughters aren't very old before they learn that in our society, fathers
are still considered to be better than, smarter than, and more competent
than mothers—and they are certainly a great deal more powerful and
privileged. Growing up with these ideas, a young girl quite naturally
wants to be associated with males. She is drawn to her father or father
substitute, and later to other men. "I adored my father," a friend told
me recently. "Growing up, he was the center of my life. In many ways,
he still is."

　　If a girl's bonding with the father-world is strong, she may become
what some feminist psychologists call a *daughter of the Fathers:* compelled
to seek her father's approval (and that of her male teachers, mentors,
and bosses), to reject feminine affiliation in favor of masculine autonomy, and to renounce her feminine self. Given the right circumstances,
a daughter of the Fathers is likely to be successful, both professionally
and in her efforts to earn male approval. She is also likely, as June Singer
puts it, to suffer the "sadness of the successful woman."

*Full fathom five thy father lies;
Of his bones are coral made:
Those are pearls that were
　his eyes:
Nothing of him that doth fade,
But doth suffer a sea-change
Into something rich and strange.*

—William Shakespeare

　　As I write these paragraphs, my heart is heavy, for I see myself in
what I have just written. My father was not a professional man—he was
a blue-collar worker with a high school education and a serious problem with alcohol. But he loved music and books (my mother never read
anything other than the newspaper), he worked out in the world, he had
(I imagined) vast skills and authority that my mother lacked. My embrace of all he represented created a chasm between my mother and me
that has only begun to be bridged in the last few years. I see myself in
Maureen Murdock's story of her flight to the fathers, recorded in her
book *The Heroine's Journey:*

　　　　As a young girl I saw my father as a god. I couldn't wait for him to
　　　　come home from work; he was funny, intelligent, creative, and, as an
　　　　advertising executive, he had power in the world . . . His mysterious
　　　　comings and goings early in the morning and late at night gave him

mythic proportions in my young eyes. He must be doing "important work," I thought—probably the work of gods! When he was home, I wanted his attention, his approval, his conversation. . . . I performed well the role of the pretty, intelligent daughter, waiting for my prince to come. He never succeeded in rescuing me, however. I realized many years later that he had abandoned both me and my mother so that he could do important things in the world.

In one sense, Murdock did the right thing—the healthy thing—when she identified with masculine power and authority. A nurturing, supportive father can use his daughter's need to identify with him to help her gain a sense of her own physical and mental power, as well as her emerging attractiveness. In fact, psychologists who studied career women occupying positions of power in the sixties and seventies found that their fathers had actively nurtured their skills, encouraged their successes, and had high expectations of them.

But not all fathers are nurturing. Many are too weak to support their daughters. Some (like Murdock's work-oriented, detached father) may be absent, or separated from their families by divorce, addiction, illness, war. Others may be indulgent, or unhealthily attracted to their daughters. Or too critical of their decisions and overly strict, limiting the daughter's ability to learn responsible independence.

Father-wounding has many serious consequences. A woman whose father was easygoing and indulgent may lack the ability to set standards, to create structure and discipline in her life. Or she may drive herself to success at all costs, trying to succeed for him. An angry or violent father creates much pain for his daughter, who may forever after associate "love" with anger or violence, or both.

I don't mean to suggest here that fathers are solely responsible for their daughters' difficulties in the world. The truth is that the patriarchy damages men just as much as it damages women, and that it is still the rare man who has the wisdom and insight to be able to truly father his daughter. If that is the case, what's a daughter to do?

The first thing we have to do is to be clear with ourselves about our feelings for our fathers, and theirs for us. This task, while it may be painful, is necessary to telling our true story.

The life of the father has a mysterious prestige: the hours he spends at home, the room where he works, the objects he has around him, his pursuits, his hobbies, have a sacred character. . . . he incarnates the immense, difficult and marvelous world of adventure; he personifies transcendence, he is God.

—Simone de Beauvoir

To be a successful father there's one absolute rule: when you have a kid, don't look at it for the first two years.

—Ernest Hemingway

Storyboarding

If you've ever read a comic strip, you've seen a storyboard: a layout of the essential actions of a story in side-by-side frames. Storyboarding is a helpful writing strategy that allows you to tell the simplest outlines of a story without a great deal of elaboration. To use this technique, you don't have to be an artist; all you need is a pair of scissors and some magazines, or a pencil for drawing stick figures.

Let's call this storyboard "My Father and Me" and construct it in six frames. Label each frame with a particular age. (I suggest the years three, six, nine, twelve, fifteen, and eighteen. But if your father-story contains important episodes irregularly spaced through your growing-up years, feel free to choose any years you'd like to illustrate.) Clip and paste or draw the figures that are appropriate to each of the six frames. If you like, add captions or bubbles of dialogue, comic-book style.

Some father-stories are bright with love and remembered joy; others are dark with anger, pain, even violence. Storyboards are good for telling happy stories because they are usually simple; they are also useful for telling painful stories because they allow us to use images instead of words to express our feelings. The frame construction also enables us to tell stories that span a period of time: we can select the important points to illustrate and leave out the in-between. If you wish to write a narrative to accompany the storyboard, please do so.

A member of a story circle I worked with created a compelling six-panel storyboard. In the first, a man and a woman were arguing while a little girl sat on the floor, looking on. In the second, the man walked out, slamming the door, as the girl looked on. The third, fourth, fifth, and sixth frames pictured the girl still sitting in the same position, a few years older in each frame. Over the girl's head was a balloon filled with a fantasy of the man, her absent father. Her painful loss and the strategy she used to deal with it were clearly evident. Her story needed no words.

Let's Pretend Once More

When you've finished your storyboard, with or without a written narrative, repeat the "let's pretend" exercise that you did a few moments

We bear the influences of our parents, but we are not fated to remain merely the products of our parents . . . There is within us as well the positive and creative aspects of the inner archetypal father which can compensate for many of the negative influences in our actual life histories.

—Linda Schierse Leonard

ago. Go back to that council meeting somewhere in the universe, where the you-entity is being assigned its curriculum and teachers. One of these teachers is your father. Now, answer these questions, taking as many pages as you like to do so:

What are you to learn from your father-teacher?
In what way is your relationship with him essential to your soul's growth?
What is the curriculum?

Clippings: "But now I realized . . ."

When she was fourteen years old, writer Ursula Owen discovered a photograph of her father in his army uniform, which revealed something she had never before recognized:

> . . . Because it was odd, I looked at it closely. I was a teenager battling with an autocratic if benevolent father who very much expected his will to be done. And here was this same man, in uniform, looking uncharacteristically ill at ease, anxious, even sheepish. The expression on his face was one I didn't recognize. After a while I realized what it was: my father looked vulnerable.
>
> The photographer had caught him off guard. Now I'd seen it once, I began to see that expression on his face more often. The way I looked at my father altered, and the way I felt about him changed too: I still loved him very much, he still seemed an immensely powerful person, and I was still at times afraid of him. But now I realized that he wasn't always in control and what's more, that I knew things he didn't—because I was a woman.

Love doesn't just sit there like a stone; it has to be made, like bread, remade all the time, made new.

—Ursula K. Le Guin

In this excerpt, Ursula Owen writes about seeing through her father's apparent power and control to something uncertain and vulnerable underneath. Has there ever been an occasion in which you glimpsed the real person behind the picture you'd always had of your father? What was he like on the surface? What did you see underneath? Did it change your perception of the man in any enduring way? A page-long description of what you saw and the way you felt about it would be a good addition to your chapter.

Healing with Dreams

The psychologist Carl Jung taught that dreams can be a vital link in the healing process, because they give expression to hopes and fears that are buried in the unconscious. While the language of our dreams is often enigmatic and puzzling, the more attention we pay to them, the clearer their meaning will become. As we begin to understand our dreams, we see that they point the way toward healing, for (Jung says) dreams show us the potential for new growth. Sometimes they show us that we have already made substantial movement toward growth, even though we are not consciously aware of it.

If your relationship with your father (or with your mother, for that matter) has been a troubled one, dream-work can help. To get started, begin to record your dreams in a dream journal that you update early each morning, before you get out of bed. In my dream journal, I date my dream and give it a name. Then I write a brief narrative of the dream. If I have an idea about its meaning, I might include a few lines of interpretation, but I don't make a special effort to discover what it means. (Here, I'm following Jung's idea that the conscious mind has to gradually assimilate material that arises from the unconscious in dreams. The mere act of writing the dream down is enough work at this point.) If the dream seems to be connected to other dreams, I make a note of the connection, sometimes by assigning it to a particular category. I also make a note about what I was doing the day before, for the activities of the day may hold some clue to a dream's meaning.

During my midlife years, when my past and present difficulties with my father were troubling me deeply, I dreamed often about him. I noted the dreams—many of them frightening, many others angry—in my dream journal. I recorded the dreams chronologically, but I also listed them under the heading "Father-dreams." Over the two years before my father died, I noticed that the dreams were becoming less angry, less frightening. Here is the last one I recorded, a few months after his death.

Dad's Garden

In my dream, I am an adult. My father and mother have moved into a brand-new house on the lot next to the house where we lived when I was nine, when I first knew my father had what we called a "drinking problem." He asks me if I will move into the house with them and points out that there will be brand-new furniture. I thank him, but say that I have my own house now. Dad accepts my decision, although he is clearly (and surprisingly) disappointed. In the back, there is space for a garden, and to allay his disappointment, I offer to help him plant it. Dad and I stand beside the plowed ground. He says, "The soil isn't quite right yet, but it will be after we've worked on it."

I woke in tears, feeling that the father-wound had healed. My father wasn't, after all, either the god or the devil I had imagined him. He was a small, tired man whose disappointments had overwhelmed him. He was born into a society that bound men's hearts as tightly as the feet of a Chinese girl, and he could not set himself free.

I no longer live in my father's house. But I still tend the soil of our relationship, watching it become richer and more fruitful, season by season.

Clippings: "Daddy, please . . ."

Earlier, we read Anne Frank's description of her mother. This is the way she describes her father:

> I adore Daddy. He is the one I look up to. I don't love anyone in the world but him. He doesn't notice that he treats Margot [Anne's sister] differently from me . . . I'm not jealous of Margot, never have been. I don't envy her good looks or her beauty. It is only that I long for Daddy's real love: not only as his child, but for me—Anne, myself.

Hope Edelman wrote a book called *Motherless Daughters: A Legacy of Loss.* In it, she describes her feeling about her father:

> There's no way I can write this chapter without hurting my father. Or without fearing his response. Even as I type this sentence, I see his

hands trembling as he turns the manuscript pages; his mouth dropping into a frown; his face closing down like a garage door, as it used to each time a conversation reached a painful topic and he wanted it to end. Silence and departure were always his immediate defense. So over the clicks of my computer keyboard, I hear the louder click at the other end of the telephone line, brace myself for the slam of his bedroom door, and see his broad back growing smaller as he retreats down the hall. And even though I'm an adult now, the voice inside me still calls after him: *Daddy, please don't leave.*

In an essay called "Two for the Price of One," published in *Fathers: Reflections by Daughters*, writer Sara Maitland observes that she has two fathers, a biological father named Adam Maitland, a mild man who fathered six children and died of cancer, and another father.

> . . . This one is alive and well and rampaging inside me. He never goes away . . . he is never ill, never weakened, never leaves me alone. He lurks about under other names—God, Husband, Companion, and all those relationships are made possible (which is nice) and impossibly difficult and conflicting because of the Father who is in and under and through them all. In my late teens I fled away from my father's house; it has taken me a long time to realize that I carried with me the Father from whom I could not escape by escaping childhood, from whom I have not yet escaped, and from whom I have had, and still have, to wrest my loves, my voice, my feminism and my freedom. It is this Father that I have hated loving and loved hating.

My Children, Myself

Not all women become mothers. But those who do often feel that their lives are bound together with their children's lives in mysterious ways. This is often achingly clear when a mother contemplates her child's beauty, as Lenore P. does in this piece:

> I took my three-year-old son swimming in the lake on a hot July day—I remember being pregnant with my second, with Michael. When it was time to take Tommy out of the water, I began to rub

him down, and suddenly I felt how *beautiful* his skin was, and his baby-blond hair, and his arms, and his toes. But our time together was so short, like the swim in the lake, it would be gone in a blink, and I wondered how I could possibly hold on to this moment, to him, and to the baby inside me. I wanted time to stop, so I could be there forever with them, with the children I had made.

But our children sometimes teach us lessons of loss and longing. Margaret T. wrote this paragraph about her daughter, who died at eight of leukemia:

> Sara was the most courageous person I have ever met. She endured it all—the pain, the sadness, the fear, the waiting—with grace and dignity. Even in the end, with all the tubes sticking in her and the machines hooked up to her, she could smile. For a long time, whenever I felt as if I couldn't stand another minute without her, I would remember that smile. If Sara could stare at death and be that brave, so could I.

And Mary K. ended a ten-page history of her troubled relationship with her son Todd with this paragraph:

> I ask myself over and over what I would do differently if I had known how it was all going to turn out. Would I have stayed with Todd's father, hoping that having a man in his life would give Todd a better chance? Would I have gotten counseling for him? Would I have put him in a different school, or moved to a different neighborhood? But when I get tangled up in these questions, I tell myself, stop. Todd's life is *his* life. It's his lesson. My lesson is Todd. It's loving him and watching him struggle with drugs and alcohol, and letting go of him. It's trying to remember that he is the one who is choosing, not me.

As a daughter, your task has been separating yourself from mother and father and becoming your own authentic self. If you are a mother, your task is to support your child's efforts—whatever they are, however you feel about them—to become his or her own self, separate and independent from the parents who gave life. If you have a child or children, this is a good place to write about your experiences and the soul lessons you have exchanged. To do this, I suggest that you begin by writ-

Your children are not your children.
They are the sons and daughters of Life's longing for itself.

—Kahlil Gibran

ing a brief narrative chronology of your life with each of your children. (The important word here is *brief*. One way to pace yourself is to write no more than a paragraph about each five-year period of your child's life with you, and to summarize in a single paragraph the years since the child left home. If you like, you can always come back later and expand the narrative.)

When you've finished your narrative, repeat the "let's pretend" exercises that you did with your mother and father. Return to the council meeting somewhere in the universe, where you are being assigned your curriculum and teachers. One of your teachers is your child. Now, answer these questions, taking as many pages as you like to do so:

What are you to learn from your child-teacher?
In what way is your relationship with him or her essential to your
    soul's growth?
What is the curriculum?

My Loves, Myself

Earlier, you wrote a brief history of your heart. In that summary of your relationships, you probably covered the most significant loves of your life: those relationships that challenged you to enlarge your sense of self. In the history of my heart, I can read the story of my soul's lessons in intimacy. Lovers, spouses, children—my strongest connections to others are here on the page before me. And as I glance over it, I can see quite clearly what and how I have learned, and how I have grown in an inward direction, into the soul's dimension.

The Soul's Intimates

The word *intimacy* comes from a Latin root that means "innermost." An intimate relationship is one in which the innermost self is connected to the innermost self of another—parent, child, friend, and most particularly lover or life partner.

In our society, true intimacy is difficult. Where parents and children are concerned, issues of power and control get in the way. In romantic relationships, we may confuse intimacy with the sudden and intense experience of "falling in love." The truth is, though, that the chaotic feelings of new love may be a barrier to intimacy. And if the relationship is brief, as many of our dating and love relationships are, how are we to reach the stage where we can even begin to practice intimacy? Many of us, particularly if we want to build a successful professional career before embarking on marriage, find ourselves involved in one superficial, short-term relationship after another, none of which can be truly called intimate.

There may be a greater barrier to intimacy. In order to be truly intimate with another, I must first be intimate with myself. I must know that I have an interior life—a life of the soul—and be familiar with it. I must know who I am, what I need and want, where I have been, where I am going. Intimacy with another begins in the depths of my own soul. And if I don't know the difference between the outer and inner parts of me—if I confuse my exterior and interior lives—how am I to be clear about the outer and inner parts of somebody else? I may think I am intimately related to another person when it is my outer self, which we call the ego, that is connecting with his or her outer ego-self. If this is true, I have a great deal of work to do on *myself*—getting to know the many parts of me, cultivating my inner life, becoming conscious of the difference between inner and outer and the vibrant interplay between both—before I can expect to be intimate with someone else.

Looking back over your life, you may see periods of time when you could not be truly intimate with another because you were not intimate with yourself. Most of your energy may have been devoted to developing your outer ego-self, in order to achieve career success or to accomplish some other important goal. During that time, your relationships (both short- and long-term) may have been superficial and unsatisfying, hardly touching the soul. Or you may see relationships in which you confused intimacy and sexuality, or in which intimacy was compromised in a struggle for control.

Look again at the history of your heart. Which of the relationships was (or is) the most intimate? For a moment, think quietly about it—about the other person, the time and the place, your feelings, the other person's feelings. Try to re-create in your mind the "feel" of it, as much

Women's great desire for affiliation is both a fundamental strength, essential for social advance, and at the same time the inevitable source of many of women's current problems.

—Jean Baker Miller

It is not the quality of the love, or even the quantity of the love; it is the consistency of the loving that makes the difference.

—Peg Armstrong

Women are quite validly seeking something more complete than autonomy . . . a fuller, not a lesser, ability to encompass relationships to others, simultaneous with the fullest development of oneself.

—Jean Baker Miller

as you can, including its joys and sadnesses, its honesties and dishonesties, its dreams and illusions. What were the soul-lessons involved in it? Perhaps you were changed by its pains as well as its pleasures; for intimacy necessarily involves pain, just as it involves growth.

Now, still quietly thinking about the relationship, write out your responses, in as great length as they seem to require, to these questions:

What was at stake in this relationship?
What did I want from it in the beginning?
What did I give to it?
What did I lose to it?
What was its most important gift to me?

These are important questions. In them are clues to the mysterious soul of intimacy, the core of the interior life. Here is a brief answer, written by a woman named Celeste, who said that her most significant relationship was an obsessive love affair that compelled her to see that her life had been one long string of obsessive relationships—none of them truly intimate. The relationship she writes about here, however, forced her to become intimate with herself for the first time.

What was at stake in my relationship with Rick was my life, I think. If I hadn't gotten so *fiercely* involved with him, I might have gone on repeating my obsessions forever! I might never have gone deeply enough inside myself to find out what I was doing to myself, or why.

In the beginning of our relationship, I wanted (or thought I did) love, devotion, somebody to care for me. Somebody who would be there for me, through thick and thin. Somebody I could count on. Funny thing, though, I had always picked the kind of man I *couldn't* count on, so maybe what I really wanted, deep down, was somebody like my father, who left my mother when I was twelve but came to visit on Christmas and birthdays, bringing me an armload of presents.

When Rick came into my life, I was eager to give him anything he wanted and willing to wait forever for him to make up his mind that he wanted me. Looking back, I know I gave far too much, and that the more I gave, the more I hated myself for giving.

What did I lose? Here's the odd part. For a long time, I knew I'd lost Rick. That was why I went into therapy. I kept asking, What's wrong with me, that I keep losing the men I love? But now that I've come through the healing and seen why I was connecting with men as I did, I know that what I really lost in the relationship was my own way of relating. I don't have to do that anymore—what a relief!

Looking back, I can see that the relationship brought me many things—none of which Rick had much to do with. It brought me self-knowledge (so *this* is what I'm really like!). Self-appreciation (you've got a lot of guts, Celeste!). My *self* (I've done a lot of inner work since then). And the ability to have a healthy (i.e., nonobsessive) relationship with somebody else. (Odd that I thought of that part last.)

—Celeste J.

If you choose, you could write about each of your soul relationships in this way, answering the questions suggested on page 116 or answering questions of your own. Or you might write a letter to one of your soul mates, or record a conversation exploring the relationship, or compose a poem. Or you might do one or both of the following exercises.

Writing from a Photograph

For this writing, you'll need a photograph of yourself with the other person—preferably an action photograph that shows the two of you doing something together. Using the photograph, you could

— write a dramatic scene, complete with dialogue, that reveals the soul of the relationship
— describe yourself and your soul mate first from your point of view, then from the other's viewpoint
— imagine how the other person would have answered the questions you dealt with a moment ago. (What was at stake? What did I want? What did I give? What did I lose? What was the most important gift of the relationship?)

Replying to a Love Letter

For this writing, you'll need an old love letter from one of your soul mates. If you don't have a letter, try writing one. Imagine that you are your soul mate, and say something about how you feel, what you want out of the relationship, what you are prepared to give, and so on. Reply to the letter, being as clear and honest as you know how to be. Include some or all of the following:

—a paragraph about what the relationship means to you now. (If that's different from what the relationship used to mean, tell the person how it's different.)

—a paragraph about how the relationship changed you. (What are you doing or feeling now that you wouldn't be doing or feeling if the relationship hadn't occurred?)

—a paragraph about your feelings now about the person. (If those feelings have changed over time, say how.) You might find it useful to repeat this writing for all the people you included in your "history of the heart."

Clippings: In Praise of Aphrodite

The feminist theologian Carol Christ writes movingly about the power of Aphrodite, the goddess of love, in this excerpt from an article entitled "In Praise of Aphrodite," published in the magazine *Women of Power*.

Though I had no idea where the reinitiation into the power of the erotic which I experienced with my lover would lead, I knew at some depth of my being that my life would change dramatically. I would no longer be able to continue to do work that did not give me joy, and I would no longer settle for relationships in which the erotic's power was not manifest.

Like all lovers, I prayed that the relationship we had would last for us. And when it didn't, at least not in the way I had imagined it would, I was devastated. It was little consolation to remind myself that the reason Aphrodite's powers are called "divine" is because they are transformative, not because they promise the "happily ever after" of a fairy tale. . . .

Now, as I look back on the relationship I had with my lover, I understand that Aphrodite brings transformations in our lives that are deep and lasting, but not necessarily those we would knowingly choose. At the moment . . . I am in bed alone. And at the same time, I know more deeply than ever that I am Aphrodite's priestess. I am learning, not without difficulty and a great deal of stumbling along the way, to trust the power of the erotic in my life.

In *Henry and June,* the novelist Anaïs Nin (then married to a banker) gives us a glimpse into her turbulent feelings for her lover June, the wife of writer Henry Miller. The passage rings with the elation of a transforming, and taboo, eroticism:

> I was terribly happy. June was exultant. We talked simultaneously . . . Our fears of displeasing each other, of disappointing each other were the same. She had gone to the cafe in the evening as if drugged, full of thoughts of me. People's voices reached her from afar. She was elated. She could not sleep. What had I done to her? She had always been poised, she could always talk well, people never overwhelmed her.
>
> When I realized what she was revealing to me, I almost went mad with joy. She loved me, then? June! She sat beside me in the restaurant . . . I told her, "We have both lost ourselves. I am not trying to think any more. I can't think when I am with you. You are like me, wishing for a perfect moment, but nothing too long imagined can be perfect in a worldly way. Neither one of us can say just the right thing. We are overwhelmed. Let us be overwhelmed. It is so lovely, so lovely. I love you, June."

Both of these writings are testimony to the power of the erotic in our lives, the renewing strength of Aphrodite. "Let us be overwhelmed," Nin says. Let us learn to "trust the power of the erotic," Christ says, for in that power is the potential for change and growth. As you look back over the history of your heart, do you see relationships in which you yielded to the power of the erotic? How important were they in your life's curriculum? What did they teach you? How were you transformed?

Putting Your Fourth Chapter Together

In the three main sections of this chapter, I've suggested ways to write about your family, your parents, and the loves of your life: your soul mates. For your chapter, you've composed a history of your heart, a conversation, a storyboard, a reply to a letter. You may also have illustrated your chapter with photographs of yourself and others.

There are other things you might want to include in a chapter called "Soul Mates." Your family may have a collection of mementos that tell an important family story: a land grant or a property deed, birth certificates, obituaries. Or you might include a selection of personal letters—letters from your father, mother, children, friends, lovers, partners—or love poems, your own or others'. Or you may have kept some mementos that recall a long-ago tryst; these could spark several pages of recollections. This chapter can open up in a variety of ways, depending on your inclination. I hope you'll play with it, and see where it can take you.

Meditation

The Heart of Love

This exercise is based on the Buddhist "loving-kindness meditation." Its purpose is to make us aware of our intimate connection with all beings through the heart of the universe, which is love. It allows us to experience our connection to the entire universe, to feel the energy of loving-kindness that breathes life into and through all creatures, the energy that *is* life. When I practice the meditation regularly—three or four times a week—I find that it brings me closer to the people I hold in my heart. It makes me more mindful of them, more compassionately attentive to them, and, importantly, less anxious about their welfare. It encourages me to trust that their lives will unfold beautifully without my telling them how, for they are, as I am, held in the loving heart of the universe.

Close your eyes and relax, feeling your weight pressing into your chair, exhaling gently, exhaling the tension and nervous energy from your body. Observe the tension slowly drain away, from the top of your head to your toes, as if it were water moving through you. . . . Feel your weight, the full, firm stillness of your body, erect in your seat. . . . Let go of all the busy thoughts and simply watch your breathing, breathing in, breathing out.

Now, call to your mind someone you love dearly . . . see the face of the one you love . . . silently speak your loved one's name. . . . Picture yourself embracing your loved one, and imagine that person's body warm against you. Feel your love for this person, like a warm current of electrical energy coming through you to the other. . . . Feel the other's love for you, that person's loving energy, flowing into your body. . . . And feel, in your heart, in your mind, in your body, how much you want your loved one to be released from anxiety and stress, from confusion, from sorrow. That desire, strong and sincere, comes from the loving heart of the universe. That desire is the true heart of love.

Now, continue to feel that warm, strong pulse of energy flowing through you, arising from the heart of love. As you sit quietly, see in your imagination the faces of your family, your parents, your friends and co-workers, your neighbors. . . . Imagine them with you, and seeing each face, silently speak each name, quietly touch each person on the face, the shoulder, the hand, whatever is appropriate . . . Among these people will be some with whom you've been in conflict . . . but regardless of the tension between you, wish each one well, feeling the desire that he or she will be free of anxiety, free of sorrow, free of fear. . . . With each one, share the generous current of loving energy that flows through you. . . . Feel the current of their energy, like rays of light or a pulsing energy, moving from them to you. . . . Feel yourselves held, together, in the loving, energetic heart of the universe. . . .

Now, imagine your larger family, friends you haven't seen in a while, members of your community. . . . And as you see them, as you feel their presence and imagine their faces, let the current of loving energy pass through you to all of them, and receive the current that returns to you from them. Wish them well. Feel your desire that each one of them shall be free of stress, of fear, of grief. . . .

And beyond this group of people you know are all the unknown peoples of the earth, all the countless creatures of the earth, every earth dweller. . . . Feel their presence, feel the many ways you are interconnected on this small planet. . . . And feel your wish, your strong desire that all shall be free of fear, free of grief, free of suffering. . . . With all these beings, share the current of loving energy, the lifeblood of the cosmos, flowing through you, through them, from the warm heart of the universe.

And as you sit quietly with this multitude of beloved fellow-creatures, feel your place among them, seeing yourself small and vulnerable, alone and yet not alone. . . . See your face, call your name, the name of this person that you know more intimately than any of the others. . . . feel your wish for love, your need for peace, your desire to do well and be well. . . . Feel your own wish that you be free of anxiety and fear and confusion. . . . And feel the universe enfolding you in its warm embrace, in its loving heart. Feel yourself connected, intimately, with all other beings in the warm heart of the cosmos. . . . You are loved. . . . We are all loved. . . .

And now, bring your attention back to your breath, to your body in its sitting posture, to your place in the room. Open your eyes, take a deep breath, and know that all is well. Sit quietly for as many moments as you like. If you wish, you may add to your chapter anything you have drawn from this meditation.

Celebrating the Completion of Your Chapter

Our relationships with others are at the center of our lives, and a chapter about them is at once difficult and rewarding. Congratulations on having finished it! Here are several things you might do to mark the completion of this part of your soul's story.

1. Share parts of your chapter with the members of your Story Circle. One way you might do this: each person could distribute a copy of her history of the heart, then choose one relationship to talk about, using the questions on page 116 as a framework. Or, since the chapter is a long one, you might break it up and spend three meetings on it: one session on mothers, another on fathers (bring your storyboards!), another on romantic love.

2. Arrange a special celebration with one of your soul mates. If the person is available, share some time together. If not, perhaps you can connect long-distance, via telephone, E-mail, or letter. As you celebrate, be mindful of the special quality of this relationship. Let the other person know what he or she has meant to you.

3. Create a "soul shelf," with photographs of your soul mates, special mementos of your relationship, and symbols of what you have learned from your experience together. Decorate your shelf with fresh flowers and spend a few minutes every day arranging it and thinking about the relationships it honors.

4. Make a "soul album," using photographs and other mementos, perhaps including, as well, some of the material you've written. You might want to decorate the pages of your album with drawings or cutouts. You could share your album with your Story Group, or with the soul mates it honors.

Chapter Five

Journeys

If you travel far enough, one day you will recognize yourself coming down the road to meet yourself. And you will say—YES.

—Marion Woodman

Lady Tourists

Until the late 1800s, journeying was a men-only activity. Explorers, traders, soldiers, adventurers, tourists, men have always been free to trek off into the exciting unknown. They left to escape from failure or from their wives. They embarked to make war, discover new territories, conquer new terrain, find new trading products. History is one long adventure story, told by men on the go.

Women have had a different experience. Until fairly recently, most of us stayed home, minding children, tending livestock and garden, doing "women's work." If we traveled, it was to establish a new home somewhere else—usually at the behest of the man of the family. (When I read between the lines of the much-loved *Little House* books, for instance, I see long-suffering Caroline Ingalls, following her footloose husband, Charles, up and down the Great Plains, patiently creating one "little house" after another for her family.)

By the middle of the nineteenth century, however, women began to

You are destined to fly, but that cocoon has to go.

—Nelle Morton

travel where *they* wanted to go. Upholstered in woolens and strong boots and armed with hat pins and umbrellas, genteel ladies—caricatured as "globe-trotteresses"—set off around the world. They bicycled across Europe, safaried across Africa, trekked the Gobi Desert, climbed the Swiss Alps. For the most part, they weren't adventurers, and they weren't looking for love. (May French Sheldon departed to Africa wearing a sash that read *"Noli me tangere"*—don't touch!) They were able to go because they were free of responsibility: as Mabel Sharman Crawford says in her *Plea for Lady Tourists*, they were of "independent means and without domestic ties." When they came home, they gave magic-lantern lectures and wrote books with exotic titles—Flora Tristan's *Peregrinations of a Pariah*, Amelia Edwards's *A Thousand Miles up the Nile*, Mrs. F. D. Bridges's *Journal of a Lady's Travels Round the World*. They told of a life of adventure and freedom that most women of their time could scarcely comprehend.

Clippings: A Lady's Life Abroad

Until she was thirty, Mary Kingsley tended her elderly parents and surreptitiously read as much as she could about Africa. In 1892, a year after they died, she went to the jungles of West Africa to collect fetishes and fish. In *Travels in West Africa*, she described the treacherous mangrove swamp through which she traveled in a "suitable small canoe" in the mid-1890s. Her unique voice is that of a traveler who is both an absorbed participant in her experience and a wryly amused observer of it. To achieve the immediacy of participation, she uses present-tense verbs; to achieve the ironic distance, she uses the pronoun *you*:

> But [canoeing through the swamp] is a pleasure to be indulged in with caution; for one thing, you are certain to come across crocodiles. Now a crocodile drifting down in deep water, or lying asleep with its jaws open on a sand-bank in the sun, is a picturesque adornment to the landscape when you are on the deck of a steamer, and you can write home about it and frighten your relations on your behalf; but when you are away among the swamps in a small dug-out canoe, and that crocodile and his relations are awake—a thing he makes a point of being at flood tide because of fish coming along, he is highly interesting, and you may not be able to write home about him—and you get frightened on your own behalf. . . .

*A Lady an explorer? a
traveller in skirts?
The notion's just a trifle too
seraphic;
Let them stay home and
mind the babies, or hem
our ragged shirts;
But they mustn't, can't, and
shan't be geographic.*

—*Punch, 10 June 1893*

*Doubtless, in the twentieth
century, enterprising lady
tourists will not feel it need-
ful to preface the published
records of their travels with a
plea in vindication of the act;
for ladies continuing to do
what daily experience proves
they can safely do, with high
enjoyment, will soon be safe
from ridicule or reproach,
since the unfamiliar, passing
into the familiar, invariably
becomes a recognized social
law.*

—Mabel Sharman Crawford
(1863)

In addition to this unpleasantness you are liable . . . to get tide-trapped away in the swamps . . . and you find you cannot get back to the main river. For you cannot get out and drag your canoe across the stretches of mud that separate you from it, because the mud is of too unstable a nature and too deep, and sinking into it means staying in it, at any rate until some geologist of the remote future may come across you, in a fossilized state, when that mangrove swamp shall have become dry land.

In 1873, the Englishwoman Isabella Bird made an extended tour of the Rocky Mountains—"no region for tourists and women," she wrote in *A Lady's Life in the Rocky Mountains.* One day in early autumn, unaccompanied, she rode her horse fifty-six miles along the Denver stage road—"the worst, rudest, dismallest, darkest road I have yet traveled on, nothing but a winding ravine." She spent the night at a log cabin along the way. With the temperature dropping below freezing, her drunken host gave her a bed in a canvas-sided shed. The next day, she wrote to her sister:

> I once gave an unwary promise that I would not travel alone in Colorado unarmed, and in consequence left Estes Park with a Sharp's revolver loaded with ball cartridge in my pocket, which has been the plague of my life. Its bright ominous barrel peeped out in quiet Denver shops, children pulled it out to play with, or when my riding dress was hung up with it in the pocket, pulled the whole from the peg to the floor; and I cannot conceive of any circumstances in which I could feel it right to make any use of it, or in which it could do me any possible good. Last night, however, I took it out, cleaned and oiled it, and laid it under my pillow, resolving to keep awake all night. I slept as soon as I lay down, and never woken till the bright morning sun shone through the roof, making me ridicule my own fears and abjure pistols for ever!

Bird's voice, like Kingsley's, is that of an ironic observer who can describe her fears while she makes gentle fun of them.

In the years since the Victorians, women travelers have become so numerous that no one thinks twice about them—except perhaps to calculate, happily, how much their travel expenditures add to the gross national product. The tourist industry is a multibillion-dollar enterprise, and women account for a significant share of it. In the span of only a hundred years, they have taken on men's itinerant habits.

Once, when I was a young lady and on a night express, I was awakened by a man coming in from the corridor and taking hold of my leg. Quite as much to my own astonishment as his, I uttered the most appalling growl that ever came out of a tigress. He fled, poor man, without a word: and I lay there, trembling slightly, not at my escape but at my potentialities.

—Sylvia Townsend Warner

Like many women, I have become a journeyer. Some of my journeys aren't long (many are only two or three days), few are elaborate (one was a no-frills camping trip to the mountains, another a two-week silent retreat in a room with only a bed, a desk, and a chair). I've frequently been a tourist, although I've never actually been on a tour bus with a tour guide. I've been on quests in search of information and background for my writing. I've gone on pilgrimages to sacred places that gave me a new awareness of the sacred in my life. And I've gone on soul journeys that opened me to a new understanding of the world around me and the landscape of my spirit.

In this chapter of your book, you will explore your own journeys—tours, quests, pilgrimages, and soul journeys. You will see where you've been, imagine where you might like to go, reflect on what it all means. Your reflection, your writing, your chapter, will be your journey into journeying.

Bon voyage!

Travel Log

Let's start your chapter with a travel log—a list of all the journeys you have taken in your life. It will probably be easier if you do this chronologically. You may find it best to organize your list by five-year periods. Then, as you prod the details out of your memory, try to pin each trip down to its particular year. Most people have to make several passes at this task before they consider it complete, so don't be discouraged if you can't recall every journey right away—even the important ones. They'll come to you.

What constitutes a journey? You'll have to be the judge of that. For some people, a journey might involve thousands of miles, a dozen different countries, and months away from home. For others, a journey might be a few days' stay in a cabin on a nearby lake. If you regularly travel for business, you may want to exclude routine trips, or include only those that also became quests, pilgrimages, or soul journeys.

However you define your journeys, make your list as complete as possible. Include the dates, the names of the people who traveled with you, where you went, how you traveled. You can continue to add to your list as you remember journeys you've temporarily forgotten. When

Journeyer: one who whirls through Other worlds, Spinning/Spiraling on multidimensional Voyages through Realms of the Wild, which involve Quests, adventurous Travel, the Dispelling of demons, cosmic encounters, participations in Paradise.

—Mary Daly

you've finished your personal travel log, set it aside for the moment.
We'll come back to it later.

Clippings: Becoming the World

In her book *Wall to Wall*, Mary Morris writes about her mother's yearn-
ing to leave the cocoon of home, family, and the suburbs and see the
world:

> It was my mother who made a traveler out of me, not so much be-
> cause of the places she went as because of her yearning to go. She
> used to buy globes and maps and plan dream journeys she'd never
> take while her "real life" was ensconced in the PTA, the Girl Scouts,
> suburban lawn parties and barbecues. . . . Once, when I was a child,
> my parents were invited to a Suppressed Desire Ball. You were to
> come in a costume that depicted your secret wish, your heart's desire,
> that which you'd always yearned to do or to be. My mother went into
> a kind of trance, then came home one day with blue taffeta, white
> fishnet gauze, travel posters and brochures, and began to construct
> the most remarkable costume I've ever seen.
>
> She spent weeks on it. I would go down to the workroom where
> she sewed, and she'd say to me, "Where should I put the Taj Mahal?
> Where should the pyramids go?" On and on, into the night, she
> pasted and sewed. . . .
>
> The night of the ball, she descended the stairs. On her head sat a
> tiny, silver rotating globe. Her skirts were the oceans, her body the
> land, and interlaced between all the layers of taffeta and fishnet were
> Paris, Tokyo, Istanbul, Tashkent. Instead of seeing the world, my
> mother became it.

A workshop participant remembers her grandmother, whose imaginary travels were lived out in the lives of her sons. The writer nicely captures her grandmother's unexpressed longing in the last sentence.

> When I was a small girl, my grandmother had a world map and a
> scrapbook. The map hung on the wall over the kitchen table. It was
> stuck all over with pins, red, blue, green, yellow. A different color for
> places where each of her four sons had lived. The scrapbook was di-

vided into sections with different colors of construction paper, red, blue, green, yellow. Into each section she put the postcards and pictures that her sons sent her from their travels. She used to look at the scrapbook longingly, turning the pages, studying the pictures of palm trees and skyscrapers and Old Faithful.

"It's like being there myself," she'd say wistfully. "Just think of all the things they've seen."

"Why don't you go, Grandma?" I'd ask.

She'd scoff. "What, an old lady like me? What business do I have gallivanting all over the world? Anyway, who'd feed the cat?" But the next minute, she'd be gazing up at the map with a faraway look in her eyes.

—Carole D.

How did your grandmother feel about traveling? Your mother? What held them at home? Or, if they were able to travel, what gave them that freedom? How did their traveling or stay-at-home habit affect you? Write a page or two here about your grandmother's or mother's experience of travel.

Lady Tourists and Journeywomen

What's the difference between a lady tourist and a journeywoman? For a tourist, I think, travel is ladylike, entertaining, amusing, diverting, while a journeywoman's motives are deeper, more complex. Usually, a tourist lets someone else—a travel agent, a tour guide, a guidebook— "package" (what a wonderful word!) her travel, while a journeywoman follows her own itinerary, makes her own choices. (Not that guides and guidebooks aren't helpful when judiciously consulted.) With the advent of multinational hotel and food cartels, a tourist can insulate herself against the dangerous foreignness of a place at the same time that she gingerly exposes herself to it. Almost never surprised, a tourist knows what to expect because she brings her expectations from home. A journeywoman, on the other hand, joyfully embraces the intriguing strangeness of a place, innocent of expectation, always surprised by what she sees.

We don't have to be one thing or another all our lives. We can be

My heart is warm with the friends I make,
And better friends I'll not be knowing;
Yet there isn't a train I wouldn't take,
No matter where it's going.
—Edna St. Vincent Millay

both tourist and journeywoman. Going somewhere for the first time, especially if I have only two weeks' vacation and I'm on a tight budget, I might choose to go as a tourist. Another time, under other circumstances, I might journey to the same place in a more leisurely, open way, letting myself experience whatever happens, continually surprised along the way.

A Tourist's Tale

All of us have been tourists, at one time or another, usually on vacations. We all have stories about the Hotel From Hell, the tour guide who didn't speak English, the baggage that went to Brazil. Here's one that's a bit startling:

> Sandra and I had been in New York since Monday, shopping, taking in shows, gawking at the sights—typical tourist stuff. It was early Wednesday morning, gray, drizzly and cold. I was standing on the sidewalk beside a fountain, showing my teeth to Sandra, who was shooting me with the videocamera. We were both a little cross, not having had our second cup of coffee. Suddenly there was a rush of air and a massive thud, and Sandra screamed and turned white. A man had jumped out of a tenth-story window and landed on the sidewalk behind me. You know the phrase, "Every bone in his body was broken"? They were.
>
> "To hell with the coffee," Sandra said as the police sirens began to wail. "I'm ready for a good, stiff bourbon."
>
> One thing about the Big Apple. It's not hard to find a bourbon, even at eight in the morning.
>
> —Kim L.

Your tourist's tale may not be as deadly as Kim's, but chances are that you recall something out of the ordinary, something interesting or challenging or frightening, about one of the trips you listed in your travel log. Write it down, including as many details as you can: where you were, who was with you, what happened, what you did. Keep your verbs in the active voice and try to write as if you were basically seeing what you remember. (If you have more than one good tourist tale, this is the place to write them down.)

All adventures, especially into new territory, are scary.
—Sally Ride

Snapshots

How many travel snapshots do you have stuck away in a drawer or an album? Take them out and choose a half-dozen that prompt an especially vivid memory. Write one or two paragraphs, more if you like, about each photo, being as specific and detailed as you can about the scene. Were you traveling as a tourist or a journeywoman? What made the place memorable for you? What strong feelings and memories do the snapshots reawaken? Attach the photos to the pages with your writing and put the pages with the other writing you've done for this chapter.

Clippings: Fried Locusts and Other Exotic Delights

Our modern tourist tales may not be as hair-raising as those told by earlier travelers:

> The locusts fried are fairly good to eat.
> —Lady Anne Blunt, *A Pilgrimage to Nejd,* 1881

> We enjoyed washing our faces very much, having had but one opportunity of doing so before, since we left Cabul. It was rather a painful process, as the cold and glare of the sun on the snow had three times peeled my face, from which the skin came off in strips.
> —Lady Sale, *A Journal of the Disasters in Afghanistan,* 1843

> The wretched thing [a snake] had bitten me below the knee . . . With my scalpel I cut across the bite and pushed in two halves of a tablet of permanganate of potash. I wasn't happy for a little time, and though trying hard not to find myself panicking, having searched through my baggage I eventually found a mirror; I hadn't used one for months. I examined my face carefully to see if I was going black or grey or had a queer colour on my lips. Except I seemed a great deal thinner, with big dark rings under my eyes, nothing seemed to be amiss . . . I decided on coffee, a walk and sleep, and if I was going to die it was a fine spot for it and I was at peace with the world—so any way there was nothing to worry about.
> —Violet Cressy-Marcks, *Up the Amazon,* 1932

One of the things I find interesting about these passages is the wryly courageous face these travelers present to their audiences as they understate their reactions to events that must have been difficult or painful. They seem to me to be making a special effort to convince the reader (and perhaps themselves) of their bravery in the face of various exotic adversities. Perhaps you will notice something of the same tone in your own tourist tales.

Quests

A quest is a journey inspired by a purpose, often modified by the word *heroic*. We may use the word in its literal sense. The Crusades were a heroic quest to quell the Infidel. Columbus's voyage to the New World was a quest for trade routes to the Orient. Star Trek's *Enterprise* was on a quest in galaxies beyond our own. Or we may use the term less literally: you might say, for instance, "My friend Maggie went on a quest for her birth mother." Or we may use the word with intentional symbolism. For example, I think of the first part of my adult life as a quest for career success, which was fueled by my desire to be a university professor and administrator.

But a quest, which is aimed at a specific outcome and driven by the promise of reward, may be disappointing—even when it is successful. I am reminded of Joseph Campbell's famous remark about ambitious, desire-driven men suffering midlife crises: "They've gotten to the top of the ladder and found it leaning against the wrong wall." Reaching the goal of the quest is no guarantee of satisfaction.

For many women, questing itself seems to be an alien journey form. As Maureen Murdock suggests in *The Heroine's Journey*, the "heroism" of the quest is a masculine concept, built on the principle of competition: climbing higher, going farther, going faster, doing more, having more. Before the quest can be a soul-satisfying model for women's journeys, we may have to redefine the word *heroic*.

Yet many women have gone on quests, spending their lives in search of a dream, holding up their hope as a candle to their path. Fifty years after the Victorian women trekked around the world, Amelia Earhart died trying to fly around it. Less than fifty years later, Sally Ride orbited it in *Challenger 6*. In the early 1990s, breast cancer survivor Laura

The literature of women's lives is a tradition of escapees, women who have lived to tell the tale. . . . They resist captivity. They get up and go. They seek better worlds.

—Phyllis Rose

To gain that which is worth having, it may be necessary to lose everything.

—Bernadette Devlin

Evans led an expedition of women climbers—also cancer survivors—to the top of 22,834-foot Mount Aconcagua in Argentina. "It was the most important thing in my life," one climber said simply. "I *had* to do it."

And there are other kinds of quests. Marie Curie's lifelong scientific quest ended in the discovery of radium. Dian Fossey died protecting the primates to whose study she had devoted her life. Hillary Rodham Clinton, Barbara Jordan, Sandra Day O'Connor, Ruth Bader Ginsburg—each is a remarkable hero of a quest she defined for herself. Open a copy of a magazine that features people in the public eye and you will find other examples of women who have been successful, at some level, in their quests.

Clipping: "I don't have to walk uphill anymore."

Naturalist-photographer Vivienne De Watteville (1900–57) wanted more than anything else to film rhinoceroses—something that had not been done before. On a filmmaking expedition to Kenya, arranged at great cost and effort, she found what she was looking for. Seen through the viewfinder, one of the rhinos seemed far away, but when she lowered the camera, she saw that he was ready to charge:

> He was standing squarely upon a flat boulder that raised him like a pedestal, and he seemed to tower up rugged and clear-cut as a monument against the flying clouds . . . Before I had time to skip out of his sight he had made up his mind to charge me. The angry thunder of his snort, mingled with a screech like an engine blowing off steam, lent me wings . . . The boys [camera bearers] had a start of me, and as I raced after them across the vistas of stone bare as asphalt without a blade of cover anywhere, conviction swept over me that this time the game was up.
>
> Though I ran and ran as I had never run in my life before, and my heart pounded in my ears and my lungs stiffened with the pain of drawing breath, time went suddenly into slow motion. Each step was weighted with lead; I wanted to fly over the ground and, as in some horrid nightmare, I felt as though I were scarcely moving.

De Watteville escapes unharmed, and enjoys a self-congratulatory moment—until she checks her camera:

There was nothing like an escape to give you the feeling of exhilaration. The pleasant glow of it was stealing over me when I made a crushing discovery. In changing the film I found I had overshot the end by fully six feet. This meant that the rhino's mad rush and the dramatic moment when he had stood silhouetted against the sky, were recorded on nothing but blind, red paper. The disappointment was bitter, so bitter that there were no words for it. The boys still talked of the marvelous picture, and I had not the heart to undeceive them.

Arlene Blum went on a quest to climb Annapurna I. After many setbacks, she reached the top. In *Annapurna, A Woman's Place*, she includes this passage from her journal:

> The summit of Annapurna I at last! At 3:30 P.M. on October 15, 1978, we are at 26,334 feet on top of the world's tenth highest mountain— on top of the world . . .
>
> How do I feel? Partly an incredible sense of relief because I don't have to walk uphill anymore. And a sense of accomplishment for myself and the whole team. We've done what we set out to do— there's no point higher. But mostly, I know that it's 3:30 in the afternoon, and we're going to have to make tracks to get down before dark.

Photographing a charging rhino or climbing Annapurna may not be your dream, but these two quests aren't so different from our own. Our hearts hunger for something—to discover, to know, to achieve, to be known for our achievement. We make plans and sacrifices, prepare ourselves, and meet enormous challenges on the way to our goals. Sometimes we succeed in capturing the prize our hearts are set on and sometimes not. But even when we do, the victory may not fully satisfy. "The trophy itself falls short of the imagination of it," De Watteville wrote later, explaining—sadly—why she had abandoned filmmaking for writing. How do we feel when we've reached our goals? Some of us may immediately establish another goal, set out on another quest. Others may feel like Arlene Blum: incredibly relieved that we don't have to walk uphill anymore. And whatever the summit of our quest, we all have to find a way to integrate our success into ordinary life—to "get down before dark."

There is something I have noticed about desire, that it opens the eyes and strikes them blind at the same time.

—Jane Smiley

Writing about Your Quest

Think back over your life. Have you ever embarked on a quest? Has there been anything in your experience—any goal, any purpose—that commanded an intense effort from you? The wings of your desire might have carried you on a journey to exotic places, in search of strange experiences. Perhaps you quested for new creations: new forms of art, dance, music. Or perhaps you were carried in another direction, into the world of ideas. How did you prepare yourself? What were the costs of your quest? How successful were you in achieving what you set out to do? Did you experience disappointment along the way? How did your quest fit into the framework of your ordinary life? What did you have to give up in order to make the journey? What other women did you meet along the way, taking the same path, going in the same direction?

Defining and describing your quest might take just a few pages or many more. Whole books have been written by women about their quests. But however many pages it takes, the effort is well spent. And when you are finished writing, sit back and think—and then write—about another question: Did the trophy fall short of the imagination?

And if it did, what does that tell you about the difficulty of satisfying the heart-hunger we call desire?

Clippings: "That grim shadow . . ."

Isabel Savory traveled to escape the sad truth that she, like many of the Victorian upper class, had nothing else to do. In *A Sportswoman in India*, we see that while an expedition might be temporarily entertaining, it could not erase the reality of her life.

> Travelling is a Fool's Paradise. I am miserable; I want to get out of myself; I want to leave home. *Travel!* I pack up my trunks, say Farewell, I depart. I go to the very ends of the earth; and behold, my skeleton steps out of its cup-board and confronts me there. I am as pessimistic as ever, for the last thing I can lose is myself; and though

I may tramp to the back of beyond, that grim shadow must always pursue me.

This paragraph was written by a woman in one of my classes:

I've gone on cruises, taken a dozen tours, and been to all the trendy places—Nepal, Singapore, the Greek Isles. But I am like a wandering ghost, hungrily hoping that the next magic mountain will fill my desire for something beautiful and new and different. Somehow it never does, though. By the time I come home, I'm running on empty.

—Dot M.

Pilgrimages

A pilgrimage is a journey to a place where the human soul encounters the sacred. Churches, cathedrals, shrines, temples, mosques, holy cities: these are spaces designed to ritually separate the sacred from the secular, from the profane. They are experienced as centers and sources of enormous spiritual power, charged with an energy that can redeem human life. They have been the goals of countless searchers over the centuries, pilgrims who set aside special hours in the day, special days in the year, and even special years in their lives, to worship there. Or if not to worship, to simply experience the grandeur of the place and reflect on the dreams and desires of the long-dead craftsmen who built it, the artists who decorated it, the ordinary people whose tithes paid for it. These sacred places moor the drifting human community. They are the bridge between earth and heaven, the still point on which rest both time and eternity.

But because cathedrals, temples, mosques, and shrines are seats of political power and because patriarchal religions have refused to allow women to participate significantly in that power, many women and some men have begun to seek their own holy places. Some celebrate the sacred places of the earth—mountains, deserts, rivers, springs, groves of ancient trees—that strike the soul with awe, with a sense of the numinous. In Native American traditions, these are "power places." Alone

The spiritual journey is one of continually falling on your face, getting up, brushing yourself off, looking sheepishly at God, and taking another step.

—Aurobindo

All the way to heaven is heaven.

—St. Catherine of Sienna

on a sacred mountain or deep in the desert, a human being can find herself touched and transformed by the ancient wisdom of the Grandmothers and Grandfathers, by the sacramental vitality of the natural world, by her own physical and spiritual connection to the planet, her home.

The following passage was written by a woman who, the week after her divorce from her husband of twenty-five years, decided it was time to get reacquainted with her soul. She got in the car and drove west, hardly knowing where she was going. The most powerful place she visited—"it was a shrine, really," she said—was Chaco Canyon. This is what she wrote about it.

> To get to Chaco, you turn off New Mexico Highway 44 at the trading post at Nagiezi and drive twenty-seven miles across sagebrush flats. If you're looking for something spectacular, the canyon itself isn't much—sandstone cliffs and a dry, rocky wash. But the prehistoric Anasazi ruins are wonderful. They are communal buildings built of masonry, three and four stories high, and underground ritual chambers, *kivas.* There is a mystery in the dusty silence of the abandoned buildings, and in the shadows of the sandstone cliff. It seems to touch the mystery that my life has become.
>
> Sitting quietly in the dimness of the Great Kiva, I was moved by the presence of the human beings who lived here before me. They had a spiritual vision of wholeness that brought them into harmony with the rhythmic flow of nature and enabled them to live in this arid and desolate landscape. My life felt very fragmented, not at all whole, and I wanted desperately to share their vision. I camped for a few days and watched the sun move across the sky and began to feel peaceful, calm, whole. That was what I took with me when I went home. The feeling of wholeness. I have a picture of a *kiva* on the wall over my bed. It reminds me that there is a place, a very sacred place, where I felt one with all of nature. I'd like to feel that way more of the time.
>
> —Elizabeth P.

The sense of unity, of participation, is one that we often experience in a sacred place. Sometimes it is the whole goal of our pilgrimage.

Writing about Your Pilgrimage

Look back over your travel log. Does it contain any journeys that you think of as pilgrimages? Perhaps you have traveled to a traditional spiritual site—a cathedral, a temple, a mosque. Or perhaps you have made a pilgrimage to a sacred place: a mountain, a spring, a river—a site that is felt to have a special spiritual energy, like the one Elizabeth recalls in the passage above. Take several sheets of paper and write about your experience. Here are some questions to help you organize your writing:

What was the sacred place? For whom was/is it sacred? What is there about this place that makes it so special?

Why did I decide to make a pilgrimage to this spot? How did I learn about it? Was something going on in my life that made this journey possible or necessary—or both?

What was my experience of the place? What did I see, hear, smell? What dreams did I dream?

Did my pilgrimage make a difference in my life? Did I return from it with any kind of changed awareness? How have I integrated that awareness in my everyday life?

Clippings: A Listening Heart

Lebh Shomea—the words mean "Listening Heart"—is a silent monastic community in South Texas. Susan Hansen, a Texas journalist who frequently goes there on retreats, writes that in its silence, "the slightest sound reverberates. Even the whispers have echoes."

The white stucco ranch house rises three stories above the south Texas brush and mesquite. Capped by a red tile roof and tower, the Big House is a place that invites wandering, a mystery that begs for exploration. On my first morning here, I pull back the shutters and find thirty wild turkeys—give or take—nibbling on the lawn below. Later, wearing my poncho against the cold March rain, I will stand down there myself, training my binoculars on a small flock of kiskadees. Browsing in the library, hiking the nature trails that wind through a thousand acres of wild terrain, listening to the coyotes

I live my life in growing orbits
which move out over the things of the world.
. . . I am circling around God, around the ancient tower,
and I have been circling for a thousand years,
And I still don't know if I'm a falcon,
or a storm,
or a great song.

—Rainer Maria Rilke

howling in the distance, or just listening in silence—I sense that there is time for it all . . .

On my final afternoon, I pick up a book and head for the cool veranda. Instead of reading, though, I find my eyes drawn to a row of white stone arches. As much as anything, I realize it is their shadows that intrigue me. Ever fluid, the arches speak to me of the mystery of life, of sun and shade, of appearance and its shadow underside. They are beautiful, in part, because they are true. Unabruptly, gently, they lead my eyes in and hold me there. They are a moment, but a moment that has only depth and no length.

Tempted to analyze, to find some message in this wilderness, I tell myself that, for this week, at least, these are not my tasks. And so I sit and watch and listen in the silence of spring.

Joan Halifax is known for her study of the shamanistic practices of native cultures. In her book, *The Fruitful Darkness: Reconnecting with the Body of the Earth,* Halifax describes her pilgrimage to the desert on the day following her mother's funeral:

> As I entered Joshua Tree National Monument at midnight, lightning turned the landscape bone white . . . As I wandered around among the rocks and crevasses for hours looking for a protected place, I realized that the protection I sought was her. The womb that had given birth to me was gone . . . the body I had been written from was dead . . .
>
> I returned to base camp and the fire, the hearth, another place where mother-comfort is found. There I watched her life in the fire . . . After the moon set, I had the following dream: My mother is on an operating table. A friend, a surgeon in the dream, has his scalpel on her belly. I turn away in horror, but he reaches across her body to comfort me as he cuts into her. From the pool of blood in her abdomen rises a small human figure with its eyes wide and awake. Coming out of the dream with a start, looking at the night sky and tasting the desert in my mouth, I decided to continue the journey of mourning for my mother. I also discovered I was grieving for Earth. At that moment the two, the Earth and my mother, were one body.

A pilgrimage need not be a long journey. The one Linda Hogan describes in her essay "Walking" spans only a few minutes, but it takes her deep into the heart of the sacred.

Tonight I walk. I am watching the sky. I think of the people who came before me and how they knew the placement of stars in the sky, watched the moving sun long and hard enough to witness how a certain angle of light touched a stone only once a year. Without written records, they knew the gods of every night, the small, fine details of the world around them and of immensity above them.

Walking, I can almost hear the heart of redwoods beating . . . It's winter and there is smoke from the fires. The square, lighted windows of houses are fogging over. It is a world of elemental attention, of all things working together, listening to what speaks in the blood. Whichever road I follow, I walk in the land of many gods, and they love and eat one another.

Walking, I am listening to a deeper way. Suddenly all my ancestors are behind me. Be still, they say. Watch and listen. You are the result of the love of thousands.

I have not ceased being fearful, but I have ceased to let fear control me. . . . I have gone ahead despite the pounding in my heart that says: turn back, turn back, you'll die if you venture too far.

—Erica Jong

These three pilgrims share a common experience: a sense of heightened perception, of sharper hearing, clearer sight. It is as if the act of pilgrimage itself opens us to the sacred. "Walking, I am listening to a deeper way," Linda Hogan says. That is what pilgrimage is about.

Soul Journeys

Pilgrimages can put us in touch with the energy that moves the cosmos, the power that generates life. When I go on a pilgrimage, I often return with a new consciousness of my place in the cosmic scheme of things, a renewed sense of grace. But there is another journey that also renews me. It is the soul journey: the journey in which I leave home as one person and return home as another. My destination and purpose do not have to be special, and I may not intentionally set out in search of a spiritual goal. I might be traveling to the faraway mountains of Nepal, or to some place nearby. It is the journey itself—my *interior* journey—that resizes my soul.

When I go on a soul journey, I travel through the outer world along the paths of my inner landscape. For me, one of the most moving accounts of this kind is *The Snow Leopard*, which tells the story of Peter Matthiessen's trek through Nepal after the death of his wife, Deborah.

The path is whatever passes—no end in itself.

—Gary Synder

At once a pilgrimage to a holy city and a quest for a rare creature, Matthiessen's journey is a spiritual adventure that takes us through the mountains and gorges of his soul. By the end of the trek, he says, words have become a clutter, do not say the simple truth that he means to say: "I am moved from where I used to be, and can never go back."

The soul journey moves us from where we used to be. One such journey, for me, took place at the intersection between my academic career and—what? I didn't know. I had taken a leave of absence from my administrative position and had to decide whether or not to return to the university as a faculty member. The week before my decision was due, I went to the Great Smoky Mountains. It was early November and the park was remarkably empty, the campgrounds closed to all but primitive camping, the water and electricity turned off in the restrooms. The afternoon air was quite chilly, the evening air, cold. The sun, when it shone, was a pale, water-color silver in a sky brushed with haze. I pitched my small tent in a deserted campground and watched autumn die into winter.

As I watched, I wrote in my journal about the long way I had come, the distance I had traveled from graduate school through the teaching years, through the administrative appointments, always pushing, striving, achieving, one of only a few women in what was still a man's profession. I sensed that it was time to end the fierce questing that had made the last two decades so exhilarating. But was I ready to give up the excitement of career success, the challenge of juggling dozens of tasks successfully, the triumph of carving out a place for myself in a male-dominated world? If recognition and achievement no longer motivated me, what did? And practically: if I didn't teach, how would I make a living?

As I wrote in my journal, I realized that I didn't know the answers to any of these questions, and I shivered with fear. What was coming? A cold time, a dark time, without the stimulation of work and career? Not knowing what lay ahead, I could only look around. At a brown squirrel eating an acorn as jauntily as a small boy eating corn on the cob. At a fat black bear stuffing wild berries into his mouth with both paws. At brown corduroy leaves, pewter-colored skies, the glaze of stream-spray on a granite rock.

And as I sat in the doorway of my tent, watching the mountain ready itself for winter, I slowly became aware of my own changing rhythms. I

The fear of going too far keeps us from going far enough.

—Sam Keen

was here in these mountains because I had arrived at a point in my life when it was time to *mark* time, not spend it, when it was time to do one thing with attention—watch a squirrel, follow the fall of a leaf—rather than everything at once. What I saw around me—a withdrawal of energies, a turning from the bright exuberance of summer to the darker solitude of winter—was inside me. I realized that it was time to direct my journey inward, and that there was nothing out of the ordinary about this. It was a common miracle, a seasonal grace, a natural turn of events.

The next morning, I woke to the first snowfall, a blanket of unblemished brilliance covering the browns and grays, the fallen leaves, the skeletal trees. I started my fire and brewed coffee in my blue enamel pot. I felt clear and transparent, and the cold light poured through me as through a crystal. It was time to go home.

But the I who returned was not the I who had left.

It had been a soul journey.

Walk on the right,
watch your step,
don't get off on the wrong
*   foot*

The poet says: forget all that
*   stuff*
about how to get there.
You are who you are right
*   here.*
Stand on that.

—Susan Albert, after Kabir

Your Soul Journeys

Look once again at your travel log, and think back over the course of your life, considering these questions. Is there a journey that reshaped your life, that marked a passage? Where did the exterior journey take you? Interiorly, where did you go? From what to what? Why? Looking back on the journey from the distance of time and space, what did it mean? Where would you be if you had not journeyed?

When you have considered long enough, write.

Clippings: Nowhere to Go

I went on a soul journey last weekend, but I didn't go anywhere. I just sat. Not doing anything, not going anywhere. I went to a Vipassana [a style of Buddhist meditation] retreat. We sat on round hard cushions on a bare wooden floor in an empty room in a lodge surrounded by trees, and all we did was pay attention to our breathing. Every now and then the leader would strike a gong, and we would get up and

Without going out of my door

I know what the countryside is like.

Without glancing out of my window

I know the color of the sky.

The farther you travel,

the less you know.

If you are wise,

you can arrive without going,

see without looking,

do everything while you are doing nothing.

—Susan Albert,
after Lao Tzu

Journeys start from where we are. Everything starts from where we are. Where we are is where we're supposed to be.

—Evelyn Eaton

walk outside under the trees, very slowly, paying attention to our walking.

Doing nothing, going nowhere, all day, two days. Thoughts came up, lots of thoughts, thoughts of all that I *should* be doing, places I *should* be going. But after a while the thoughts went away. And after a longer while, I realized that the longest journey of all is letting go of my thoughts and my habits and what I have learned to do and be. It's not a journey I can make all at once, or overnight. But getting started is a journey by itself. After that, everything is something new. After that, each moment is a journey.

What did I do last weekend? I did nothing. I went nowhere. I took a soul journey.

—Ruth S.

I don't think soul journeys have to involve big, important changes all at once. I think I make little soul journeys (baby soul journeys?), and that one journey is connected to another. Last month I went to see *Schindler's List.* It was a soul journey. I wasn't the same person coming out of the movie theater that I was going in. The next day, I volunteered for hospice work, and last week, I went to a day-long training workshop, where I met people who have worked for years with dying people. Just meeting them, hearing their stories, seeing what a difference compassion can make—that was a soul journey. Next week, I get my first assignment. I wonder where that soul journey will take me. . . .

—Jean A.

In August of 1994, I made a journey which marked a solemn passage in my life, a journey from which I returned forever changed. I traveled with my husband's body back to the place of our birth and growing-up years, to the family plot in the old cemetery by the river. I remember vividly the cedar tree next to his space, the stones naming his parents, grandmother and sister. There is one space left and, when I let myself, I can see my name next to his. My life ended that autumn day in the company of priest and relatives saying a last good-bye. I died to the safety of thirty-four years of marriage and was newly born into a strange, frightening, sometimes exciting world. For the first time in my 56 years of life, I was alone.

Today, a year later, I feel that I am on another journey, one that has shown me glimpses of adventures ahead. I am finding new friends to travel with and am learning to trust myself to do what needs doing. I venture daily into unknown territory both physically and spiritually. No one walks so closely with death without being forever changed, but I find I am moving forward more easily every day. Like Robert Frost, I have miles to go before I sleep.

—Marjorie C.

The first two writers remind us that this kind of journey may not look like much on the outside. We may look like we're going through the ordinary movements of our ordinary lives—"doing nothing, going nowhere." Yet on the inside, we are taking big steps. The third writer reminds us that the end of one part of the journey is the beginning of another. Yes. We have miles to go before we sleep.

Getting Lost, Paying Attention, and True North

Journeys are various, and there is perhaps only one true thing that can be said about all of them. They take us away from home. Home, home base, home ground, home territory: the space I know so well that I can walk through it blindfolded, can tell from the sound of my footsteps and the faint, familiar scent of kitchen and bedroom and bath exactly where I am. Home, where I don't have to make an effort to find my way around. Home, where I am safe, comfortable, rooted, never lost.

In the last analysis, that may be why journeys are so important to us. Being safe and comfortable can mean that we aren't compelled to look around us because we already know what we'll see. That we don't make ourselves listen because we know what we'll hear. Home is a place where we don't have to be always on the alert.

But when I go on a journey, I *have* to pay attention. Traveling to a truly alien place switches off my autopilot. "I don't like to travel abroad because I always feel so out of place," a woman friend said to me once. "I don't know what to expect." But feeling out of place, not having any expectations, is a good reason for journeying. At home, I know my place, more or less. I know who I am. Traveling in strange places, meeting people who lead foreign lives, I wonder: *Who am I? Where do I belong? Which way back? Which way forward?* As I journey, these questions require

Maybe "journey" is not so much a journey ahead, or a journey into space, but a journey into presence. The farthest place on earth is the journey into the presence of the nearest person to you.

—Nelle Morton

She gave herself up to the feeling of being at home. It went all through her, that feeling, like getting into a warm bath when one is tired. She was safe from everything.

—Willa Cather

me to pay attention to the place where I am and to my interior terrain, to the people around me and the self inside me. I open my inner map and find there the directions for seeing the real world. I begin to question my social conditioning, my expectations and prejudices, my fears, my plans—the social compass my culture has given me. And then I look up and set my course by the polestar, by true north, rather than by some false, drifting signal I've been programmed to receive.

True north? It's worth a soul journey or two to find out where it is.

Clippings: True North

These two stories may not seem to have much in common on the surface, but look deeply enough into them, and you'll discover how they're linked. The first one is about a woman who went camping in a place where she'd never been, sprained her ankle, lost her way, and found something unexpected.

Suppose it is not possible to be lost, and that feeling lost is simply an interpretation of how I do not know where I am. Suppose that you are right here where you are.

—Dianne Connelly

I wasn't lost, exactly. I knew where I was going, more or less. The problem was, I didn't know how *far* it was, or exactly which way to go to get there. I'd gone camping alone for two spectacular nights under a West Texas sky studded with stars. I'd eaten all my food, and, since it was only a couple of hours' hike back to my uncle's ranch house, I'd drunk almost all my water. On the way back, I turned my ankle, which swelled so that I had to unlace my boot and break off a limb to use as a crutch. Then I took what I thought was a shortcut and wound up in a blind canyon thick with sotol and yucca and hot as the hind side of hell. The gravelly streambed was dry, and I had no water. I'll never get out of here, I kept thinking. I was crying. My ankle hurt like blazes and I thought, I'm not strong enough, I don't have enough stamina, I can't. . . .

Six hours later, back at the ranch, I realized that I'd met a different *me* out there in that blind canyon. She's tough and she has endurance. She can take a lot of pain. She's not very experienced in the wilderness, but she's got good survival instincts. Knowing her, I can rest easy. It's taken me awhile to find her, but I have the feeling she's my True North.

—Pam J.

In 1957, Evelyn Fox Keller was admitted to Harvard's graduate program in theoretical physics. "I was on a quest," she says, in *Working It Out.* "I wanted to succeed in an area where women had rarely ventured." But the male faculty and students refused to accept her. By the end of the first year, she was "totally lost"—and things got worse.

> My second year was even more harrowing than the first. I had few courses and a great deal of time that I could not use without guidance. I had no community of scholars. Completing the orals had not served in any way to alleviate my isolation. I was more alone than ever. The community outside of the physics department, at least that part to which I had access, offered neither solace nor support.... Such support might have made a big difference. As it was, I had neither colleagues nor lovers, and not very many friends ... And I wept because I had no friend whose ambition I could identify with. Was there no woman who was doing, had done, what I was trying to do? I knew of none.

But Keller refused to give in. She moved to molecular biology, was awarded her degree, and went on to teach at a liberal arts college, marry, have children. She finishes her story:

> After many years, I have carved out a professional identity very different from the one I had originally envisioned, but one that I cherish dearly.... It has meant acquiring the courage to seek both the motives and rewards for my intellectual efforts more within myself. Which is not to say that I no longer need affirmation from others; but I find that I am now willing to seek and accept support from different sources—from friends rather than institutions, from a community defined by common interests rather than by status.

Writing about Getting Lost

Look back now at your travel log. As you glance over it, do you see a journey that took you so far away from your usual life that you felt lost, out of place? Or, now that you have read Keller's story, perhaps you realize that you were once lost in the labyrinth of a large institution or an

What's ahead of me and what's behind me are nothing compared to what's inside me.

—Jean Shapiro

It would be nice to travel if you knew where you were going and where you would live at the end—or do we ever know, do we ever live where we live? Or are we always in other places, lost, like sheep?

—Janet Frame

impersonal corporation or a career. How did it feel to be lost? What did you lose, along with your sense of direction? What did you gain from getting lost? How did you correct your compass? How did you find true north?

Take a sheet of paper and fill at least one side with your story; use additional sheets if you need to. When you're done, add your writing to the other pieces you've been collecting.

Clippings: "If I am lost, I am lost"

This excerpt comes from Natalie Goldberg's *Writing Down the Bones.* In it, she leads us to understand why being lost is an essential condition for creativity:

> I don't fear being lost. If I am lost, I am lost. That is all. . . . In the same way I need to wander in the field of aloneness and learn to enjoy it, and when loneliness bites, take out a map and find my way out without panic, without jumping to the existential nothingness of the world, questioning everything—"Why should I be a writer?"— and pushing myself off the abyss.

Agnes de Mille, the famous dancer, also reminds us that our truest learning comes when we are lost in the dark:

> Living is a form of not being sure, not knowing what next or how. The moment you know how, you begin to die a little. The artist never entirely knows. We guess. We may be wrong, but we take leap after leap in the dark.

After I asked a writing class, "When did you last feel lost?" a seventy-something woman wrote this paragraph:

> I've just started taking a pottery class and I feel *very* lost in the process. But when I plunk the clay on the wheel and start to turn it, holding my hands the way the teacher holds hers, the wheel and the clay and my hands seem to know what to do. In fact, now that I think about it, maybe being lost is an essential part of learning. When I'm lost, I listen and look harder.
>
> 　　　　　　　　　　　　　　　　　　　　—Jane B.

Creating a Soul Map

Take a clean sheet of paper and some colored markers. Imagine what your soul would look like if it were a feature on a globe of the world, and draw it. Are you a continent all to yourself? An island? A peninsula? What is your political organization? Are you a principality? A democracy? A state within a nation? Is your climate temperate, tropical, equatorial, arctic—or a mixture? What is the nature of your soul's terrain? Are there mountains, deserts, valleys, rivers, farmlands, orchards, vineyards? Are there cities? As you draw these features, name them. (Here are some from my own map: the Peak of Career Success, the Yellow Brick Road to Fame and Fortune, Bridal Veil Falls, the Geyser of Father-Anger, Freedom Bridge.) If you have visited places like these on your soul's journey, you might want to take a pencil and trace out your path from point to point.

When you have finished your map, look it over. Where are you located right now? How would you describe your current soul-status? Write a page or two that describes the weather, the terrain, the political or economic climate—the pertinent details about your personal landscape as it is today.

As you have the time, create your own personal travel guide. For each of the features you have drawn, write a paragraph telling when and how and under what conditions you discovered it (or settled it or crossed it); something of its natural, social, economic, and/or political history; and one or two important memories of your stay there. Who was traveling with you on this leg of your journey? Were you on a tour or a quest or a pilgrimage? Would you like to return there?

A soul map can become an extensive project and involve many different creative skills. One woman painted hers on a large canvas. Another made hers into a quilt, with appliqué and fanciful embroidery. Another drew a map of the three acres on which she lives, located her soul features on the map (the Tree of the Knowledge of Power, the Crossroads of Indecision) and is in the process of building paths, creating markers, and planting little gardens to mark and honor each important site. Your work with your soul map is limited only by your creativity!

There are outer mountains and inner mountains. Their very presence beckons to us, calls us to ascend. Perhaps the full teaching of a mountain is that you carry the whole mountain inside yourself, the outer one as well as the inner.

—Jon Kabat-Zinn

Putting Your Fifth Chapter Together

In this chapter on journeys, we've looked at ourselves as tourists, as questing women, as pilgrims, as soul journeyers. For your chapter, you've collected at least one tourist's horror story (maybe more), several annotated travel photos, and narratives of a quest and a pilgrimage. You've composed an account of a soul journey, remembered how it felt to be lost, and created a map of soul-territory. When you have assembled these pieces of writing and artwork, your chapter will be finished—for the moment, that is. When you undertake another journey, you'll have more to add. Life is like that—one journey after another.

Meditation

A Journey in One Step

In Eastern monastic settings, sitting meditation is punctuated by walking meditation. Both kinds of meditation are designed to quiet the mind, to shift from doing to being, to allow us to be present, to come to a stop. Perhaps this seems a little ironic. What can walking teach us about stopping? What can stopping teach us about our journeys?

A great deal, I think. Most of the time we run frantically from place to place, doing things. We are always going somewhere. We are always on one trip or another, checking our watch, anticipating the next place we're supposed to go, thinking about what we'll do when we get there. Even when we're sitting down, our minds are racing, full of plans for the next move. Most of the time, we live in the future, not in the present moment.

Walking meditation—walking slowly, paying attention to sensations of physical movement—helps our bodies slow down. With practice, our mental processes slow down, too, and eventually the mind stops racing for future destinations. We begin to understand what it means to have nowhere to go, nothing to do. "Each step we take in walking meditation," says Thich Nhat Hanh, a Zen Buddhist monk, "makes a flower bloom under our feet. We can do it only if we do not think of the present or of the past, if we know that life can only be found in the present moment."

Yes, it is true. Our journey—yours and mine—consists of one step only: the step we take right now, where the flower blooms under our feet.

You may do this meditation indoors or outdoors. It is best to move in a circle (around the room or the patio or yard) or in a straight line, with a turning point (to the end of the hall and back). I like to use a timer, and set it for ten minutes or fifteen minutes, even a half hour, if my schedule allows it. The time you spend in this meditation is less important than the quality of attention that you bring to it.

Stand comfortably. Close your eyes, straighten your spine and shoulders, letting your arms relax at your sides. Stand quietly for a moment, becoming aware of your breathing. Inhale gently, exhale slowly, letting your breath move through the whole length of your body, from the top of your head through the soles of your feet, and into the floor or the earth. Listen to the body, allowing yourself to feel whatever you feel. There's no reason to hurry. You have nothing to do, nowhere to go.

When it feels right, begin to walk slowly, taking each step as it falls and being fully mindful of it. *Feel* the sensations of walking: the lifting and placing of each foot, the flexing of the knees, the shifting of the hips, the body's balancing. You don't have to look at your feet, though. You're watching your step in a different way. You're paying attention to sensations, not to where you're going.

Continue to walk slowly, maintaining your focus on the physical sensations of walking. As you walk, thoughts and feelings will come to you, competing for your attention. When this happens, simply recognize that your attention has been pulled away—"Ah, thinking again!"—and bring your attention back to the physical sensations. To the present step, the present moment, where the flower blooms under your feet. If you become impatient, simply observe—"Ah, impatience again!"—and bring your attention back to your step. "You are here now," meditation teacher Jon Kabat-Zinn says. "When you get there, you will be there. If you miss the *here,* you are also likely to miss the *there.*" In this meditation, we are learning not to miss the *here*—the precious moment of journeying.

When your walking meditation is over, stand still for a moment, feeling the sensations of being at rest, in feet, ankles, knees, hips, back, shoulders. Breathe quietly, inhaling and exhaling gently, simply being where you are, knowing that being still is a great journey.

If you wish, you may add to your chapter whatever you have drawn from this meditation.

A traveler is to be reverenced . . . going from—toward; it is the history of every one of us.

—Henry David Thoreau

Celebrating the Completion of Your Chapter

To mark the completion of this part of your book (past the midpoint in your autobiographical journey!), you might:

1. Share your soul map with others in your Story Circle by choosing a partner and taking a tour of each other's soul country. Your aim here is not to do therapy, but to simply hear another woman's journey story. Share other stories, too: the tour from hell, the quest, the pilgrimage. Perhaps each member could bring several photos or slides and use them to illustrate the journey-story she has to tell—a version of the magic lantern shows our Victorian foremothers gave when they returned from their journeys.

2. Look back over your journey log. Who was your journey-mate on an important journey? If possible, contact the person and arrange to do something special together to commemorate the experience. Compare notes on your recollections of the trip, look over travel photos or souvenirs, reminisce. Let the other person know what the journey meant to you, discover what meaning it held for him or her. What can you learn from this exchange?

3. Find a large map of the world and pin it to a wall. With colored markers (or colored pins and matching yarn) mark out the course of your travels. For each important journey, pin photos, mementos, and more detailed maps on the wall, color-keyed to the larger map. Study the map. Where would you like to travel next? Will your trip be a tour, a quest, or a pilgrimage? Are you up to a soul journey? Begin to plan, remembering that every journey consists of one step only, the step you take right now. And have a good trip, wherever in the world you're off to!

Chapter Six

Writing Home

Home is all-embracing, a continuous inclusion of all events: this too and this too and this too. Home en route. Home is the place from which I have come and to which I return. Home is where I always am.

—Dianne Connelly

Home Is . . .

Before we do anything else, let's write.

Begin by writing down every place you have called home and the approximate dates you lived there. Annotate your list with as many identifying characteristics as you need to create a picture of it in your mind. Perhaps you will remember the number and street and city. (My mother made me learn my first address—1933 South Fourth Avenue—so that if I wandered away, I could be returned home expeditiously.) Perhaps you will recall the way the house looked: "A shingled cottage, gray, with a white porch and a maple tree with a swing hanging from it." Or perhaps you will remember it by the people you lived with: "the one-bedroom apartment where Jerri and Tina and I were crammed together like sardines."

This task may take awhile, and if you've lived in dozens of houses (as I have) you may not want to do it all at once. But perhaps you don't think of every house you've lived in as a home. If the word has a special meaning for you, take a moment before you make your list to define what you think it takes for a house (or an apartment or a tent or whatever) to become a home.

Home is_____

Home is_____

Home is_____

When I was writing my definitions, I was struck by the fact that the lines looked and sounded like poetry.

HOME IS

Home is why I bother

Home is what I've searched for
And found when I didn't expect it

Home is where I find myself
When I've been lost for so long
I've forgotten where I was going

Home is when I'm so tired
I can't take another step
and there's a bed to welcome me

Home is who's hoping to be there with me

Home is how I begin and end

Perhaps you would like to make a "Home is . . ." poem out of your definitions. Rendered in calligraphy or embellished with appropriate sketches or snapshots, it would be the perfect beginning for your chapter.

After you've written your poem and with your definitions in mind, go back to your list of homes and finish it. It is a powerful tool that will help you recall not only places, but people and events as well—an indispensable guide for creating your own home-chapter.

At-home-ness

As you made your list of homes, you probably began to get a sense of the different qualities of "at-home-ness" that you experienced in each of them. Sometimes these qualities have a sharp, compelling distinctness. The seven homes of my childhood were definitely not upscale, and we didn't live in any of them very long. My alcoholic father moved from job to job, and we moved from house to house. But in my memory, these homes are rich with images of mother and family, with recollections of my much-loved dollhouse and books. My own first home, into which I moved when I was eighteen, also reminds me of mothering and dollhouses. But in this small "starter" home *I* was wife and mother, and it was my children and their collections of toys and books and clothes that I recall. Eight homes and twenty years later, a busy, successful professional woman, I was living alone, and my house (where I spent very little time) was full of books and works of art I had brought back from various journeys. Now, another decade has passed and I live in the country, in a house that is furnished with old, comfortable furniture, including some of my mother's antiques. It is surrounded by gardens, and I am more at home out of doors, in the wind and the weather. Different homes, each with its own distinct quality of at-home-ness, each revealing something significant about me: about my life phase and circumstances, about the way I connect to the world at a particular point in my journey.

Direct your eye right inward, and you'll find
A thousand regions in your mind
Yet undiscovered. Travel them and be
Expert in home-cosmography.

—Henry David Thoreau

Writing about At-home-ness

What qualities of at-home-ness distinguish the homes you have lived in? Look back over the list of homes and choose those that represent markedly different qualities, different ways of being "at home." If your life feels to you as if it's had a strong continuity, that it's all of a piece, you may find yourself choosing only a few—two or three, perhaps. If you've moved from here to there and your life has been composed of discontinuous elements, you will probably choose many more.

Using one sheet of paper for each home, write as much as you can remember about it: where it was, what it looked like, who lived there with you, how you felt when you were "at home" there. Include photographs, if you have them, and a floor plan of the house (as much of it as you can remember). If you recall the details of a favorite room, sketch it. Your finished pages will comprise the first section of your chapter.

Clippings: Writers at Home

In *An American Childhood*, Annie Dillard writes about the room she occupied when she was nine:

> The attic bedroom . . . was a crow's nest, a treehouse, a studio, an office, a forensic laboratory, and a fort. It interested me especially for a totemic brown water stain on a sloping plaster wall. The stain looked like a square-rigged ship heeled over in a storm. I examined this ship for many months. It was a painting, not a drawing; it had no lines, only forms awash, which rose faintly from the plaster and deepened slowly and dramatically as I watched and the seas climbed and the wind rose before anyone could furl the sails. Those distant dashes over the water—were they men sliding overboard? Were they storm petrels flying? I knew a song whose chorus asked, What did the deep sea say?

The wanderer seeks many ways.

Sooner or later, she comes home.

—"The Wanderer,"
Hexagram 56, I Ching

Nature photographer and writer Anne LaBastille built a log cabin in the Adirondack wilderness. She tells about it in her book *Woodswoman*:

> A twelve-by-twelve cabin is hardly a mansion. I had hundreds of books to move in and a desk to install. I needed a dresser for clothes, cupboards for gear . . . I suspended a ceiling across the open back porch and framed in one end with a wide window. Nailing a rustic log ladder on the inside wall, I had easy access (by possessing the agility of a red squirrel) to my bedroom, snug with mattress and goose-down pillows . . . The newly hung door and window frames had to be painted dark green before hand-woven red and white Guatemalan Indian curtains could be hung. Cabin posts needed a good soaking in creosote to prevent rot or decay. The kitchen was stained dark brown so muddy boots would not discolor the plywood . . . I nailed up deer antlers as gun, fishing rod, and clothing racks. A Mexican guitar and Colorado coyote pelt decorated one long wall. On the front porch, a couple of Adirondack-style rocking chairs and a Brazilian hammock swayed back and forth . . .

Be it ever so humble, there's no place like home.

—John Howard Payne

In 1961, poet Sylvia Plath wrote to her mother about her new home:

> Well, I am writing this from my big "back kitchen" (not really a kitchen, for I cook and wash up in a small room across the hall) . . . surrounded by my copper saucepans and the Dutch tea set you brought, all displayed in the various lovely nooks and crannies . . . and at last, I have all the room I could wish for and a perfect place for everything. . . . The place is like a person; it responds to the slightest touch and looks wonderful immediately. I have a nice, round dining table . . . and we eat on it in the big back room, which has light-green linoleum on the floor, cream wood paneling to shoulder height, and the pink-washed walls that go throughout the house . . . really the heart-room of the house, with the toasty coal stove Ted keeps burning.
>
> My whole spirit has expanded immensely—I don't have that crowded, harassed feeling I've had in all the small places I've lived in before. . . . What is so heavenly here is the utter peace.

From 1983 to 1986, Cynthia Rich and Barbara Macdonald lived in a trailer in the Anza-Borrego Desert. In *Desert Years: Undreaming the American Dream*, Macdonald writes:

> Sometimes our home is as large as the desert, doors and windows flung wide, expanding us to the top of the Vallecitos, opening up to a puffy white cloud or down the washes where the smoke trees grow. Outside and inside are almost one, and I move my yellow writing pads from the kitchen table to the picnic table under the awning . . . Making dinner, I slice off a carrot top at the sink and with one step toss it to a rabbit who is sniffing the sand at the front door. Later at night, I look up from my book to meet the shine of raccoon eyes through the screen, checking me out . . .
>
> Sometimes we're trapped inside our eight-by-twenty-four-foot trailer walls. When the summer heat is 110 degrees or even 120, we shut our windows and doors, drape them with kitchen foil, and turn on the air conditioner. Even so, every surface is hot to the touch—a glass, a pillow, the Formica tabletop. The water from the faucet scalds our hands. Our bodies and minds slow to a dreamlike pace . . . After a cold night, we hear a crackling as the metal walls of the trailer expand in the morning sun. Those walls become a kind of skin connecting us to the new rhythms we are learning.

It is necessary to have a hundred a year and a room with a lock on the door if you are to write fiction or poetry.

—Virginia Woolf

Anne Truitt is a sculptor. In 1974, she spent the summer at Yaddo, the artists' community in Saratoga Springs, New York. Her *Daybook: The Journal of an Artist* contains these paragraphs about her studio and sleeping room:

> It is a joy to be here, set free, anonymous within a shelter . . . My studio here is peacefully widening out. The green shades are furled, the windows are open onto a sweet-smelling meadow with purple martin houses stalking among fruit trees. A grapevine flourishes against the gray stones of the south wall—the studio is called Stone South—and meanders in tendrils over my screens. A wide vegetable garden lies beyond a stout privet hedge to the east. Two triangular skylights allow the northern light to flood in, and me to see the changing clouds. My drawing table stands free to itself. In another area there is room for two sawhorses to support an 8' x 4' piece of ¼" plywood on which I can paint, and other surfaces on which I can spread finished work.
>
> My bedroom is small and white and has a turret and a narrow green-tiled adjoining bathroom. . . . Pine-scented wind sings gently within my shell. I am alone, acknowledged in a silent community.

As you write about your homes, try to use as much detail as possible. Did you, like Dillard, find some metaphoric significance in the space around you? Did you take pride in building your home, as does LaBastille? Perhaps you will focus on the effect the space has on you, as do Plath and Rich and Truitt. Whatever approach you take, anchor your description with detail.

Suppose we are already home and this is what home looks like.

—Dianne Connelly

Homes with Dark Corners

Not all homes are happy. Three statistics tell the bitter truth: close to two million women a year are beaten by their husbands; 35 percent of women who visit hospital emergency rooms exhibit symptoms of on-going domestic abuse; and six out of every ten married couples have experienced violence at some time during their marriage.

Many homes have dark corners, closets, closed doors behind which secrets are hidden. In some families, the secret is anger, rage, violence. In others, it is sexual molestation, rape, incest. In my childhood homes, the secret was alcoholism. When I was a girl, loving my father but terrified and shamed by his out-of-control behavior, the corners seemed to me to grow darker and more terrifying every year. I carried the shadows with me into my own adult homes. I was forty-five years old before I could talk openly about my fear or begin to understand the truth—that my father had been a sad, sick man. Lighting up the old shadowy corners illuminated my fears and allowed me to deal with them, and my dwellings became more comfortable.

If there are dark corners in any of your homes—and for most of us there are—now is the time to open the doors and turn on the lights. Hidden wounds cannot heal. Unspoken, unshared pain festers in silence. Give your dark corners a name: Mother's unpredictable anger, Dad's inexplicable absence, Uncle Jim's inescapable hands. Write about them. Write what you remember, what you guess, what you suspect, what you feel. Keep your writing short and to the point: you are writing about feelings, but they are also facts. And as you write, let the light shine in.

Clippings: Dark Corners

My stepbrother Mark was my dark corner. He was seventeen and I was twelve. It always happened on Friday night, when Mother and my stepdad went to the movies, and on other nights, too. The first time, I didn't know what was happening. I just knew that it was wrong, and I was so ashamed because I thought it was my fault. Mark said it was, and he said that if I told, he'd say I was lying. I knew they'd believe him, too, because he was their favorite, so good-looking and he always made the honor roll at school.

I thought the dark corner would go away when Mark went to Vietnam, but it didn't. I was still ashamed, and I had this terrible secret that I couldn't tell anybody. When he was killed, I was glad. And then I was ashamed of that, too, especially when I saw how sad Mom and Ron were. So even his being dead didn't help. One way or another, I've lived in Mark's dark corner my entire life. I've never written this down before. It helps.

—Lynette J.

In *The Wounded Woman: Healing the Father-Daughter Relationship*, therapist Linda Shierse Leonard describes her own dark corner:

Domestic violence is the leading cause of injury to women and girls, accounting for more visits to hospital emergency rooms than the combined total of automobile accidents, muggings, and reported rapes.

—Committee on Family Violence

One does not love a place less for having suffered in it.

—Jane Austen

My father often came home late at night when he was drunk and threatened to hurt my grandmother (his mother-in-law). My mother and I often had to call the police to get him out of the house. Usually I was the one to make the call. Sometimes if my father was so violent that I couldn't get to the phone, in my fright I would run out on the porch screaming for help. On one of these especially violent nights the police arrived to find me sobbing and huddled in the corner. One policeman turned to my father and said, "How can you do this to your daughter?" The memory of this stranger's concern and his question to my father echoed in my mind for many years . . .

Another woman, frequently molested by her mother's brother, writes about feeling "at fault" for what happened:

I was eight. I loved and respected grown-ups, because they knew so much, were so important. My mother and father taught me to listen to them and obey them. Why shouldn't I listen to my uncle? Why shouldn't I obey him? He was an adult. My parents loved him. They respected him. So how could I think differently, even after what happened? He was so important, he knew so much—I must have been the one who was at fault.

—Tracy O.

Rewriting Our Dark-Corner Stories

In an essay entitled "Living Our Stories: Discovering and Replacing Limiting Family Myths," Nancy Napier writes about the importance of rewriting the old, dark-corner stories of pain and fear—what she calls the "negative programming" of our childhood. She says:

The more you know about how you got to be who you are, the greater your ability to decide which story you want to live: your own or a limiting one left over from childhood . . . You might start by thinking of a theme or message . . . that you might be truly ready to give back. When it comes to mind, write it down and take a look at what you've written. See if you are ready to say, "Okay, I've had enough of this. I don't want this anymore."

If you can reread your dark-corner story and say to yourself, "I'm tired of hearing this old story," it's time to rewrite it. No, you can't change events that happened in the past. They happened, and that's that. But you *can* change the way you feel about those events, and you can keep your old stories from coloring your perceptions of the events that are happening now. The rewriting of your dark-corner stories is an important first step in the healing process. Once you've started it, it will continue to develop, allowing you to revise more and more of the old script, the negative programming.

Many women have discovered the importance of writing themselves out of their dark corners. In the previous Clippings section, Linda Schierse Leonard wrote about her father's drunken violence. When she was in her thirties, her father fell asleep while drinking and smoking and started a fire that resulted in her grandmother's death, and his own, two years later. Shortly afterward, Leonard began writing. The book, which became *The Wounded Woman*, healed her, she says. Whether the book would ever be published wasn't an issue. She simply needed to write, to tell her story.

> Perhaps the act of writing could bring my father and me closer together. . . . Perhaps on the inner level, through this writing, I could redeem my "inner father.". . . Writing has required a commitment and an act of faith that something will appear from the depths of my psyche that I can name, that I can express, however momentarily, in words. At the same time I know that whatever I write, although it may illumine the father-daughter wound, it will also cast its shadow. . . . In the process, I have often become angry; I have often cried as well. My rage and my tears are behind every page, no matter how serene the final result may seem.

The act of writing, full of rage and tears, finally redeems not only Leonard's inner father, her negative concept of fathering, but her understanding of her real father as well, giving her the compassion she needs to understand the paradoxes that damned him—and nearly destroyed her, as well. "I began to see him whole," she writes, "and the vision healed me."

Allowing ourselves to see into our dark corners and writing down what we see opens us to a redemptive grace. One way to begin is to write a letter—you don't have to send it—to your dark-corner person, laying out your feelings, speaking the truth.

Tracy, whose writing appeared on page 160, wrote the following letter to her uncle:

> Dear Uncle Matt,
>
> All these years, I've been wanting to tell you how I've been hurt by what you did. You stole something from me that can never be returned. You took my innocence and my trust in others. You stole my belief in myself. You cost me years of pain and heartache. But worst of all, you made me think it was all my fault, and I grew up believing that I was totally, completely bad. I know better now. I know I'm good, and that you were a bad thing that happened to me. . . .

And another woman testified to the power she gained in writing a letter, even though she didn't send it. In this excerpt, she points out that sometimes we don't know the truth until we have written it:

> Writing my truth lets me say what I need to say when it's too frightening for me to confront the person. In fact, writing is sometimes the best way for me to figure out what my truth is. How do I feel? What do I want? Just answering those two questions lets in a lot of light. And I've noticed that even though I don't send the letter, the next time I think about that dark corner or see that person, I feel much more in control. I'm closer to the truth, and that helps.
>
> —Elise R.

Clippings: "After Great Pain"

In *After Great Pain*, Diane Cole writes about the dark corner—a closed room—that remained in her home and her life after her miscarriage:

> Peter and I had redecorated our home in such a way that my old study—the room that was to have been our baby's room—was left suspended in a kind of limbo, as an extra den. Slowly it had become a storage room, its closet filled with my maternity clothes, a place to store our future dreams as well as those that had died. This room, filled equally with sad reminders and with poignant hope, was a part of my home, a part of my life. But in the same way that there can be

a break in the music, a rest between movements, I saw that even if I closed this room's door for a time, glancing within only now and then, I could still live in the other rooms of my home, and in the rest of my life.

As I imagined the music of my life unfolding, I also saw that, eventually, I would clean out that room and make it a new room—whether a child's room or a different kind of room, I did not yet know. But I would be content to wait out the music, for life had also taught me that there were notes and turns in every song that no one could predict . . .

For Cole, the room intended for the baby became a metaphor for the place in her life the baby would have filled. But a room can have several functions, as she begins to realize in the second paragraph. We can clean out our corners and turn them to another use.

Home Truths

For most of us, *home* is a word that represents a deep connection to what is basic and most essential in our lives: a feeling of being centered, grounded, belonging. This sense of home is probably as old as the human need for dwelling. "A place to be safe in," wrote Charlotte Perkins Gilman, in her 1898 feminist study, *Women and Economics*:

> a place to be warm and dry in; a place to eat in peace and sleep in quiet; a place whose close, familiar limits rest the nerves from the continuous hail of impressions in the changing world outside; the same place over and over—the restful repetition, rousing no keen response, but healing and soothing each weary sense—that "feels like home." All this from our first consciousness. All this for millions and millions of years. No wonder we love it.

We *do* love home, and for us as women it has a special meaning. But Gilman's wry "no wonder we love it" gives a clue to her ambivalence about home—and our own. For with the home came housework, women's unpaid labor, which was devalued to the extent that men's paid labor in the productive economy was valued.

The problem is, of course, that since the industrial revolution, home

Look you, I keep his house, and I wash, wring, brew, bake, scour, dress meat and drink, make the beds, and do all myself. 'Tis a great charge to come under one body's hand.

—Clarissa Packard, 1834

has meant different things to women than it has to men. For men (according to a popular magazine of 1830), home was a "sanctuary where sympathy, honor, virtue are assembled"—a place to get away from the hurly-burly of life, rest, relax, and be cared for. For women, home was a "gathering place of the deepest and purest affections," but it was also the place of the never-ending, backbreaking work involved in caring for children and husbands: washing, ironing, mending, cleaning, cooking, washing dishes. Those who could, of course, hired others to do the work—other women, whose place in domestic service was poorly paid and very little valued. Housework was—and is—among the largest service industries in America, but to this day it has been excluded from the gross national product.

Now, at the end of the twentieth century, machines and commercial services perform many of the tasks that were once carried out by women in the home, while those women have moved *en masse* into the labor force. But while the nineteenth-century idea of home as a man's palace and a woman's place has faded from our conscious thoughts, it continues to operate in the lives of many two-income families. Women retain the responsibility for home and family as they take on paid work. According to economist Juliet Schor, in her book *The Overworked American*, women with families work at least one hour a week at home for every hour they work on the job. And although men are beginning to take on more of the household chores, the major burden of the "second shift" (as sociologist Arlie Hochschild has called it) falls to the wife. Women find themselves in a dilemma, Hochschild says: how to preserve the domestic culture of their mothers and grandmothers while they work eight to twelve hours a day outside the home. To encourage this domestic culture, consumer magazines are full of images of the beautiful home: a commercialized glorification of the surroundings, if not the spirit, of home. (The irony is, of course, that many women work long hours outside the home in order to purchase the furnishings and decor that make it comfortable and beautiful.) No wonder, then, that many of us have a great many deep-down ambivalences about home!

Clippings: House Proud

In *The Overworked American,* Juliet Schor writes about changing American expectations of their homes:

> In the 1950s, when developer William Levitt created Levittowns for ordinary American families, his standard house was 750 square feet. In 1963, the new houses were about twice as large; and by 1989, the average finished area had grown to almost three times the Levittown standard—2,000 feet. At the same time, fewer people were living in these dwellings. Fifty years ago, only 20 percent of all houses had more rooms than people living in them; by 1970, over 90 percent of our homes were spacious enough to allow more than one room per person.

The cost of housing has also changed:

> In 1949, a thirty-year-old worker could purchase [i.e. get a mortgage on] a median-priced home for about 14 percent of his gross monthly income. By 1985, the cost had risen to 44 percent. (*New York Times*)

What role has "house pride" played in your life? What trade-offs has your family chosen to make between the size of your house and the amount of time you have to enjoy it? Have your views on this question changed over the years? Have your changing views resulted in altered living arrangements? If so, write about it.

Things fill up empty spaces in our lives. Many couples concentrate on owning a house or filling it with nice furnishings, when what they really crave is an emotional construction—home.

—Juliet Schor

Writing about Home Truths

This is a good place for you to write down some of the feelings and thoughts you have had about your own work at home and how it relates to paid work outside the home. One way to do this is by writing a retrospective summary that focuses on the way your housekeeping has changed over the years. Here is a paragraph written by a government worker in her late thirties:

> I began keeping house when I married Matt at twenty-five. Things were easy the first couple of years—we were gone a great deal and both of us were working and we weren't too particular about keeping the apartment spotless. But after the twins came, things changed.

I was working a forty-hour week and spending the rest of the time either taking care of the children or the house. Matt would change diapers, but that's about all.

When the twins were three, we moved to Grand Valley, to a bigger house with a yard. So there was a lot more house to take care of, plus the yard. Matt started mowing the grass, but that was basically all he did except for making spaghetti—his specialty—a couple of times a month. That was kind of a game of "let's pretend." I pretended to think that his contribution was to make great spaghetti. It seems pretty silly now, but I guess I thought it was a way of breaking him into the housework, and that his attitude would change over time. It did, but not enough.

The boys are ten now, and I decided last year that we had to make some changes. I'm making enough money to hire a woman to clean twice a week, and a man comes to do the yard. And Matt will occasionally put the dirty clothes in the washer. But I still feel pretty angry about this whole thing. I carry a lot more of the workload than he does, and it's not fair.

—Jessica J.

When Jessica read what she'd written, there was a buzz of agreement around the room—especially when she described the "let's pretend" game. Many of the other women agreed that when it came to the distribution of home work, they too had often concealed the truth. "It was a myth," one woman said when we shared our stories. "My husband always said we split the housework and family stuff fifty-fifty and I agreed, even when I knew in my heart that it wasn't even close to being true. I guess I needed to believe that we were partners. I couldn't face the fact that I had married somebody who would take advantage of me."

If you would like to write about this subject, here are four questions to help you structure your writing:

In your family, what is the present distribution of responsibility for home and family care?

What was the situation five years ago? Ten years ago? Fifteen years ago?

Has your family created any myths about these situations?

How do you feel about this?

If you do not do paid work outside the home, you may not have experienced much tension over this particular problem. But for women who work exclusively at home, there is another important issue: the question of the appropriate value of what they do. When I was doing the research for my book *Work of Her Own*, one full-time mother wrote to me about the frustration she felt when other people disparaged the work she had chosen:

> I'm a wife, a mother, and a homemaker, and I take my job seriously. The problem is that nobody else does. When I go to a party and I tell somebody what I do, I get this little smirk. In most people's estimation, women choose to stay home because they can't compete in the world out there.

And another wrote comparing her present at-home work with her previous paid work:

> I left my sixty-thousand-dollar-a-year job to stay home with my two children. What I've discovered is that being a full-time mom and housewife is the lowest-paid, most difficult, and most rewarding job there is. Day to day, I work harder and face more problems than I used to when I had twenty people working for me.

Perhaps your experience has shifted between being a career woman and being a full-time mother, full-time homemaker, or both. If so, you may want to write a narrative about the change. Here are some questions you could consider:

> What was my career experience like? What did I find rewarding about it?
> What made me decide to leave my career and come home?
> What was it like to make the change? What was best about it? What was most difficult?
> How has the change affected my life? How has it affected my family?

Or perhaps yours has been the opposite scenario: you stayed home to raise children, only to discover at some point that you wanted to work, or that a second salary in the family was a necessity:

And do you know where I can get a steady body? A cook is of the most consequence. I must not have one who will be put out of humour by company comeing in unexpectedly. She must be willing upon washing & Ironing days to assist in the after part of the day to fold cloaths & to help Iron if necessary, to keep every thing clean and neat in her department.

—Abigail Adams, 1800

The cave of womanhood feels cozy to me, and I shall always, I think, retreat to it with the comfortable feeling that I am where I should be in some sense deeper than words can articulate . . . But because womanhood is "home" to me does not mean that I wish to stay home all the time.

—Anne Truitt

What compelled me to decide to change my work?

What was it like to go outside to work after years at home with the family? Were there unexpected dividends in the change? Unexpected losses?

How has the change affected my life? How has it affected my family?

Clippings: Holding the Center, Climbing the Stairs

Anne Morrow Lindbergh wrote her classic *Gift from the Sea* while she was alone at a Florida beach house, searching for a balance between the space she needed for herself and the demands of her home and family. Written in 1955, before women began to move in large numbers into jobs and careers, Lindbergh anticipates the problems many contemporary women face.

For to be a woman is to have interests and duties, raying out in all directions from the central mother-core, like spokes from the hub of a wheel. The pattern of our lives is essentially circular. We must be open to all points of the compass: husband, children, friends, home, community; stretched out, exposed, sensitive like a spider's web to each breeze that blows, to each call that comes. How difficult for us, then, to achieve a balance in the midst of these contradictory tensions, and yet how necessary for the proper functioning of our lives. . . .

The problem is . . . how to remain whole in the midst of the distractions of life; how to remain balanced, no matter what centrifugal forces tend to pull one off center; how to remain strong, no matter what shocks come in at the periphery and tend to crack the hub of the wheel.

Do the circle, the wheel, the compass, the web seem to be metaphors for your life, as Lindbergh suggests? If so, what is the center of your circle, the hub of your wheel? What are the points of your compass? Or perhaps another metaphor would serve you better. Storm Jameson uses this one in *Journey from the North*:

There is a sense in which it is true that we only live in one house, one street, one town, all our lives. I have no memory of the first house I lived in, though I ought to be able to remember an afternoon in my sixth month when I began climbing its dangerously steep staircase on hands and knees: I set off six times, and was fetched back and whipped six times. Have I been doing anything ever since except setting off again up those infernal stairs?

Choose a metaphor that seems to describe your efforts to find your balance, to create your place, and use it to structure a page or two.

Coming Home to Hestia

We've been discussing home work in terms of its gender shadow—clearly an important issue as partners struggle to achieve the fair, right balance of livelihood and family. But there is another way to think about home, a way of imagining it that deepens and enriches our experience of it, that allows us to hold home in our hearts with fewer reservations, with less ambivalence. That is to invoke the goddess Hestia: the thirteenth divinity in the Greek pantheon, the goddess of hearth and home.

In *Journey through Menopause*, Christine Downing writes about Hestia as a sacred figure who is present, not in the most exalted moments, but in the most mundane and ordinary tasks of life. The other goddesses—Demeter, Hera, Athena, Aphrodite, Artemis, Persephone—lived lives of storied excitement that made for thunderous drama and heart-wrenching suspense in the tales of the gods. But Hestia's story is different, for the home she rules is a place of calm, quiet groundedness. And that is all there is to tell.

Hestia is the goddess who never goes anywhere or does anything special, except to be enduringly present. "Hestia alone abides at home," Downing quotes Plato as saying. His observation, she says, expresses both Hestia's hiddenness—her life is carried on within the private refuge of the home—and her continual availability. Hestia is waiting at the end of every journey, the moment of every homecoming, whether we have only stepped across the street or crossed continents and oceans. As Downing says:

> I see now that my journey was all along a journey toward her, a coming back, as T. S. Eliot puts it, to the place from which I started and

It was wonderful to be able to shut my door and keep my daily life free of other people's inquisitiveness. . . . To have a door that I could shut was still the height of bliss for me.

—Simone de Beauvoir

knowing it for the first time. The journey toward Hestia is not a journey toward a luminous unknown but toward a luminous known, toward the holiness of the most familiar. . . .

Hestia makes a house a home by endowing it with soul. It is her gift to reveal how my dwelling serves as an outward expression of my inward self and how the image of the inmost center of a dwelling, its heart, serves as the most adequate, the almost inevitable, image of the essence of self.

To honor this undramatic goddess, then, to incorporate her story into my story, I need to learn from her all that is sacred about my homing, my home making, my life at home. I need to bring my story home and find the depths of its meaning in that quiet centeredness. Hestia asks us to reimagine our place in the world, to see our story as something other than the masculine journey epic, the heroic quest, the glorious tragedy, the thrilling adventure, the generational saga. These action stories take us away from the center, into contest and conflict, into the world. Hestia's story—her "unstoriedness," as Downing puts it—represents the opposite movement, from the world and its visible achievements, into the whole, unfragmented, unconflicted center, into the dark, the place of soul.

But incorporating Hestia's story into my own isn't an easy task. Her plots are not charged with the excitement of the chase or the exhilaration of sexual triumph or the thrill of novelty. "I struggle," Downing says, "to stay with a perspective that pays homage to the holy in The Ordinary, The Boring, The Everyday." Staying with this perspective, finding the greatest significance in the commonplace and unexceptional, can be a very difficult task for those of us who have grown up with soap operas and shoot-'em-ups.

Hestia's perspective reminds me of that of a seventeenth-century Christian monk, Brother Lawrence, who wrote about what he called "practicing the Presence." Practicing the presence is the simple art of finding the sacred in every little homely thing:

The time of business does not with me differ from the time of prayer, and in the noise and clatter of my kitchen, while several persons are at the same time calling for different things, I possess God in as great tranquility as if I were upon my knees at the blessed sacrament.

Don't bother to run outdoors for a better view.
Don't hang out of a window.
Stay put. Look inside.
The way to do is to be.
—Susan Albert,
after Lao Tze

Putting clean sheets on a bed . . . , in fact making order out of disorder any time, anywhere, can be regarded as a sacrament.
—May Sarton

It is also very like the teaching of the contemporary Zen Buddhist monk Thich Nhat Hanh. In his book *The Miracle of Mindfulness*, he writes about the power of conscious awareness to bring us home:

> While washing the dishes one should only be washing the dishes, which means that while washing the dishes one should be completely aware of the fact that one is washing the dishes. At first glance, that might seem a little silly: why put so much stress on a simple thing? But that's precisely the point. The fact that I am standing there and washing these bowls is a wondrous reality. I'm being completely myself, following my breath, conscious of my presence, and conscious of my thoughts and actions. There's no way I can be tossed around mindlessly like a bottle slapped here and there on the waves.

Hestia reminds me, too, of what Dianne Connelly calls "the practice of being home," in her book *All Sickness Is Homesickness*: the mystical awareness that any small, any ordinary act—washing the dishes, making a bed, answering the telephone—can open a path to the extraordinary.

> The paradox of practice is the paradox that all is in all, that the flow of life is evidenced in everything and in nothing in particular, in the guest house of the mystic, the whiteness of a washed pocket handkerchief, in all the events of the whole day long. The practice of being home is an ongoing kindling of the life quality. It is the practice of finding our way home in every moment, every condition, every symptom and every circumstance . . . It is the place of the mystic. The practice of being home *is* being home.

And all of this reminds me of my favorite cookbook, *Laurel's Kitchen*, where, in an introductory essay called "The Work at Hand," Carol Flinders writes about the way home work, and particularly working with food, can enrich and transform our lives:

> Only last week I read of one homemaker's discovery that eggs are cooked to perfection after three Hail Marys. "I use the boiling time," she adds, "to place myself in touch with earlier generations of cooks who measured their recipes with litanies, using time to get *beyond* time."
>
> We are so oppressed by time these days . . . At moments of deep

I don't clean house . . . to please others. I do it for myself. It does for my soul what prayer does for others. And it takes so much less faith. House ordering is my prayer, and when I have finished, my prayer is answered. And bending, stooping, scrubbing, purifies my body as prayer doesn't.

—Jessamyn West

I mark Henry James' sentence: observe perpetually. Observe the oncome of age. Observe greed. Observe my own despondency. By that means it becomes serviceable . . . And now with some pleasure I find that it's seven; and must cook dinner. Haddock and sausage meat. I think it is true that one gains a certain hold on sausage and haddock by writing them down.

—Virginia Woolf, Journal, Mar 8 41

concentration, though, we are lifted clear *out* of time, and for a few minutes the stress of the day slips away . . .

"I don't know, really, what changed," reflects my longtime friend Beth Ann. "I just know that one evening I walked into the kitchen grim as usual, determined to get it over with, and instead I found myself relaxing—accepting that I was there and willing to do it as well as I possibly could. And ever since then, it's been completely different.

"You know, partly I think it's the food itself. If you watch, so much beauty passes through your hands—of form, and color, and texture. And *energy* too." Abruptly her hands flew up into the air as if an electric current were passing between them. "Each grain of rice, each leaf of kale, charged with life and the power to nourish. It's heady, feeling yourself a kind of conduit for the life force!"

Of course, we don't experience a spiritual exaltation every time we pick up a potato. But potatoes and rice and kale—and Hestia—can teach us some important home truths. That we need to become conscious of the importance of small things, of the power of routine; that we need to put down deep roots where we live, to become intimately connected to the land. That we need to turn our homes into places that heal and nourish our souls. That this necessary home work is not woman's work, or man's work, but work for *all* of us.

Clippings: Sacred Dailiness

The sense of sacred dailiness comes through very clearly in the excerpt from Susan Ackley's essay "A Meditation on Diapers," in which she describes a task that most of us view as pure drudgery in terms that allow us to see it as a sacred act.

It is two or three days since the last time I did this—fill the washing machine, rinse out the poopy diapers in the tub (hope for no raisins!), then dump the soggy mass in the hot water and soap. I use a wringer washer to save our primitive septic system, so I have a lot of time for contemplation as the process goes on.

So I meditate on diapers. . . . Because what is happening here, after all, but renewal—"Behold, I shall make all things new." Here is

*I was passionate,
 consumed with longing.
I searched from horizon to
 horizon.*

*But the day
the Truthful One found me,
I was at home.*

—Lal Ded, fourteenth-
century Kashmir poet

heat, and the earthy rubbing of matter on matter, but above all here is water, water freshening, refreshing . . .

Of course, all the time, from diaper change to diaper change and wash day to wash day, there is more profound change happening—the diapers are softening, becoming more and more absorbent and forgiving, and finally wearing out to rags. And the baby grows. But this small, quotidian access to the sacred mystery of renewal returns wash day after wash day, reminding, guaranteeing that renewal is possible in the universe we belong to. And this is because the tedious, smelly process of diaper washing reveals what in our universe can be done—the world gives renewal to us as a gift. It is *that sort of universe.*

The next piece, "Cleaning the Stove While Listening to Bobby McFerrin," was written by Jon Kabat-Zinn and is included in his book, *Wherever You Go, There You Are.* (In the process of creating this book, my editor, Robin Cantor-Cooke, wrote a note in the margin: "A man who cleans the oven? I'm in love!") It is harder for men to be lured by Hestia's magic, but it can happen:

> I use a scrubber which is abrasive enough to get the caked food off if I rub hard enough with baking soda, but not so abrasive that I scratch the finish. I take off the burner elements and the pans underneath, even the knobs, and soak them in the sink, to be tackled at the end. Then I scrub every square inch of stove surface, favoring a circular motion at times, at others, a back and forth. It all depends on the location and topology of the crud. I get into the round and round or the back and forth, feeling the motion in my whole body, no longer trying to clean the stove so it will look nice, only moving, moving, watching, watching as things change slowly before my eyes. At the end, I wipe the surfaces carefully with a damp sponge.
>
> Music adds to the experience at times. Other times, I prefer silence for my work. One Saturday morning, a tape by Bobby McFerrin was playing in the cassette player when the occasion arose to clean the stove. So cleaning became dancing, the incantations, sounds, and rhythms and the movements of my body merging, blending together, sounds unfolding with motion, sensations in my arm aplenty, modulations in finger pressure on the scrubber as required, caked remains of former cookings slowly changing form and disappearing, all rising and falling in awareness with the music. One big dance of presence, a celebration of now. And, at the end, a clean stove. . . .

This is so clear that you might miss it.
The fire you're looking for
Lights your own lantern,
Your rice was already cooked
The day you went looking for food.

—Chinese poem

Mindfully speaking, I can't get away with claiming that "I" cleaned the stove. It's more like the stove cleaned itself, with the help of Bobby McFerrin, the scrubber, the baking soda, and the sponge, with great appearances by hot water and a string of present moments.

And here is my own reflection, a hymn to Hestia:

Welcome, dear heart.
Using chopsticks,
picking up each white seed
I am nourished by the life of small things.
Folding sheets,
shaping each into a true square,
edges aligned, cotton smoothed,
I am attentive and careful,
amazed at my pleasure in such an ordinary act.
Scrubbing the floor, routine labor,
I am surprised
when I turn the corner
and find joy there:
Welcome, dear heart.

Writing about Coming Home

How about you? Have there been moments in your life when you saw, mirrored in some simple, homely act, the essential nature of things? Have there been homecomings when you encountered Hestia, or days when you discovered the peace and calm of practicing the presence, practicing being home? To complete your chapter on home and homing, you might choose one or more of the questions below and use it to write several pages, a meditation, or a few little hymns to Hestia.

1. What daily task do you do that is like Ackley's washing diapers or Kabat-Zinn's cleaning the stove? How does it renew or transform you as you do it? What kind of attention must you bring to it? What does it teach you about the nature of the task, and about the present moment?

I have possession of my Aunt's chamber in which you know is a very conveniant pretty closet with a window which looks into her flower Garden. . . . I should like to be the owner of such conveniances. I always had a fancy for a closet with a window which I could more peculiarly call my own.

—Abigail Adams, 1776

2. Looking back over your life, when did you come closest to the practice of being home? Where and how did you live then? What enabled you to achieve that perspective?

3. When in your life did you, like Christine Downing, come home to Hestia? What were the circumstances? What did you learn? How did your homecoming affect your life?

Putting Your Sixth Chapter Together

In this chapter, you have made an inventory of all the homes in which you have lived, defined what home means to you, and written about different ways of being at home. You have remembered that homes have dark corners, and you rewrote your dark-corner story. You wrote about home work and the way your family handles the "second shift." You also wrote about coming home to a new understanding of home: as a place to be continually present, to celebrate the dailiness of your life. This chapter is a crucial one in your story, because home is one of the most powerful images we hold in our hearts.

Meditation

Being Home

The imagination is a powerful tool that can help you create the life you want to lead—an important truth I discovered for myself. In 1982, living in an apartment, I began to think in specific terms about where and how I would prefer to live, and the kind of home and intimate relationship I wanted. As I thought, often with a great longing and a deep intensity, I recorded my thoughts in my journal, filling dozens of pages with hopes for home. Now, as I write this chapter on homes and homing, my own new home is just being completed—very nearly the home I envisioned. This is a marvelous, grace-full synchronicity that reminds me to be grateful for the gift of hope and the ability to clearly express my desires.

This guided meditation asks you to imaginatively create the kind of home and way of being-at-home that you would like. Repeated frequently and remembered with respectful attention, it can help you shape your life in the direction of your dream. But please, don't think that you have to come up with "the" perfect home all at once. Repeat the meditation frequently, allowing yourself to experiment with different creations, to see yourself in different surroundings, until you have explored enough to know what you want. Then work with that vision, gently, never forcing it, repeating the meditation until you have refined your dream. And as you repeat it, write it down, articulating your desires. To acknowledge what we want and need is the first step toward attaining it.

Sit quietly in a cushioned chair or sofa. Allow yourself to relax, breathing gently, evenly. Feel how your body is supported by your chair. . . . Relax into it, letting go all that you are holding on to, allowing yourself to simply be held and supported, cradled by a loving and beneficent universe. . . .

Bring your attention to your breath, simply observing it as it comes and goes. . . . Now, imagine that your breath is a cleansing stream, moving through your body like a calm, slow tide, picking up and taking with it all the old anxious thoughts, sweeping out all the old fears. As you exhale, imagine that you are breathing out all your old thoughts, old dreams, readying yourself for new ones. . . .

Now, imagine that you are traveling to the home you would like to have. . . . Are you driving through the country? Stepping off the metro? Bicycling through a small college town? What is the landscape around you? If there are people, who are they? . . . Now you are going up to your house. What kind of house is it? What shape is it? What size? What color? What are its immediate surroundings? . . .

Now you are opening the door and walking in. . . . What do you see? . . . Walk from room to room, seeing each room fully as you walk. . . . Walk all through the house, slowly and mindfully, until you have come to the part of it that you like best, where you have a favorite place to sit and relax. . . .

Now, sit there for a moment and imagine being at home in this house. . . . What kind of life will you lead? . . . Will anyone share this house with you? . . . Will it be a place where you can celebrate Hestia? . . . Imagine waking up in this house and going to bed in it . . . bathing and dressing in it . . . eating breakfast in it, and lunch and dinner . . . doing chores indoors and out . . . enjoying your house, being at home in it. . . .

When you have thought as long as you want about being at home in this place of your dreams, look around you and choose one thing to take back to the present with you, a symbol that can lead you from the home where you live now back to this place. Perhaps it is a picture from the wall, a book from a shelf, a piece of art from a table, a rose from the garden. . . .

When you are ready, return the same way you came, noting once again the landscape you're moving through, the people you see, the sounds you hear. Return to your present home, to your chair, to your breath, to your body. . . . Slowly open your eyes and stretch. . . .

But before you leave your chair, there is one last thing. . . . Recall the symbol you took from the house of your imagination. . . . In your mind, turn it over, looking at it carefully, seeing its shape and color, feeling its weight, its texture. . . . Hold it in your mind and in your heart, to remind yourself that your dream is real. . . .

If you wish, you may add to your chapter anything you have drawn from this meditation.

Celebrating the Completion of Your Chapter

To commemorate the completion of this important chapter, you might do one or more of the following things:

1. Share a part of your chapter with your Story Circle. You might share a dark corner and read the letter you wrote to the person involved. Or you might share your feelings about housework and your solutions to the problem of the "second shift."

2. Looking back, choose your favorite house and create a wall collage with photographs, floor plans, snapshots of the people with whom you shared it, and mementos of your time there. If possible, contact one of your housemates or family members who lived there with you and reminisce. What does the other person remember about the house? What makes it memorable in both your lives?

3. In your meditation, you chose a symbol of your imaginary home.

You can use that symbol as a key to making your dream real. Find or draw an object that replicates the symbol. Place it on a shelf, along with a few other special objects that would belong in your imaginary home. Begin to collect photographs or clippings that remind you of your meditation, and allow these to clarify your vision of the home and way of life you want. What would you have to do to achieve it? What kind of timetable would you set? In what small ways can you begin to live now as you imagined yourself living in your dream home?

4. Choose some small, repetitive task—cleaning the bathroom sink, washing the dishes, making tea—and allow it to become a celebration of home, of being home, of practicing the presence. For a week, every time you repeat this task, use it to remind you of the importance of Hestia in your life. Is there a way that you can enlarge this special feeling to more of your home tasks, even to all of them?

Chapter Seven

Valley of Shadows

The soul presents itself in a variety of colors, including all the shades of gray, blue, and black. To care for the soul, we must observe the full range of all its colorings, and resist the temptation to approve only of white, red, and orange—the brilliant colors.

—*Thomas Moore*

The Way of the Dark Angel

Our journeys take us far and wide—and high and deep. For every sunlit peak of confident success that we ascend, there is a place of shadows, where we feel anxious and uncertain, confident only of failure. We experience warm love for someone, and anger toward the same person. We have high-energy days when we sail happily and competently through our work and our play, and days, weeks, even, when we are deeply depressed, lethargic, sad, sensitive to every slight, vulnerable to every hurt.

These periodic alternations of mood, our experiences of the darkness and sadness of life, are natural to our human nature and necessary to the full realization of our beings, Thomas Moore suggests in his book *Care of the Soul*:

> Some feelings and thoughts seem to emerge only in a dark mood. Suppress the mood, and you will suppress those ideas and reflec-

tions. Depression may be as important a channel for valuable "negative" feelings, as expressions of affection are for the emotions of love. . . . Depression has its own angel, a guiding spirit whose job it is to carry the soul away to remote places where it finds unique insight and enjoys a special vision.

Everything terrifying is, in its deepest being, something helpless that wants our help.
—Rainer Maria Rilke

But most Americans would not agree that the dark angel permits us to *enjoy* a special vision. Depression and its cousins, fear, anger, grief, and pain, do not have a place of honor in our culture, which values the light and bright and upbeat. Contented, happy, successful, pleasure driven—these are the adjectives that characterize the ideal personality in our culture. "Happiness at all costs" is a motto for many of us.

But happy hedonism has its downside. "What price have we paid as a people for all this light?" asks theologian Matthew Fox. "We have become afraid of the dark. Afraid of no light, of silence, of imagelessness." As a consequence, we spend billions of dollars annually on entertainment that makes us smile, medication and therapy that ward off the dark, and alcohol and other substances that give us a high. It is hard to estimate costs, but some economists say that the "feel-good" industry is the largest in America.

Some believe that we are overdoing it. In his arguments against the mood-brightening drug Prozac, psychiatrist Richard Schwartz points out that our society has a low "affect tolerance"—a difficulty with acknowledging our emotions. We need to learn to feel what we feel, he says, without attempting to lessen the feeling. We also need to respect those who deviate from our cultural norms, recognizing that those standards are not universal. For instance, Americans who suffer from bereavement for longer than a year are thought to be suffering from depression, while in rural Greece, someone who grieves for less than the five-year period of formal mourning risks social censure. It is important, Schwartz adds, to allow people to experience grief, pain, and loss for as long as it takes to heal, rather than labeling them as emotionally ill and then curing them with a mood-altering drug.

University of Michigan psychiatrist Randolph Nesse goes further, arguing that our "bad" feelings can be helpful. For example, pain, diarrhea, and nausea may distress me, but the sensations carry vital information about the state of my body; if I ignore or suppress them, I may be seriously harmed. In the same way, feelings of anger, sadness, and grief may help me adapt to the world—or prod me to adapt the world to myself. (The organization Mothers Against Drunk Drivers, or MADD, is a famous example: a mother's anger at the death of her daughter moved her to work for change in state and local drinking laws and in people's alcohol-related behaviors.) If I anesthetize myself with a mood brightener or amuse myself with entertainment to the point where I have forgotten my "bad" feelings, I may miss the full range of human experience, may rob myself of emotional elasticity, and may fail to develop the capacity to bear troubling emotions. My emotional life may be brightened and lightened, but the variety, richness, and subtlety of my emotional experience has been drastically reduced.

This is not to say that people should not seek treatment for long-term, disabling depression, or that chemical mood brighteners such as Prozac are not useful. People who have been mired in depression for months or years may find relief in a therapeutic drug's capacity to heighten their optimism and expand their sense of what is possible in their lives. Through its use, people who have been severely damaged by childhood trauma may recover their equilibrium long enough to allow them to change outworn, inhibiting ways of confronting the world.

But the rest of us need to come to terms with the dark angel who accompanies us on our journey, rather than blind ourselves to her challenging, grace-full presence. The path she invites or compels us to take, a dim, shadowy way illuminated only by starshine, is as interesting and beautiful as the road that takes us through daylight.

In this chapter, we will become better acquainted with our dark angel and explore some of the somber valleys through which we have journeyed in our lives. We will discover that we have a great deal to learn from the dark.

Fear is a basic emotion, part of our native equipment, and like all normal emotions has a positive function to perform. Comforting formulas for getting rid of anxiety may be just the wrong thing . . . To be afraid when one should be afraid is good sense.

—Dorothy Fosdick

Those who don't know how to weep with their whole heart, don't know how to laugh either.

—Golda Meir

Glimpses of the Dark Angel

The poet Sylvia Plath struggled for years with her dark angel. In 1957, she wrote these compelling lines in her diary:

Tuesday, October 1

Letter to a demon:
Last night I felt the sensation I have been reading about to no avail in [the novels of Henry] James: the sick, soul-annihilating flux of fear in my blood switching its current to defiant fight. I could not

sleep, although tired, and lay feeling my nerves shaved to pain & the groaning inner voice: oh, you can't teach, can't do anything. Can't write, can't think. And I lay under the negative icy load of denial, thinking that voice was all my own, a part of me, and it must somehow conquer me and leave me with my worst visions: having had the chance to battle it & win day by day, and having failed.

I cannot ignore this murderous self: it is there. I smell it and feel it, but I will not give it my name. I shall shame it. When it says: you shall not sleep, you cannot teach, I shall go on anyway . . . Talking about my fears to others feeds it. I shall show a calm front & fight it in the precincts of my own self . . . My demon of negation will tempt me day by day, and I'll fight it, as something other than my essential self, which I am fighting to save. . . .

The Swiss psychologist Carl Jung was the first to name the nameless part of ourselves—the "demon" whom Sylvia Plath addresses in her journal. It is our *shadow*, he said: "To become conscious of it involves recognizing the dark aspect of the personality. This act is the essential condition for self-knowledge and wholeness."

Recognizing the dark aspect of the self is difficult, though, for the shadow is made up of the things we don't want to know about. It is the self we are afraid of, the self that might get out of control and do something terrible if not carefully watched. Secret and unrevealed, it is the self we are ashamed of, the self that is unacceptable to those whose expectations we try to meet: parents, children, friends, teachers, mentors. It is the self that is *opposite* to the light, the rebellious self that may wreak havoc when it erupts into everyday life, disrupting our normal behavior, frightening us and startling those around us. Because it is so unpredictable, so formidable, we often think of this part of ourselves as a devil. We demonize it.

*Y*ou can't keep a good monster down.

—Poster for *The Ghost of Frankenstein*

Like Plath, who was constantly striving to meet impossible expectations, we may experience it as the "murderous" self—a devil, utterly opposite to the good, competent, cheerful persons we expect ourselves to be. Like Plath, we may defend ourselves against this murderous being by trying to confine it, with the predictable result: like a coiled spring, its power is increased by being pressed down, and it erupts into our lives with a destructively explosive force.

But the shadow has spontaneity, creativity, and imagination. Ironically, its creativity in part derives from its very nonconformity, for creativity is related to new and unique and often socially unacceptable ways of seeing, thinking, feeling, doing. Its creativity is also related to its energy, for the shadow has a great natural force, deriving in part from its own wild, uncontrolled, uncensured potency. Further, the shadow contains repressed ideas and desires, and its energy is like that of a tightly coiled spring: it is often released only when we can't be held back any longer, and its impact in our lives can be explosive. This kind of natural energy is very different from the controlled social behavior that we learn in our families, schools, and churches. If we learn to effectively release the shadow's potency, it can renew our lives and awaken our true individuality.

That is why Jung says we must explore the dark side of the self, get acquainted with the shadow. For the truth is that the murderous self and the good self are *both* part of the whole self. Even if I could banish my shadow, I would be cutting off a vital part of myself. It possesses extraordinary energy, vitality, and creativity, and trying to get the better of it (so to speak) only intensifies its darker power. If I stuff all this energy down inside me and put a lid on it, it will still lurk like a genie in a bottle, waiting for a moment when I am feeling weak and vulnerable, when it can overwhelm me. (As it did Plath. Six years after she determined to banish her shadow, she committed suicide.)

There is another important thing we must know about the shadow. If we defend ourselves against it by refusing to recognize and acknowledge it, we are destined to meet it in other people and in events. If we don't see our own competitiveness, all of our co-workers will seem like competitive cutthroats. If we don't acknowledge our fears, we will find ourselves in one threatening situation after another. If we fail to see our desperate need for love, we will continue to meet others who seem to need us desperately. Because we project onto others what we ourselves are experiencing, the shadow multiplies its power manyfold: not only does it exist in our minds and souls but in the world out there. And if we are seeing only our projections, we can never see the truth.

The healthiest response to your shadow is to get to know it and resist making it into a demon. With that in mind, I think it is helpful to imagine your shadow as your dark angel. Give her a name and get to know her personal history, her likes and dislikes, her fears, her needs. Recognize and greet her when she appears in your consciousness or in your projections onto other people, without imposing a negative judgment on her: "Oh, *there* you are!" you might say. "How interesting that you should show up just now." Try to discover her hidden potential, tap

There is the "I," the ego, that represents what I call myself; then there is the persona, the mask that I wear to show to the world; and there is still another part that I know, or partly know, exists but which I prefer to keep hidden because it is usually almost entirely forgotten— that is, it becomes unconscious to myself, although it may be quite obvious to others.

—M. Esther Harding

Let us rejoice in our sufferings, knowing them to be symptoms of our potential health. Pain is a script, and as we learn to read it, we grow in self-knowledge.

—M. C. Richards

If you do not tell the truth about yourself, you cannot tell it about other people.

—Virginia Woolf

her resources of energy and creativity. See how much of her spontaneity, individuality, and originality you can integrate into your everyday self. And as you do, see how this effort can help you become *all* you truly are, instead of being only the person others expect or want you to be.

The Life Story of a Dark Angel

One way to get to know your dark angel is to write her life story, using her voice and her point of view. Here are excerpts from the "Life History of Lilith," written by twenty-five-year-old Andrea K. Judging from Andrea's account, the name she gives to her dark angel is appropriate. Lilith was the enterprising trickster of Jewish myth who was created simultaneously and coequally with Adam, before Eve came on the scene. She tricked her creator into revealing his secret name and was banished from Paradise.

LIFE HISTORY OF LILITH

I've been in Andrea's life since the very beginning. In fact, I was probably the cause of all those temper tantrums that made Andrea's mother decide to tell the doctor that there was something dreadfully wrong with her little girl. I was definitely the reason why Andrea ran away from home when she was five. We hid in the neighbor's garage all night and played with the white rabbit who lived there. . . .

I talked back, too. In fact, my radical nature and my tendency to challenge authority were always getting Andrea into trouble at school. When she was eight, I said a "bad" word to Sister Anne and Andrea got labeled as a troublemaker. When she was fourteen, I refused to go to Catholic school anymore, which caused her mother to get sick (at least that's what her mother says, although I've never believed it). . . . Andrea was the first girl in her family to graduate from public high school—and it's all my fault. It's my fault, too, that Andrea became a vegetarian (and pretended to be a Buddhist) when she was twelve. You can bet *that* made the family go up in flames!

In Andrea's junior year at the state university, I decided to become an art major. That wreaked even more havoc, because if I hadn't pushed her, Andrea would have gotten an M.B.A. and gone into the family business, even though the thought of it made her terribly depressed. . . . After she graduated, I egged her into spending a year traveling across Europe, sketching. Now she's a graphic artist and I make exotic jewelry. We get along together better than we used to because Andrea listens to me more. But life is getting to be a bore again, and we're thinking about quitting our job and moving to California. She wants to go to the art institute. I want to study with a shaman.

Andrea tells Lilith's life story in a slightly humorous tone that conceals the very real internal conflict she suffered—and the unrestrained, self-destructive ways she found herself behaving—until she began to accept and acknowledge the part of her that was not the nice girl her strict Catholic parents expected her to be.

"I felt a lot like Sylvia Plath did," she told our group, which had read the excerpt from Plath's diary. "I thought I had a 'murderous self.' Sometimes I knew I was so evil that I didn't deserve to go on living. I hung out with a gang, I took antidepressants, I got involved with drugs. But things improved when I listened to Lilith and decided to get an art degree."

The dark episodes of Andrea's life, which also included a short stay in jail for shoplifting, were the expression of a nonconforming part of her that rebelled against any learning, any work, any lifestyle except that which she chose for herself. For Andrea, "listening to Lilith" meant choosing her own learning, work, and lifestyle. When Andrea began to make those choices and declare herself independent from the wishes of her parents, Lilith's behavior ceased to be so deeply self-destructive, although she continued to experience dark times, lapses into behavior she later regretted, and moments of real despair. Over time, Andrea began to act more and more often out of her own strengthening sense of personal autonomy and to incorporate Lilith's chaotic, spontaneous impulses more productively in her life. For Andrea, it is important to recognize when she needs to learn to experience something new and different, something that is on the fringes of "social respectabilty," and act on that need in a way that does not disrupt the stability of the life she has worked to create. For instance, after she wrote the passage above, Andrea decided to take graduate courses in graphic arts at the local university, get involved in a local Wiccan group, and postpone the move to California.

The unending paradox is that we do learn through pain.

—Madeleine L'Engle

Do not be amazed by the true dragon.

—Dogen Zenji

Were it possible for us to see further than our knowledge reaches, and yet a little way beyond the outworks of our divining, perhaps we would endure our sadnesses with greater confidence than our joys. For they are the moments when something new has entered into us, something unknown.

—Rainer Maria Rilke

Writing Your Dark Angel's Story

Like Andrea and Sylvia Plath and the rest of us, you have a dark angel—more than one, perhaps. Or perhaps your dark angel has more than one face or guise. When she is isolated and unheard, she may manifest herself in rebelliousness, anger, fear, sadness, depression, anxiety, or lowered self-esteem. She may also show herself in various compulsions and addictions, including food and substance addictions and workaholism—even in an addiction to success. When her needs and desires are listened to and integrated into your life, she may show herself in creative, spontaneous, imaginative, and enterprising ways.

To begin your seventh chapter, write the story of your dark angel in two or three pages, letting her speak in her own words and sign her name to the writing. Here are some questions you might consider in your writing:

> What is your dark angel's name? Is there any special significance
> behind the name?
> When did she first appear in your life? How did she manifest herself? Has she changed since you first met her? If so, how? Does
> she have more than one face or appearance? If so, what are they?
> What are her likes and dislikes, her habits, her needs, her wants?
> What happens in your life when she doesn't get her way?
> Has your dark angel brought you experiences that you otherwise
> wouldn't have had? How have these experiences changed you?
> What have you learned from them?

Your dark angel's personal history will become the first section of your chapter.

Valleys of Shadows

In your sixth chapter, you wrote about dark corners: times and places where you experienced pain even in the safety of your home. Sometimes your anguish isn't confined to a corner, though. Sometimes it seems to extend to the horizon itself. Extended periods of severe illness, of loss, grief, anger, and despair are like valleys. We descend into them, confused and groping, not sure of the path, not sure if we will ever find the way out.

Clippings: Valleys of Shadows

When she was nineteen months old, Helen Keller was struck by an illness that robbed her of the ability to see and hear. She lived in what she later called "this black hole" until she was almost seven, when she had her first miraculous experience of language. In this passage from *The Story of My Life,* she describes her valley of shadows:

> Have you ever been at sea in a dense fog, when it seemed as if a tangible white darkness shut you in, and the great ship, tense and anxious, groped her way toward the shore with plummet and sounding-line, and you waited with beating heart for something to happen? I was like that ship before my education began, only I was without compass or sounding-line, and had no way of knowing how near the harbour was. "Light! give me light!" was the wordless cry of my soul. . . .

Keller's metaphor—her life as a ship in a dense fog, without compass or depth gauge—describes a common perception of the valley of shadows. We feel as if we're drifting, but we can't tell whether we're making progress or moving backward. We have no point of reference.

Recovering: A Journal is the account of poet May Sarton's difficult sixty-sixth year. Her dearest friend was ill with Alzheimer's and she herself had had a mastectomy. On January 5th, 1978, she wrote:

> The worst thing right now is that I no longer have any distant hopes, anything ahead that I look forward to with a leap of the heart. What I have lost this past year is the sense of a destiny, the belief that what I have to offer as a human being in love or as a writer with a great deal of published work behind her, is worthy . . . which means worth all the struggle and pain that has gone both into love and work. In naked terms, I simply feel a failure. Too old to hope that things will ever get any better. . . . A trajectory, the sense I had of myself and my own powers, has been broken.

Life presents us with repeated opportunities to face what we fear, what we need to become conscious of, or what we need to master.

—Jean Shinoda Bolen

We have all had valley experiences like Keller's and Sarton's. Some of them continue for a long time, others are relatively short; some are darkly anguished or lit by fearful lightning, others are monotonously gray. It is hard to see the valley when we are in it, of course, or to appreciate the very real learning that goes on there. One experience of despair or grief or anger may be so overwhelming that we can feel nothing but the emotion itself, like a giant storm raging around and within us, or a flat, dry desert spread out under a searing sun, or a frigid arctic waste.

But when we have climbed out of the valley—when the storm has abated, the desert has turned green, the polar ice floes have thawed—it helps to look back and see where we have been.

Down in the Valley

We have to make myths of our lives, the point being that if we do, then every grief or inexplicable seizure by weather, woe, or work can—if we discipline ourselves and think hard enough—be turned to account, be made to yield further insight into what it is to be alive, to be a human being.

—May Sarton

Spend a few minutes now thinking back over your life. What have been your valley experiences? Choose one that you recall with special vividness—perhaps one that seems to you to have special significance—and imagine it as if it were an actual valley. What was its name? What was its topography, its climate? Did a gentle slope pull you downward, or was the plunge sudden and sharp? What colors and shapes did you see in your valley? How did you feel, moving through it? What emotions were involved? How long did you stay there? Were you alone in the valley, or were others there too? How did you find your way out?

After you have thought about these questions, and perhaps jotted down some of your own, give yourself an hour or so to sit quietly and write about your valley experience. As you do, be aware that you are *revisiting* the valley, rather than experiencing it for the first time, and that you can recall both the valley experience and the landscape beyond. This suggests two other questions you might consider as you write the final paragraphs of your "valley story":

What did you learn while you were in the valley?
Did your valley experience change you in any important way?

Writing about and Writing Through

Your valley story is a story about suffering and pain. Writing about such past experiences is helpful. Through retrospective writing, the kind we're doing here, you can put your experience in perspective, can see what it has meant to you. But writing *through* the present experience is even more helpful. In my own life, my daily journal has been my constant, faithful friend. I've recorded in it all my valley sojourns as they happened, so that it is a day-to-day, sometimes even a minute-by-minute, account of my wanderings. Now that I am safely out of the valley, I don't have to try to remember what it was like—it's all here, in the pages of my journal. I can revisit the valley whenever I feel there's something new to be learned there.

But a journal is more than a record of experience; it is also a *shaper* of experience, a guide and a helper. Especially in times of stress and pain, writing brings unconscious materials to the surface, helps us communicate with the dark angel. By writing your way through pain and anguish, through anger and grief and loss, you can reach a quieter, calmer place. Here is May Sarton again, on October 12, 1978:

> I began this journal ten months ago as a way of getting back to my self, of pulling out of last year's depression, and now I am truly on a rising curve. What has changed in a miraculous way is the landscape of the heart, so somber and tormented for over a year that I was not myself. . . . What has happened, that quite suddenly some weeks ago the landscape became luminous and peaceful, no anger, no irritation. . . .

For Sarton, for me, and perhaps for you as well, the daily business of writing through our feelings can change the "landscape of the heart" and point us toward the road that rises out of the dark valley. And as we leave, we carry with us the record of our wanderings, so that when the next valley beckons and the road dips once more—as it inevitably will—we can face the darkness with the knowledge that it holds lessons for us.

Be patient toward all that is unsolved in your heart and try to love the questions themselves like locked rooms and like books that are written in a very foreign tongue. Do not now seek the answers, which cannot be given you because you would not be able to live them now . . . Live the questions now. Perhaps you will then gradually, without noticing it, live along some distant day into the answer.

—Rainer Maria Rilke

No soul gives itself more work to do than it is fully equipped to accomplish.

—Emmanuel

Pain, Ritual, and Community

Living in a culture that prefers to shut out the dark, avoid shadows, and anesthetize pain means that many people are isolated. In our society, those who experience psychic or physical suffering, including the ache of old age and illness and sad memories of the devastation of war, are often exiled from healthier, younger members of the community. Families, friends, and co-workers, fearful of the dark, are reluctant to participate in our shadow experience and may urge us to be done with the dark before it is done with us.

Lacking a supportive community, many people turn to therapy as a way of sharing the dark. Even there, however, we are too often urged to turn our backs on the pain, to get on with the business of healing, to take a pill to lighten our moods. Our society defends itself against the tragic, and those of us who experience it deeply may feel that we are culture expatriates.

Not all cultures exclude the tragic. Jewish rituals are often designed to explicitly re-create the tragic event. In the Passover meal, or *seder*, for instance, salt water commemorates the tears, spilled wine the suffering of the plagues, ground nuts the mortar with which the Jewish slaves were forced to work; all symbolically reenact and honor the experience of slavery in Egypt. The ancient Jewish holday of Purim commemorates the courage of Esther, the girl who saved the Persian Jews from annihilation; Jews of the Middle Ages added a "second Purim" to commemorate their escapes; and modern families have created their own "third Purims." In an article in the magazine *Common Boundary* ("Walls for Wailing," May/June 1994), psychiatrist Jeffrey Jay writes about a Jewish man who was taken hostage by terrorists and forced to witness the murder of several other hostages. After the rescue, the man's children asked him to write about his experience, agreeing that they would write their recollections of the trauma as well, and all would read their stories each year on the anniversary of the event. The ceremony became a "third Purim," aimed to help the family commemorate and remember the tragedy that changed their lives.

Grief, sadness, loss, fear—these are solitary emotions that isolate and alienate us. Shared, they can be powerfully uniting. In the last few years, some in our own culture have begun to see the importance of building communities within which we can share our individual and common experiences of the dark. Support groups have been created for

I have a duty to speak the truth as I see it and share not just my triumphs, not just the things that felt good, but the pain, the intense, often unmitigating pain. It is important to share how I know survival is survival and not just a walk through the rain.

—Audre Lorde

abused children, recovering alcoholics, survivors of incest, and victims of crime and their families. As a nation, we have built the Vietnam wall, a powerful symbol of our collective grief about the war, a recognition of our obligation to honor the terrible truth of our memory of that long, dark valley.

Our lives after trauma become a struggle to give meaning to what has happened, to redeem our experiences by seeing them within a larger context. As individuals, families, and communities, we need to create places where we can cry out our grief, open our memories, and speak the truth of our experience.

I have thought for as long as I can remember that the asking of unanswerable questions and the facing of irreparable truths is our only consolation for having to live them.

—Catherine Madsen

Clippings: "Whenever I See a Bag Lady"

Some part of our shadow often belongs to the community as a whole. In this excerpt from a "Hers" column in the *New York Times,* writer Barbara Lazear Ascher gives us a glimpse of a shadow we fear talking about:

> Whenever I see a bag lady, I see myself slipping past the edge of time and space into an abandoned doorway. "We are all bag ladies in our souls," says a friend who has certainly had her successes. She tells me of riding a bus recently when a bag lady climbed on, heaving herself and her possessions through the door and up the steps . . .
>
> The men continued to read their papers. "But the women became very tense, as if she were sending a current through them," my friend recounted. "We sat up straighter, drew our knees together and clutched at whatever was in our laps. When she got up to leave, there wasn't a woman on that bus who didn't turn to watch her safely down the steps, and gaze after her until she was no longer in sight. But she left behind a scent of vulnerability."
>
> It is a fearful scent of our own . . . We can see ourselves rummaging through trash cans, reaching for a tin can because it will make a perfect cup, rejoicing in rags because they warm the feet. Even women with regular jobs can imagine this. Even those with five-piece place settings for twelve.

"Whenever I see a bag lady, I see myself," Ascher says. The homeless, the poor, the gang member, the criminal, the AIDS sufferer (and perhaps also the atheist, the homosexual, the radical, the revolutionary)— why do we fear these members of our community? What elements of their experience frightens us? How can we bring the shadows they represent into the light of our individual and community consciousness? If these are questions that concern you, write about them here. As Ascher has done, choose a symbol that repels or disgusts you, and use it to explore your own secret fears and the hidden or repressed fears of your community. How do you feel when you are forced into contact with this symbol? How do others around you feel? How can you use this experience to change yourself or your community?

Seeing the Valley from a Distance: A View from the Mountain

From the higher elevations of our later experience, we can look back and see the many valleys we have passed through. The soul map you drew for chapter 5 can be useful to you here. Look at it now. If you were to stand on one of the mountains you drew in your map, what valleys would you look out upon? This is how one writer answered this question:

> When I stand on My-Own-Business Peak (the highest point in the Career Mountain Range), I can see three or four deep valleys, stretching end to end along my eastward route to the mountains. The first one was M.B.A. Valley. It took me two long, hard years to climb out of it, but the reward (my degree, making me a certified survivor of a really demanding valley) was worth it. After that, I had to cross Glenda's Glade. That was a pretty valley, though, with lots of pleasant side trips—playgrounds and zoos and afternoons at the beach with my daughter Glenda. The road was rough, but I loved every minute of it. (Well, maybe not *every* minute.) Then I got my first job on Big Blue Mountain. But just when I got within sight of the first peak, Big Blue was downsized, and I took the trail to Motorola Mountain. But then I fell into a really deep valley I just couldn't get out of. It had a glass ceiling over it, and no matter how hard I pushed, I couldn't budge it. So I left and started my own desktop publishing company. That's where I am now: My-Own-Business Peak. It's scary up here, and pretty lonely, and I worry about falling off. But the view is great!
> —Mary Jean T.

Writing a View from the Mountain

Write a page or two of your own "View from the Mountain," describing the valleys you have traveled through. Once you have sketched out your general route of travel, you might want to go into more detail about each of your valleys, pointing out their most important features. It would be especially helpful to remind yourself of what you gained in your valley experiences, and see how they helped you reach the point where you now stand.

Putting Your Seventh Chapter Together

Throughout this chapter, you've been writing about the dark experiences that every person who wants to be deeply involved in life must confront. You have written about the dark angel, revisited a Valley of Shadows, and viewed several valleys from a mountaintop.

There are several other things you might do if you would like to extend this chapter. In your book, you might include accounts of valley journeys from your journals or letters. If your valley journey involved an accident or a death, you may have newspaper clippings, obituaries, funeral momentos, or other materials that could be included here. If it involved a larger, more public tragedy—the loss of several lives, or a long and painful trial—you may want to create a much more extensive archive. You may extend the scope of your inquiry and find yourself becoming interested in a family trauma of a generation or two ago, such as the loss of a business or way of life. Many children of Holocaust survivors, for instance, have found this kind of exploration essential to understanding their lives, and the same thing is true for children of displaced Native Americans, emigrants, pioneers, and victims of war or natural catastrophe.

What you have done in this chapter is vitally important to the human task of growing through your experiences—*all* of them. Recognizing aspects of the self you do not want to acknowledge, giving your traumatic memories the honor of recognition—these gestures toward

What stays with us isn't
*   art,*
or smiles or tears or some-
*   body's good word*
or somebody else's criticism.
These things come and go.

This is the presence
that stays the same.
  —Susan Albert, after Rumi

the dark help allay ancient nightmares and lessen the chances that an old ghost will disrupt your present life. They also help prepare you for the other dark places and difficult times that you will inevitably encounter on the way ahead.

Meditation

Letting Go

Once we have allowed ourselves to feel the pain and trauma of our dark angel, it is time to release the old anguish and prepare ourselves for new experience. In *The Grandmother of Time: A Women's Book of Celebrations, Spells, and Sacred Objects for Every Month of the Year,* Zsuzsanna Budapest describes a meditative ritual for letting go. This meditation is modeled after that one.

Before you begin, create an altar upon which you can burn several pieces of paper. This might be in your fireplace, or on the ground in your backyard, or in a hibachi. Create your altar with a piece of black cloth (black represents the color of chaos, from which all life comes and to which it must return). Place on it some fallen leaves to suggest the natural cycle of the seasons; a rock (a sedimentary rock, like sandstone, if possible) to remind you of the earthy truth that all experience is created out of tiny elements of former experience; and a piece of outworn or outmoded clothing or jewelry, representing the fact that human artifacts last for only a short time before their usefulness and attractiveness fade. You may also want to add a goblet full of water to your altar, a candle, and some incense. (Good choices might be sandalwood, frankincense, myrrh, or cedar.) Place a sheet of paper on your altar and a writing implement.

Sit quietly before your altar and bring your attention to your breathing. . . . Let the breath flow through you, evenly, quietly, bringing you to balance. . . . When your mind is quiet, bring your thoughts to those shadowy things, the valley experiences, that you feel you have lived with long enough. . . . the old fears, old anxieties, old desires that you no longer need or want. . . . Now, take your writing materials and make a list of those things you are ready to let go of. . . . As you write each item on your list, picture it in your mind for a moment, then imagine yourself letting it go, allowing it to fall or blow or float away, or crumble into pieces. . . . Experience the physical sensations of that release, and the emotional feelings as well. . . . After you have let go of one item completely, go on to the next.

When you are done, reread your list. Then, holding it and addressing your dark angel by name, you might say something like this:

> [Name], I am ready to release these valley experiences, these shadow times. I have felt them fully and lived with them long enough, and I'm ready to go on to something else. Take their heavy energy and recycle it, so that I can feel lighter as I walk along my path.

Then burn your list, watching as the flames turn your darkness into light and heat. Imagine your inner darkness turning into light and new energy in the same way. You may want to say something else:

> [Name], I feel lighter, more buoyant, ready to travel new ways, across peaks, into deep valleys, learning as I go. Thank you.

Add the leaves to the flames, and watch as the ashes of your list mingle with the ashes of the leaves, natural residue of earthly experience. Burn or bury the clothing or jewelry, and toss your rock away. When you are done, all you are left with is the memory of your ritual. If you wish, add anything from it to your chapter, then let the ritual go as well.

Celebrating the Completion of Your Chapter

This chapter may have been a difficult one for you to work with. If so, congratulations on completing it! It's time for a celebration.

1. Give yourself a small but special gift in honor of the time you have spent reliving your valley journeys. Perfume would be nice, or an herbal soap, or a cassette tape or CD of your favorite artist.

2. With your Story Circle, share one of your valley experiences, and listen to the valley journeys of others. Do the stories have anything in common? Also share the view from the mountain. Is the shadow lighter now?

3. Take your dark angel out to lunch or to a special event or place. Where would she like to go? What would she like to do? What kind of energies are released when you welcome her suggestions into your consciousness? When Marge M. did this, she reported the following:

My dark angel (her name is Samantha) has had the unfortunate habit of overusing our charge cards, so when she said her idea of a special treat was going to a bead store, I had to give her a ten-dollar bill and tell her that's all there was. She complained a lot about it but finally agreed. She bought six weird-looking African beads to string on a leather thong (might look a little strange with my power suits) and then begged to go to the Greek deli next door, where we splurged on baklava (never had it before—yum yum!) and Samantha picked up a flyer advertising a belly-dancing class. Now she wants to try belly dancing. What my husband is going to say when he hears about that, I don't know.

Chapter Eight

Common Interests,
Common Causes

The idea of strictly minding our own business is moldy rubbish. Who could be so selfish?
—Myrtle Lillian Barker

Self and World

Up to this point in the life story you've been writing and compiling, you've turned your attention on yourself as an individual: your birth and birthings, your achievements, your body, your homes, your journeys. You've focused on your efforts to recognize yourself and be recognized as an independent and autonomous person, capable of minding her own business and minding it with competence and flair.

There's good reason for focusing on the self. Declaring our independence—"becoming individuated," in Carl Jung's phrase—is a vital step in life's journey. Until recently, women were defined by their relationship to parents, husbands, and children. To separate ourselves, to be responsible to ourselves, and to engage the world on our own terms are critical life tasks. Strong ego boundaries, clearly marked separation, emphatic individuation—these are all aspects of the successful individual in our society.

But there is a problem with this behavioral model. Some psychologists have recently suggested that pronounced individuation is an aspect of male development, not necessarily a path for women. In fact, says Carol Gilligan, author of *In a Different Voice: Psychological Theory and Women's Development*, masculinity is commonly defined through separation from others and the development of the autonomous self, while femininity is defined through connection with others, making women appear psychologically undeveloped and less mature than strongly individuated males.

The truth is otherwise, Gilligan says. Women's need to care, our sense that it is more satisfying and responsible to form attachments with others rather than separate ourselves from them, is a psychologically and morally mature pattern of human development. This maturity is based in what she calls "an ethic of care"—our responsibility to care for ourselves as individuals and for the other persons to whom we are connected—and it is vital to the health and welfare of the human community. Our male-oriented, male-dominated society needs to value what women have valued all along, Gilligan adds. "The truths of relationship return in the rediscovery of connection, in the realization that self and other are interdependent and that life can only be sustained by care in relationships."

Gilligan's idea of interdependency is echoed from a different point of view by another thinker, Buddhist teacher and philosopher Joanna Macy. Macy believes that none of us, female or male, can ever be truly separate from the universe in which we live. We cannot define the self as unconnected and autonomous. In *World as Lover, World as Self*, she says:

> I used to think that I ended with my skin, that everything within the skin was me and everything outside the skin was not. But now you've read these words, and the concepts they represent are reaching your cortex, so "the process" that is me now extends as far as you. And where, for that matter, did this process begin? I certainly can trace it to my teachers, some of whom I never met, and to my husband and children, who give me courage and support to do the work I do, and to the plant and animal beings who sustain my body . . .

From this point of view, the individual is not a self-created product but part of a continuing *process* of energy exchanges with numberless other selves, past, present, and future, in ever-widening circles that ulti-

One day when I was feeling like a motherless child, which I was, it come to me: that feeling of being part of everything, not separate at all. I knew that if I cut a tree, my arm would bleed. And I laughed and I cried and I run all round the house. I knew just what it was. In fact, when it happen, you can't miss it.

—Alice Walker,
The Color Purple

We are all islands—in a common sea.

—Anne Morrow Lindbergh

mately include all life on our planet: our "earth household," as the poet Gary Snyder has called it.

Physicist David Bohm has extended this idea to the universe itself. In his book *Wholeness and the Implicate Order*, he says that despite the apparent separateness of things, everything in the universe is a seamless extension of everything else. This doesn't mean that we are not unique individuals. Rather, we are like the separate whirlpools and eddies that form in a river, each one distinct from every other, each whirling at a different rate, at a different angle—but all part of the same river.

Where does all this leave us? With the understanding, it seems to me, that my story is only a chapter in a volume that contains many other chapters, many other stories. With the knowledge that while my culture might want me to imagine myself as an independent, autonomous being, I must expand my view beyond this narrow, culturally biased definition. I must define myself as a being-in-process who is part of a vast network of other beings-in-process, all of whom are constantly reshaping themselves and being reshaped through their connections to others. I must recognize that I cannot become a whole, mature person by simply minding my own business; by being separate and autonomous and successful, according to our culture's definition of success. "I" am only one of the words of my story, and "my" story is only one word of the billions that tell the story of our world. To see myself whole, to tell *all* of my story, I must look beyond myself to my community and to the world. I must see myself as part of the river.

Masterpieces are not single and solitary births; they are the outcome of many years of thinking in common, of thinking by the body of the people, so that the experience of the mass is behind the single voice.

—Virginia Woolf

"I Am——————": A Poem about Possibilities

What do you think? In your own mind, who are you? How would you complete these definitions?

I am_____

I am_____

I am_____

Doing this exercise in a seminar once, our group worked together and came up with the following lines. When we wrote them on the blackboard, they reminded us of a poem:

Stories give us our sense of identity; they define our place in the world. . . . That's because stories not only reflect who we are as individuals but also give us ever-changing kaleidoscopic glimpses of what it's like to be members of the human family.

—Anne B. Simpkinson

A Poem about Who I Am

I am the lines I read yesterday, the words I am writing this minute, the
    thoughts behind my eyes, my mind thinking, my hand moving across
    the page.
I am the orange I had for breakfast, and yesterday's sandwich. My bones
    are the milk that was once in the udder of a cow and before that was
    grass in a green meadow and water in a blue lake.
I am last night's lovemaking, and my parents', and their parents'. I am
    my children's desire, and their children's. My passion embraces the
    whole world.
I am a participating citizen of a neighborhood, a city, a state, a nation.
    I belong to a church, a political party, a gardening club, the Sierra Club.
I work in a department, in a division, in a multinational corporation.
    My influence extends to the horizon in all directions.
I am a transformer of matter and energy and information. I am a surfer
    on the vast intergalactic net of being, touching all points
I am all points, enfolded
I am all
I am
I

A poem of your "I am . . ." definitions would be a good beginning for
your eighth chapter: "Common Interests, Common Causes."

Myself, My Friend

All of this business about being part of the river is certainly intriguing,
but in terms of the way you lead your day-to-day life, it may seem abstract. The sad truth is that many of us don't actually *feel* very connected. In fact, our highly technologized society is often characterized
as "rootless," a culture in which our increasing mobility has led us to
lose touch with people and places we once held dear. Sociologists say
that our lives are characterized more by discontinuity and disruption
than by continuity and connection. Our rootlessness is one of the inevitable outcomes of an increasingly technologically based society.

    I'm not sure I agree with this assessment. The real problem, it seems to me, is that we aren't always mindful of the many ways we are connected to one another. Under the pressure of increasing work demands and decreased leisure time, we don't take the time to maintain and honor the connections we have. We fall prey to our culture's narrow definition of the self and ignore the clear evidence in and around us of our connectedness, of our expanded identity.

In this last chapter of your life's story, you will make a record of the different ways you've been connected to people. Some of those connections have been temporary and not particularly close; others have been enduring and intimate. But *all* those connections, the sum total of them, constitute what we'll call the *larger* self: the self that is you, plus all the other selves that are and have been important to you. As you follow these suggestions for writing your chapter, you will be constructing what psychologists call a relationship map.

You can begin looking at your larger self by remembering your friendships, those you have now and those you have experienced over the years. On a sheet of paper draw a small circle to represent your self. Around that circle draw four concentric rings, the last one reaching the edges of your paper. You will work with the three outer rings as you go along.

For the first step, focus on the inner ring, the one closest to the circle that is you. In it, write the names of all the people you have ever considered family, whether or not you now think of them as family, whether they are living or dead: your mother, father, sisters, brothers, children, spouses, partners. Our family members may no longer be with us, and some we may no longer think of as family. But they can be a sustaining core of kinship that lasts as long as we live, a rich source of shared memory and connection to time and place. We include them here to see, visually, the kind of grounding connections that the family can create.

Now, in the ring surrounding the family ring, write the names of as many close friends as you can remember, including those with whom you may no longer be in touch. If it is difficult to recall names, divide your life into five-year periods, remember where you lived and what you did in those years, and think of the people to whom you were close. You might cluster any names that have a special connection—three college roommates, for instance, or your four bridesmaids, or a co-worker on your first job with whom you still exchange letters. Are some of your friends closely connected to other friends or to members of your family? If so, draw lines between those names.

Now, study your drawing, consider the relationships, and decide

Friends are family you choose for yourself.

—Jane Addams

It is the friends that you can call at 4 A.M. that matter.

—Marlene Dietrich

which ones have been, over the long haul, the most meaningful to you. You could number them or mark them with a colored pen. Take more paper and write the names of your three or four most significant friendships, one to a page. (If you have any photographs or other mementos, take some time to look for them; they may remind you of the times you shared.) Then write a one-page history of each important friendship. Some things you might consider:

> how you became friends
> why you were attracted
> major ups and downs in your friendship
> incidents, anecdotes, recollections
> anything you wish you could change
> what the friendship meant to you

Clippings

> Oh, the comfort, the inexpressible comfort of feeling safe with a person: having neither to weigh thoughts nor measure words, but to pour them out. Just as they are—chaff and grain together, knowing that a faithful hand will take and sift them, keep what is worth keeping, and then with a breath of kindness, blow the rest away.
>
> —George Eliot

> I will be your friend always,
> no gaps, no forgettings.
> Not until the mountains are worn away
> and the rivers are nothing but sand and rocks,
> not until it thunders and lightning comes in winter
> or until it snows in the summer,
> or until heaven and earth are the same,
> not until then will I leave you.
>
> —First century Chinese friendship oath

> A friend hears the song in my heart and sings it to me when my memory fails.
>
> —Pioneer Girls Leaders' Handbook

We contain within ourselves a world of capacities, of possibilities, which the outer world summons forth, speaks to, releases. Perhaps this is why we learn most about ourselves through devotion to others; why we become joyful and active as we respond to the formative forces in the materials in our crafts: their potentialities call forth our own, and in the dialogue of which I have spoken, we discover our own inner vision by bodying them forth.

—M. C. Richards

Common Interests

We come together in groups because of what sociologists call "affinity"—a mutual attraction, a common interest, a shared passion. We search out others who enjoy doing what we like to do. We join with those who hold views similar to ours on important questions, such as religion and politics. We find ourselves in close physical proximity to others—in our neighborhoods, for instance. This proximity usually extends to other dimensions: our next-door neighbors probably belong to our income group, have similar consumer and lifestyle habits, and their children attend the same schools as ours.

In fact, the self you are can be defined, in part, by your membership in various "affinity" groups. At one time or another in the last dozen years, I have belonged to groups that were interested in folk dancing, sailing, gardening, barbershop singing, twelve-step work, meditation, and quilting. Some of these (folk dancing and barbershop singing) turned out to be peripheral interests that faded rather quickly. Others (gardening and meditation) continue to occupy my time and attention, and I continue to belong to groups that share these interests. As I look back over my life, I can see how I have been influenced by various affinity groups. Without them, I would be an entirely different person. They help to give continuity and purpose to the individual that I am.

To be one woman, truly, wholly, is to be all women.

—Kate Braverman

Let's return to the concentric rings: self in the center circle, family and friends in the second and third. In the fourth and outside ring, write down the names of the various groups you've belonged to in your life—church or synagogue, neighborhood associations, political parties, feminist groups, hobby or craft clubs, yoga or meditation classes, reading groups, volunteer organizations, issue-related organizations (such as AIDS groups, MADD), your story circle, and so on. (If you've been a member of dozens of groups, you may want to limit your list to the most important: those that you belonged to for a year or more, or which represented a substantial interest.) If any of the names you put down in the "friends" ring are connected to a group in the outside ring, draw a line to represent the connection.

When you're done, study the groups you have listed. Then choose the most important three or four and write a one-page history of your association with each one. Some questions you might think about:

> How did you become involved with this group?
> What attracted you to its ideas and activities?
> What does this attraction suggest about you?

When you've finished, read back over what you've written, then write one more page, considering these questions:

> How have your associations changed over the course of your life?
> What do these changes suggest about your evolving interests, your evolving self?
> Of all the groups you've been involved with, which have been the most important to you? Why? What part of you is most engaged by the interests or the people represented in this group?

If the first woman God ever made was strong enough to turn the world upside down all alone, these women together ought to be able to turn it back, and get it right side up again!

—Sojourner Truth

Common Causes

Women are passionate creatures with the capacity to care deeply. They focus their caring on what they value in a way that takes them beyond their isolated egos. Community needs have always been high on the list of our values, and our sense of connection and commitment are strong. Understanding that we have greater power when there are more of us at work on the same problem, we often band together to work for the causes we value the most. In this section, you will consider the way you have put your values to work in your life, and the way your work has shaped your family and community.

Clippings: "I was resolved"

In this excerpt from *Margaret Sanger: An Autobiography*, the founder of the American birth control movement tells about the event that made her leave obstetrical nursing to work for birth control. One of her patients, fearful of another pregnancy, had begged the doctor for help. But the doctor said only, "Tell Jake to sleep on the roof," and Sanger herself had no information to give the woman. When she died of a botched abortion, Sanger felt responsible.

For hours [after the death] I walked and walked and walked through the hushed streets. When I finally arrived home and let myself quietly in, all the household was sleeping. I looked out my window and down upon the dimly lighted city. Its pains and griefs crowded in upon me, a moving picture rolled before my eyes with photographic clearness: women writhing in travail to bring forth little babies; the babies themselves naked and hungry, wrapped in newspapers to keep them from the cold; six-year-old children with pinched, pale, wrinkled faces, old in concentrated wretchedness, pushed into gray and fetid cellars. . . .

As I stood there the darkness faded. The sun came up and threw its reflection over the house tops. It was the dawn of a new day in my life also. The doubt and questioning, the experimenting and trying, were now to be put behind me. I knew I could not go back merely to keeping people alive. . . . I was resolved to seek out the root of evil, to do something to change the destiny of mothers whose miseries were as vast as the sky. . . .

Jane Addams (1860–1935) was the college-educated daughter of a prominent Midwestern family. To her parents' dismay, she rejected marriage and turned instead to "settlement work" in the slums of Chicago, enriching the lives of the impoverished. In this excerpt from *Twenty Years at Hull-House*, she writes of the early days, when she gave up every minute to her passion:

The memory of the first years at Hull-House is more or less blurred with fatigue, for we could of course become accustomed only gradually to the unending activity and to the confusion of a house constantly filling and refilling with groups of people. The little children

Better, far, suffer occasional insults or die outright, than live the life of a coward, or never move without a protector. The best protector any woman can have, one that will serve her at all times and in all places, is courage; this she must get by her own experience, and experience comes by exposure.

—Elizabeth Cady Stanton

If you don't like the way the world is, you change it. You have an obligation to change it. You just do it one step at a time.

—Marian Wright Edelman

who came to the kindergarten in the morning were followed by the afternoon clubs of older children, and those in turn made way for the educational and social organizations of adults, occupying every room in the house every evening. All one's habits of living had to be readjusted, and any student's tendency to sit with a book by the fire was of necessity definitely abandoned. . . .

. . . We were often bitterly pressed for money and worried by the prospect of unpaid bills, and we gave up one golden scheme after another because we could not afford it; we cooked the meals and kept the books and washed the windows without a thought of hardship if we thereby saved money for the consummation of some ardently desired undertaking. . . .

Liz Walker, an activist with the American Friends Service Committee, relates this story:

One of the finest experiences I've had was going to jail with sixteen other women. This was a result of getting arrested on August 6, 1978, at a demonstration against the Diablo Canyon nuclear plant. . . . All sixteen of us found ourselves locked together in a cell for the next nine days. The experience was quite powerful and we found that even though we were jammed together in a cell not much more than ten by twelve feet, we were able to take good care of each other. We started out by telling each other our life stories, and then we did workshops. We weren't allowed phone calls, we weren't allowed medicine, we weren't allowed books; nevertheless the experience just kept getting better and better.

When Maggie Kuhn was sixty-five, she organized the Gray Panthers, which originally began in opposition to the Vietnam war and has moved on to many fronts: affordable housing, innovative work concepts, health care, the Age Discrimination Employment Act. On her eighty-seventh birthday, Kuhn said:

The adventure in my case is breaking ground, the opportunity to move in new directions, to envision what could be . . . Our philosophy was using gray power with the young for issues on the cutting edge of social change. I think we've established the fact that old age is a triumph. There's a freedom today—at my age I can speak out, be really radical. I've set myself a goal to say something really outrageous every day, and I've outlived my opposition.

A Writing Exercise: Community and Cause

Not all of us have the desire or the determination to make sweeping changes in our communities. But all of us have put our values and our caring to work in important ways, through church and synagogue, through neighborhood work groups, community organizations, and political parties. Most of us have been committed, in the course of our lives, to a variety of important causes and public agendas. We have volunteered in hospitals and hospices and rape crisis centers, worked as drug counselors and peace activists and hot-line volunteers, and helped to find housing and health care for the homeless. We have in our hearts a deep pool of compassion and wisdom, and we need to recognize it in ourselves and others.

To start thinking about the causes for which you've worked over the course of your lifetime, turn back to the page on which you drew the concentric circles: yourself in the middle, surrounded by family, then friends, then affinity groups. In the outermost circle, write down all the various causes you have supported with your time or your money or both—voter registration, for example, or victims' rights, or the Women's Shelter. Or the Nature Conservancy or People for the Ethical Treatment of Animals, or the local hike and bike trail, or environmental cleanup. As you write down the groups, notice whether there's any connection between the causes you've supported and the affinity groups you've belonged to (a hiking club and the Sierra Club, for instance), and whether there are any connections between your circle of friends and your circle of causes.

When you've set down the causes you've supported, study them for a moment. Then choose the two or three that are most important to you (those you have supported longest, or contributed most to, or care about most deeply) and write a page about each. Here are some questions that may prompt your writing:

> Why do you care about this cause? What makes it worth your
>   time and energy?
> How did you get involved? How long and in what ways have you
>   worked for it? How much of your time have you given to it?
> Are there any stories or anecdotes that illustrate your connection
>   and commitment to this cause?

I am above eighty years old . . . I suppose I am about the only colored woman that goes about to speak for the rights of the colored women. I want to keep the thing stirring, now that the ice is cracked.

—Sojourner Truth

If you want anything said, ask a man. If you want anything done, ask a woman.

—Margaret Thatcher

I am woman, hear me roar.

—Helen Reddy

When I look at the future, it's so bright it burns my eyes.

—Oprah Winfrey

When you've finished, read back over what you've written and over all the causes you've supported, then write an additional page, responding to these prompts:

How have your commitments changed over the course of your life?
What do these changes suggest about your evolving sense of self-in-community?

Clippings

I never used to care about helping anybody—it was all I could do to take care of myself. Then I was in a car wreck and had to be in the hospital for a couple of months. It changed my life. It's hard to explain, but I knew when I got out that I wasn't the center of my life—there was something larger than me, and I had to connect to it.

For starters, I didn't intend to do anything complicated, just a little volunteer work in the children's ward, because that's where the hospital needed help. Then my friend Sandi decided I should dress up like a clown. Then she decided that she'd volunteer too and that *both* of us would be clowns, so we started doing our faces. Then we created some wacky costumes—clothes from the secondhand store and wigs and weird hats. When we're all dressed up, we look pretty funny.

But what we see when we go into the ward isn't funny at all. It's horrible. Kids who are dying, kids who've been burned, kids who don't have enough face left to tell who they are, just awful. But I can't look at that. When I'm doing my clown act, I have to look in their hearts. That's where they're whole, real kids. That's what I go for, week after week. I go to look past the hurting and the dying and into their hearts.

What's next? How am I evolving in all this? I don't know. I'm still looking. All I know is that I want to help *more.*

—Joan G.

The most important thing I do with my spare time is volunteer at the nursing home. I wanted to do something constructive with my time and the nursing home is close to where I live. But more than that, I worry that we forget old people. We put them into places where they get more-or-less decent care (good enough to keep us from feeling guilty, anyway) and then we forget them. But they've got a lot of wisdom stored up inside, a lot of experiences of life. And they're lonely. The nurses don't have time to talk. Nobody listens to them.

So every Friday I do a program called "The Way It Was Back Then." Everybody sits in a circle and each one tells a story—something they remember from their past. Some of the stories are touching and others are funny, like the one about the goat that ate a straw hat with a sunflower on it. Lately, I've been taping the stories, and I've promised to put them together into a little book that they can give their relatives for Christmas.

Of course, the storytelling is good therapy for them. It helps them remember and makes them feel good that they have something to contribute. But it's even better therapy for me. I feel connected to something important—to the old people, to their lives. And I feel connected to a part of me that I used to be afraid of: to my aging self. If I live long enough, I suppose I'll be in a nursing home at some point. I'll have stories to tell. I want somebody around to listen and remember them.

—Ronnie D.

There are so many ways in which we listen to one another. "I hear you," we say to one another . . . "I understand. I'm with you." Such a message can be immensely reassuring for a person who has felt isolated or alone in their pain and suffering. The reassurance does not come from the words themselves, of course, but from what the words represent. . . . Sharing is a way of being together—heart to heart. In those moments we are no longer alone with our fear; we are reminded that we are not forgotten.

—Ram Dass

Putting Your Eighth Chapter Together

The central focus of this chapter has been the creation of a relationship map, which pictures the various ways in which you are connected to the world around you. In widening circles, you've been expanding your self-definition, seeing the experiences you've shared with friends, the interests you've shared with various groups, and the causes to which you've committed your heart. When you've finished this chapter, you should be able to see yourself in multiple dimensions, across the various communities of which you are a member.

If you would like to expand this chapter, you might want to write a longer version of any of the three writing tasks: a history of a friendship, a piece about a group to which you've belonged, a personal essay on a cause about which you feel deeply. You could include letters, newspaper clippings, or magazine articles that document the work you've done. Or perhaps you have photographs, drawings, or other material that could illustrate your chapter.

Meditation

Connections

As we have worked through this chapter, we have enlarged our sense of self, realizing that we are not isolated, separate entities. We are all integral and organic threads in a vast web of being. Our recognition that our world needs help and the pain that this recognition sometimes brings is testimony to our interconnection with others, to our place in the web. If we let this recognition move freely through us, we can open to the myriad possibilities for participating in the world. And even though what we see brings us pain, we can be confident of our resilience, our sturdiness. We are here as parts of a whole. Everything we do, everything we are, touches others, is connected to others. This meditation, which is adapted from a Buddhist meditation on compassion, helps us to experience this truth.

Sitting quietly, breathing gently. . . .

Close your eyes and be mindful of your breath. . . . Observe the tension as it drains away, as if it were water moving through your body. . . . Let your body settle into your sitting posture, erect but not stiff . . . letting go of thoughts, of plans, of memories . . . simply watching the breath . . . breathing in, breathing out.

And as you watch the breath, notice that it just seems to happen . . . that it seems to breathe without your doing it. . . . Inhaling, exhaling . . . relaxing into a natural rhythm that continues without your will. . . . It is as if you are being breathed . . . as if you are part of the breath that fills the world . . . just as all beings everywhere are breathing the same breath . . . all nourished by the breath that fills the world. . . .

Now, as you continue to be breathed by this breath, let your mind return to the pattern of circles that you drew on the paper . . . yourself in the center, connected in different ways to so many people around you. . . . Think for a moment of your circle of friends, and choose one to whom you feel close, perhaps someone you've known for years. . . . Imagine the face of your friend, and as you see your friend's face, let yourself become aware of the many connections between you, the many ways you are bound together in memory, in dreams, in hopes, perhaps even in pain. . . . Let yourself open, knowing that all those dreams and hopes are still alive in you . . . let yourself open to those connections, knowing that you and your friend are breathing the same breath. . . .

Let your awareness move now to a group that you have been connected to. . . . Imagine the members of the group, recall their energies, their enthusiasm. . . . Remember what it was that drew all of you together, your common interest. . . . Let yourself open to that energy now, feeling how good it was to join together, to work for success and to learn from setback. . . . Let yourself become aware that all those energies are still alive in you. . . . Let yourself open, knowing that you and the members of your group are all breathing the same breath. . . .

And now let your awareness move to a cause that you have been committed to. . . . Feel in your heart the urgency that pulled you to it like a magnet. . . . Recall how it was that you realized someone's need or felt another's pain or saw the terrible wounds inflicted on the earth. . . . And recall how good it felt to make a healing gesture, how another's healing healed you. . . . Let yourself open to that healing now, sensing the power of that gesture, the strength of common commitment to something larger than yourself, something worth caring about. . . . Let yourself be aware that the urgency of need and the healing of commitment are still alive in you now. . . . Let yourself open, knowing that all with whom you have joined are breathing a common breath . . . that you are all being breathed by the breath of life itself. . . .

And as you sit quietly, breathing this common breath, also feel the strength that comes from joining together. . . . In this quiet place, you are not alone, you are all the friends, all the interests, all the commitments to which you have ever given yourself. . . . In this quiet place, you are the river. . . .

And now, bring your attention back to your breath, to your body in its sitting posture, to your place in the room. Open your eyes, take a deep breath, and know that all is well. Sit quietly for as many moments as you like. If you wish, you may add to your chapter anything you have drawn from this meditation.

Celebrating the Completion of Your Chapter

This isn't a chapter you want to celebrate by yourself! Now that it's completed, you'll want to share what you've done, written, and thought about with others. Here are some things you might do:

1. Take your relationship map to a meeting of your Story Circle. Pin all the maps on the wall and share them with one another. Where does your Story Circle fit into your map?

2. Select a person from your circle of friends. Call or write to the person and share some of the things you were thinking about as you wrote that section of your chapter. If possible, do something together to remind both of you of the special bond of friendship you share.

3. On the wall of your room or on a shelf, collect snapshots, clippings, or mementos that remind you of a special group with whom you shared good times. For instance, I brought together several photos of the sailboat I once owned, snapshots of the all-woman crew I sailed with in the Adams Cup Regatta one year, and a couple of sailing trophies. (I also included my worn sailing gloves, to remind myself of the hard work!)

4. To honor the hours you have given to others, give yourself a special hour. Take a quiet walk, enjoy a simple meal, listen to favorite music, observe a beautiful flower, and know that you are blessed. Let the walk, the food, the music, the flower be a gift to you from a grateful universe.

Creating Your Own
Story Circle:

A Manual for Truth-Tellers

I need to write my story, and read it out loud. I want to hear other women's stories. I crave this chorus of women's voices, the sad and sentimental, the angry and the bitter, the happy, the joyful. My voice is stronger when it is joined to the voices of my sisters.

—Amy J.

We live the stories of our lives with such intensity and engagement that they are transparent to us. We eat, sleep, dream, breathe them. We are like fish swimming in the ocean. What fish imagines itself surrounded by water, or knows that there are creatures that breathe a lighter, brighter air?

When I write my story—the whole of it, or bits and pieces—I can *see* it, and see myself in it. When I share my story and others share theirs with me, I can see my life much more clearly. Throughout this book, we've been focusing on the task of telling the soul's story, the worthwhile work of capturing life in writing. But that's only part of the

The circle is cast. We are between the worlds, beyond the bounds of time, where night and day, birth and death, joy and sorrow, meet as one.

—Starhawk

process. The other part, equally important, is getting together with other women to share our souls' stories in what we'll call a *Story Circle*.

What Is a Story Circle?

When we cast a circle, we create an energy form, a boundary that limits and contains the movements of subtle forces.

—Starhawk

At one time or another, you may have belonged to a reading group, where you got together with other people to discuss books you had read. Or perhaps you've been a member of a writing group, where you met to read aloud and critique your writing efforts—usually fiction or poetry, sometimes journal writing or nonfiction. In the last ten years, the popularity of both kinds of groups has mushroomed, as we have begun to understand how much we can learn from exploring our inner life, pole to pole, with other intrepid travelers.

A Story Circle shares the features of both these groups. In our Story Circles, we are writers, reading aloud and discussing our own life stories—short anecdotes, longer memoirs, the chapters of our lives. We are also readers, reading and discussing the published life stories of women: some autobiographical, some biographical, some fictional—but all, in the most profound sense, true. In our discussions of our own writing and the writing of others, we come to feel the depth of our shared private and public experiences: how alike we are, under the skin, how kindred are our joys and sadnesses, our successes, our failures. What we gain from these discussions is a sense of belonging, of common purpose and common hopes. What we lose is our sense of alienation and aloneness, our separateness, our fear. But be warned: sharing your truth with other truth-telling women may enlighten and free you—and enlightenment and freedom may change your life!

The Greek word for truth, aletha, means "not hidden."

—Catherine Kober

Clippings: "Into the Plain Light"

I can subvert the power of shame by acknowledging who I am, shame and all, and in doing so, raising what was hidden, dark, secret about my life into the plain light of shared human experience. What we aren't permitted to utter holds us all, each isolated from every other, in a kind of solipsistic thrall. Without any way to check our reality against anyone else's we assume that our fears and shortcomings are ours alone.

—Nancy Mairs

For those of us who write, it is necessary to scrutinize not only the truth of what we speak, but the truth of that language by which we speak it. For others, it is to share and spread also those words that are meaningful to us. But primarily for us all, it is necessary to teach by living and speaking those truths which we believe and know beyond understanding. Because in this way alone can we survive, by taking part in a process of life that is creative and continuing, that is growth. And it is never without fear—of visibility, of the harsh light of scrutiny and perhaps judgment, of pain, of death. But we have lived through all of those already, in silence, except death. And I remind myself all the time now that if I were to have been born mute, or had maintained an oath of silence my whole life long for safety, I would still have suffered, and I would still die. It is very good for establishing perspective.

—Audre Lourde

Mairs's paragraph (from her book *Carnal Acts*) reminds me that silence isolates me, makes me believe that I am the only one who has ever felt this pain. Lourde's paragraph (from a paper she delivered at a Modern Language Association meeting in 1977) reminds me that the only alternative to speech is eternal muteness, and that if I do not dare to show myself, to share myself, I shall remain forever invisible.

Creating a Story Circle

Organizing a new group, or joining an existing one, can be a risky process—and understandably so. I may be willing to share my true story but fearful of criticism. You may welcome criticism but find yourself shy about revealing your inner life. Someone else may be anxious about the ghosts and goblins she might see if she takes a good, hard look into her darkest, innermost corners.

Fear, of course, is a natural part of any new adventure. But in my work with dozens of Story Circles, it's been my observation that the

The most important thing one woman can do for another is to illuminate and expand her sense of actual possibilities.

—Adrienne Rich

most successful participants are risk takers who acknowledge and explore their fear at the same time that they go on with the very thing they're afraid of. They're the ones who benefit the most from the risks they take—which grow into even bigger risks as they enlarge their inner and outer experiences.

Let's suppose you've finished reading this book. You've filled a notebook with your writing, photos, and other memorabilia, and you yearn to share what you've learned with others, and learn from them, as well. You look around and discover that there's no such group in your area. How do you organize one?

You might begin by imagining an ideal group and its setting. How many people would belong? How often would you meet? Where would you meet, and when? For how long? Would your meetings involve food and/or drink?

Your ideal group might take many different forms. One Story Circle, made up of women who work during the day, might meet in the local community center for a couple of hours every Wednesday evening, sharing a light potluck meal, then getting down to the serious business of writing and reading. Another group might meet on a weekend morning or afternoon and decide not to be distracted by food. A different group might meet alternate weeks, or every third Tuesday afternoon, in someone's home. One might be made up of only eight or ten people, while another might involve as many as twenty.

Where will you find the members of your Story Circle? Probably the first place to look is among your friends—four or five women you know and feel comfortable with. The members of that group could each recruit two or three of *their* friends—and your group would be under way. Some Story Circles start out as classes, sponsored by churches or temples or women's centers. For many years, I have taught organized classes in personal writing for the Jung Society in Austin, Texas. After working together for six or eight weeks in a class, participants often form their own ongoing groups, continuing to share their writing and reading.

Story is sacred, soul-speech. A Story Circle can become a self-renewing spiritual community. As community, as a hearth for our hearts, it can become essential to our lives.

I have learned not to fear, but to celebrate, the rooting of my insights in the story of my life. I have learned to trust that when my writing is most open and vulnerable, it is also most powerful, most likely to touch a chord and to influence change in others. This is not because all of our stories are the same, but rather because we are all embodied: the telling of one story opens a space for the telling of another.

—Carol P. Christ

I want to write about the great and powerful thing that listening is . . . a magnetic and strange thing, a creative force. When we are listened to, it creates us, makes us unfold and expand. Ideas begin to grow within us and come to life . . . and it is this creative fountain inside us that begins to spring and cast up new thoughts and unexpected laughter and wisdom. That is why, when someone has listened to you, you go home rested and lighthearted.

Here are some suggestions. Try to learn tranquility, to live in the present . . . Say to yourself: "Now. What is happening now? This friend is talking. I am quiet. There is endless time. I hear it, every word." Then suddenly, you begin to hear not only what people are saying, but what they are trying to say, and you sense the whole truth about them. And you sense existence, not piecemeal, not this object and that, but as a translucent whole.

Brenda Ueland

Working in a Story Circle

When we come together in a Story Circle, we take on responsibility not only for ourselves but for one another as well. My most essential obligation is to tell *my* story, with all the clarity and insight and truth I can summon. But I have another task, and that is to be present for the stories of others in the circle, to bear witness to *their* clarity and insight and truth—our common truth. Because it is *our* truth we are groping toward, we support one another's efforts, however faltering, to tell it. And we respect one another's privacy by agreeing not to reveal anything we have heard within the circle.

We are, each of us, our own prisoner. We are locked up in our own story.

—Maxine Kumin

Put simply, within the Story Circle we are safe, for we honor one another. We are safe because we may say anything and know that it will not be revealed. We listen with respect and regard, without interruption or sarcasm or envy or rivalry. We are midwives (the literal meaning of the word is "with-woman") to the vulnerable soul as it is being born, privy to all that is deep and intimate. Our relationship to one another is one of trust and mutual respect. We recognize that pain and anguish, as they are in childbirth, are signs of breakthrough, of great progress. We are witnesses to the labor, and as women, birth-givers, we know when to urge pushing and breathing and simply being still with pain. We are mutual presences, simply, and in that attentive being-with, that delicate, careful *listening*, we help one another bring forth—ourselves.

To listen. Such a small word, so ordinary. And yet, not to be listened to, not to be heard, is not to exist. So in the Story Circle, we listen one another into existence, into true life. We listen in suffering and in celebration, putting ourselves out of the way, and let others know that we have heard.

And listening completes the story. Our story. Our sacred story.

What We Do in a Story Circle*

I usually suggest that we begin our Story Circle in silence, which is a kind of gate between the chatty, casually friendly interactions that take place among acquaintances and the deeper, more meaningful communications that go on during Story Circle. The space of silence gives us a few moments to collect our scattered energies and recollect why we are here. Often, the silence is a meditation. (The meditations in each chapter are appropriate for this, or you can create your own.)

When I am leading Story Circles, I use the materials from each of the chapters of this book, beginning with the introduction, "The Power of Story." Depending on the size of the group and the interests of the participants, we discuss the chapter and take turns reading our writing aloud while the others listen. After each reading, listeners ask questions,

---

*You will find additional suggestions for groups and individual activities, as well as opportunities for sharing your writing, in the quarterly newsletter the *Story Circle Journal*. Subscription information is at the back of this book.

> *I wanted a perfect ending. . . . Now I've learned, the hard way, that some poems don't rhyme, and some stories don't have a clear beginning, middle and end. Life is about not knowing, having to change, taking the moment and making the best of it, without knowing what's going to happen next. Delicious ambiguity.*
>
> —Gilda Radner

> *Writing a book is like scrubbing an elephant: there's no good place to begin or end, and it's hard to keep track of what you've already covered.*
>
> —Anon.

offer observations, make connections—but do not criticize. Questions are helpful, especially simple, direct questions that bring us to the heart of the matter. Observations help too, because they allow the speaker to know that she is heard, and connections allow her to see that her story is *our* story. Criticism is not helpful, for it establishes a right and a wrong of something, a good and a bad. The Story Circle is not designed to improve the quality of our writing (although the more we write and share, the more proficient we become). Nor is it a confessional, where we come to be shriven and forgiven. (The verb *to shrive* originally meant "to write.") It is a place to plainly speak our truths, and in the act of intimate disclosure to find our own forgiveness, if that's what we are seeking.

Gradually, as we all join in the storytelling, it becomes clear that each story is our story. We do not need to say much, only a few brief words to make the necessary connections: "I've been there, too" is a phrase we often hear, and we recognize it as a merging of one story with another. We share laughter, which sometimes helps to puncture our self-inflated selves. We share tears, which come when we are left without words. Both the laughter and the tears are graces, shared emotions, shared compassion. They remind us that ours is a common journey. More than that, they remind us that what seems to be my soul, your soul, her soul—are *one* soul.

One soul, one story.
Our story.

Living is a form of not being sure, not knowing what next or how. The moment you know how, you begin to die a little. The artist never entirely knows. We guess. We may be wrong, but we take leap after leap in the dark.

—Agnes de Mille

Appendix Two

If You Want to Keep Writing

Writing makes a map, and there is something about a journey that begs to have its passage marked.

—Christina Baldwin

In this book, I have suggested eight ways to organize your personal memoirs—to mark your passage through the journey that is your life. If you want to keep writing, there are many other topics you can take up. Here are a few:

All My Children

You might devote one chapter to each child. Be sure to include plenty of pictures! You might want to involve the child in the creation of the chapter.

All Creatures Great and Small

Stories—humorous, inspiring, sad—of your animal companions would make an interesting chapter.

"I Take Thee"

The story of your marriage could be a chapter all by itself. You could include sections on your courtship, your early married years, and outstanding events. One couple I know created a twelve-page newsletter for their friends and family on the occasion of their twenty-fifth anniversary.

A Particular Passion

This would be the story of something you really love doing: a sport, craft, activity, cause. The chapter might focus on the history of your passion, your accomplishments in it, friends you have made through it, plans and goals, disappointments, and so on.

The Story of My Illness

Many moving memoirs have been written about encounters with illness or disability. Yours might follow the history of your illness from diagnosis through treatment, lessons you learned from the experience, people you met, ways your life was transformed.

A Memorable Experience

Writing about a compelling real-life event can help us find its deepest meaning. You might want to write about living through an earthquake or a fire, or even something exciting and unexpected—winning the lottery, for instance, or being chosen "Teacher of the Year."

Reminiscences

All of us have valuable memories. You might organize a chapter around your recollection of summers on your grandparents' farm, growing up in a small town, your college years, spending a year or two in a foreign country.

Minding My Own Business

Many women have started their own businesses. This chapter could be a chronicle of your business, from the time you felt the first inkling of ambition to the moment you opened your doors. You might write about the obstacles you overcame, the challenges you faced, the rewards you gained.

Once you've experienced the transformational magic of writing your personal stories, you will discover many more ways of organizing them. You'll read with greater enjoyment, too, with a pen or pencil in hand, copying passages that inspire you. And you'll become increasingly conscious of your life as story: as adventure story, romance, saga, tragedy, spiritual narrative. There are so many ways to create maps, to mark our passages.

There are so many ways to write the journey.

Voices of Truth and Triumph: Personal Narratives by and for Women

When a woman tells the truth, she is creating the possiblity for more truth around her.
—Adrienne Rich

Allison, Stacy. *Beyond the Limits: A Woman's Triumph on Everest.* Little, Brown, 1993. A woman's quest to reach the highest point on the globe. Read it for the excitement of the climb and the thrill of breaking into a traditionally male world—and for the personal story of the author's struggle to break out of the cycle of domestic violence.

Atwood, Margaret. *Good Bones and Simple Murders.* Doubleday, 1994. Margaret Atwood has a sharp eye and a clear, distinctive voice. The short parables, monologues, prose poems, and other diminutive masterpieces in this collection, together with Atwood's own illustrations, are a joy. Atwood gives us permission to say exactly what we think.

Baldwin, Christina. *Life's Companion: Journal Writing as a Spiritual Quest.* Bantam, 1990. My favorite journaling book, written by a compassionate, truthful woman. Baldwin's gentle insight and quiet spirituality are testimony to the deep importance of knowing ourselves fully.

Cole, Diane. *After Great Pain, A New Life Emerges.* Summit, 1992. I value this book for the author's courage. Cole writes about her mother's death, the illness of her husband-to-be, the horror of being taken hostage by a killer, and the sadness of miscarriage. But through the anguish comes a sharp, clear insight: loss leads to a new vision of who we are.

Connelly, Dianne M. *All Sickness Is Home Sickness.* Traditional Acupuncture Institute, 1993. Elegantly, intimately written, this book helps to reframe our ideas about health, healing, and home. "Suppose it is not possible to be lost," Connelly says and shows us how this is true.

Conway, Jill Ker, ed. *Written by Herself, Autobiographies of American Women: An Anthology.* Vintage, 1992. The first-person stories of over two dozen remarkable women. Valuable for what it teaches about the range of American women's experience over the last 150 years. I like Conway's brief biographical essays, which provide a context for the writing.

Curb, Rosemary, and Nancy Manahan, eds. *Lesbian Nuns: Breaking Silence.* The Naiad Press, 1985. A collection of personal narratives written by women who know the importance of speaking freely about their deepest selves. Full of insight, often painfully honest.

Dillard, Annie. *An American Childhood.* Harper & Row, 1987. A childhood memoir by an important American writer. I like this book for Dillard's ability to capture the magic of life through the perspective of a child, darting from one new revelation to another.

Downing, Christine. *Journey through Menopause: A Personal Rite of Passage.* Crossroad, 1989. Downing's experiences and reflections illuminated my own experience of menopause—and more, for her book is really about the midlife turning from the outer to the inner world.

Foster, Patricia, ed. *Minding the Body: Women Writers on Body and Soul.* Doubleday, 1994. A wonderful, readable collection of nineteen essays that address the psychological and political aspects of a woman's body in today's culture. A book for women who want to understand the relationship between their emotional and physical selves.

Friday, Nancy. *My Mother/My Self: A Daughter's Search for Identity.* Delacorte, 1977. A classic best-seller that shows how a woman's relationship with her mother affects all the passages of her life. Provocative and challenging even after two decades, this book has something to teach us all about the mother-daughter bond.

Galland, China. *Women in the Wilderness.* Harper Colophon, 1980. Accounts of wilderness experiences by a wilderness woman whose lyric voice is a pleasure to hear. I find this book valuable because it portrays women as competent, courageous, adventuresome risk takers in settings where women aren't supposed to take risks.

Gilbert, Lynn, and Gaylen Moore. *Particular Passions: Talks with Women Who Have Shaped Our Times.* Clarkson N. Potter: 1981. A collection of interviews and photographs that capture the essence of the lives of important women. These are stories about gifts and graces. They are a joy to read.

Gilligan, Carol. *In a Different Voice: Psychological Theory and Women's Development.* Harvard University Press, 1982. Simply the most helpful book on women's psychology that I know of. Gilligan helps us hear and respect our own true voices and the spirit from which we speak.

Goldberg, Natalie. *Long Quiet Highway: Waking Up in America.* Bantam, 1993. A book about a woman's spiritual journey, written in a lucid, unassuming prose style with its own natural elegance. If you haven't already, you will also want to read her *Writing Down the Bones: Freeing the Writer Within* and *Wild Mind.* Goldberg will help you find your voice.

Gornick, Vivian. *Fierce Attachments: A Memoir.* Simon & Schuster, 1987. Reviewers have called this book "blisteringly honest" and "searingly intimate." Gornick opens the depths of the passionate connection between her mother and herself. A must-read for any daughter whose mother bond feels too tight and for any mother who is afraid to let go.

Heilbrun, Carolyn. *Writing a Woman's Life.* Ballantine, 1988. "I wish to suggest new ways of writing the lives of women, as biographers, autobiographers, or, in the anticipation of living new lives, as the women themselves," Heilbrun says. If you are serious about telling your true story, you should read what Heilbrun has to say.

Hochman, Anndee. *Everyday Acts & Small Subversions: Women Reinventing Family, Community and Home.* The Eighth Mountain Press, 1994. This book contains voices we don't often hear: the stories of heterosexual and lesbian women from different cultural, racial, and ethnic backgrounds, who are finding new ways to celebrate their connections to others. They are redefining family and community, and their stories are exciting and inspirational.

Hochschild, Arlie. *The Second Shift: Working Parents and the Revolution at Home.* Viking Penguin, 1989. Hochschild tells the stories in this book, and her voice is that of the trained sociologist. I include it here because what it teaches about silence, self-deception, and outright lying about women's work in the home is absolutely crucial to all of us. Every woman who shares home and children with a partner will learn from this book how to deal more honestly with the challenge.

Jong, Erica. *Fear of Fifty: A Midlife Memoir.* HarperCollins, 1994. This is a brash, forthright personal narrative by a woman who is often outrageous and always impassioned. I love Jong for her voice and respect her for her refusal to gloss over her own internal contradictions.

Kahane, Deborah Hobler. *No Less a Woman: Ten Women Shatter the Myths About Breast Cancer.* Prentice Hall, 1990. The stories of ten women and their encounters with breast cancer. Each story opens a different kind of dark corner, faces a different shadow, and helps us understand the resiliency of women's spirt.

Leonard, Linda Schierse. *The Wounded Woman: Healing the Father-Daughter Relationship.* Painfully personal and profoundly moving, this book documents Leonard's efforts to heal her own father-wound. She shows us how our relationships with our father, and with the Fathers of our patriarchal society, can be reformed.

Lerner, Harriet Goldhor. *The Dance of Deception: Pretending and Truth-Telling in Women's Lives.* HarperCollins, 1993. Lerner shows us how and why women put on false fronts that conceal their real selves. All women are taught to lie and fake, she argues, and our silence, pretense, and self-deception damage us deeply. If you want to be challenged to tell the whole truth about your life, this is a text you will want to read more than once.

Margolis, Maxine. *Mothers and Such: A View of American Women and Why They Changed.* University of California Press, 1984. A thoughtful analysis of the evolution of women's home work in the last two hundred years. Margolis shows how our economic and social systems have manipulated the images of mother and homemaker in order to manage the behavior of women.

Morris, Mary, ed. *Maiden Voyages: Writings of Women Travelers.* Vintage, 1993. A collection of over four dozen fascinating excerpts from the writings of courageous and unconventional women travelers from the seventeenth through the twentieth centuries. If you think all Victorian women were fragile, helpless creatures, this book will change your mind.

Morton, Nelle. *The Journey Is Home.* Beacon, 1985. Nelle Morton is a distinguished theologian who came gradually to her feminist vision. This collection of her essays from the 1970s and '80s tells the story of her personal transformation, as well as documenting the slow changes taking place in patriarchal religion.

Murdock, Maureen. *The Heroine's Journey.* Shambhala Publications, 1990. In this book about personal and cultural transformation, Murdock combines her own personal experience and her background as a woman's therapist to create a map of the feminine journey to wholeness.

Rich, Adrienne. *Of Woman Born: Motherhood as Experience and Institution.* Norton, 1976. This book turned me upside down and inside out—not only because of its remarkable content (the story of motherhood in the fifties and sixties, when I myself was a mother), but also because of its method. Rich writes out of her personal experience, opening her heart, using her story to explain and illuminate the story of all of us who are daughters and mothers.

Ruddick, Sara, and Pamela Daniels, eds. *Working It Out: 23 Women Writers, Artists, Scientists, and Scholars Talk about Their Lives and Work.* Pantheon,

1977. The essays here were written from the front lines of women's advance into the work world, but they explore important issues that still challenge us today.

Sarton, May. *Journal of a Solitude.* Norton, 1977. Sarton's five journals—*Journal of a Solitude, House by the Sea, Recovering, After the Stroke, At Seventy,* and *Encore: A Journal of the Eightieth Year*—give us a stirring record of the joys and hardships of women's aging. But the pain of growing older is counterbalanced by an unexpected, exhilarating freedom from others' expectations, as well as her own. Read all the journals, in sequence, for their poignancy and insight.

Woodman, Marion. *Leaving My Father's House: A Journey to Conscious Femininity.* Shambhala Publications, 1992. This unique book is co-authored by Woodman and three women in therapy with her. All three writers (and Woodman herself) struggle with a task common to the rest of us: giving conscious voice to feminine wisdom.

Books Cited

Abbott, Shirley. *Womenfolks: Growing Up Down South.* Ticknor & Fields, 1991.

Albert, Susan Wittig. *Work of Her Own: A Woman's Guide to Success off the Career Track.* Tarcher, 1992.

Bird, Isabella. *A Lady's Life in the Rocky Mountains.* University of Oklahoma Press, 1960.

Blum, Arlene. *Annapurna, A Woman's Place.* Sierra, 1980.

Bohm, David. *Wholeness and the Implicate Order.* Routledge & Kegan Paul, 1981.

Boston Women's Health Collective. *Our Bodies, Ourselves.* Simon & Schuster, 1973.

Budapest, Zsuzsanna. *The Grandmother of Time: A Woman's Book of Celebrations, Spells, and Sacred Objects for Every Month of the Year.* Harper & Row, 1989.

Cofer, Judith Ortiz. *A Latin Deli.* University of Georgia Press, 1993.

Coman, Carolyn. *Body & Soul: Ten American Women.* Hill, 1988.

Conway, Jill Ker. *Written by Herself: Autobiographies of American Women: An Anthology.* Random House, 1992.

Cressy-Marcks, Violet. *Up the Amazon.* Hodder & Stoughton, 1932.

Downing, Christine. *Women's Mysteries.* Crossroad, 1992.

Edelman, Hope. *Motherless Daughters: A Legacy of Loss.* Addison-Wesley, 1984.

Edwards, Amelia. *A Thousand Miles up the Nile.* Tarcher, 1983.

Estés, Clarissa Pinkola. *Women Who Run with the Wolves.* Ballantine, 1992.

Frank, Anne. *The Diary of a Young Girl.* Doubleday, 1967.

Friedan, Betty. *The Feminine Mystique.* Norton, 1963.

Friedan, Betty. *The Fountain of Age.* Simon & Schuster, 1993.

Gilligan, Carol. *In a Different Voice: Psychological Theory and Women's Development.* Harvard University Press, 1982.

Gilman, Charlotte Perkins. *Women and Economics: A Study of the Economic Relations Between Women & Men.* Prometheus Books, 1994.

Grumbach, Doris. *Coming into the End Zone: A Memoir.* Norton, 1991.

Grealy, Lucy. *Autobiography of a Face.* Houghton Mifflin, 1994.

Halifax, Joan. *The Fruitful Darkness: Reconnecting with the Body of the Earth.* Harper San Francisco, 1994.

Hunter, Brenda. *In the Company of Women.* Multnomah, 1994.

Kabat-Zinn, Jon. *Wherever You Go, There You Are.* Hyperion, 1994.

Keller, Helen. *The Story of My Life.* Doubleday, 1920.

Kelly, Marcia, and Jack Kelly, *Sanctuaries: A Guide to Lodgings in Monasteries, Abbeys, and Retreats of the United States.* Bell Tower, 1993.

Kingsley, Mary. *Travels in West Africa.* C. E. Tuttle, 1993.

Koller, Alice. *An Unknown Woman.* Holt Rinehart and Winston, 1981.

LaBastille, Anne. *Woodswoman.* Dutton, 1976.

Lindbergh, Anne Morrow. *Gift from the Sea.* Pantheon, 1955.

Macy, Joanna. *World as Lover, World as Self.* Parallax Press, 1991.

Mairs, Nancy. *Carnal Acts.* Harper & Row, 1990.

Mairs, Nancy. *Remembering the Bone House.* Harper & Row, 1989.

Mannes, Marya, *Out of My Time.* Doubleday, 1971.

Matthiessen, Peter. *The Snow Leopard.* Viking, 1978.

MacDonald, Barbara, and Cynthia Rich. *Look Me in the Eye: Old Women, Ageing, and Ageism.* Spinsters Ink, 1984.

Miller, Jean Baker. *Toward a New Psychology of Women.* Beacon Press, 1976.

Moore, Thomas. *Care of the Soul.* HarperCollins, 1992.

Morris, Mary. *Wall to Wall.* Doubleday, 1991.

Munro, Eleanor. *Memoirs of a Modernist's Daughter.* Viking Penguin, 1988.

Murdock, Maureen. *The Heroine's Journey.* Shambhala, 1991.

Nin, Anaïs. *Henry and June.* Harcourt Brace Jovanovich, 1986.

Owen, Ursula, ed. *Fathers: Reflections by Daughters.* Pantheon, 1985.

Plath, Sylvia. *The Journals of Sylvia Plath*, ed. Ted Hughes. Doubleday, 1982.

Prouty, Olive Higgins. *Pencil Shavings.* Riverside, 1961.

Robertson, Laurel, Carol Flinders, and Brian Ruppenthal. *Laurel's Kitchen: A Handbook for Vegetarian Cookery and Nutrition.* Ten Speed Press, 1986.

Sanger, Margaret. *Margaret Sanger: An Autobiography.* Report Services, 1991.

Schor, Juliet. *The Overworked American.* Basic Books, 1991.

Scott-Maxwell, Florida. *The Measure of My Days.* Knopf, 1968.

Siegel, Bernie. *Love, Medicine and Miracles.* Harper & Row, 1986.

Shepherd, Laurie. *A Dreamer's Log Cabin: A Woman's Walden.* Barricade, 1981

Thich Nhat Hanh. *The Miracle of Mindfulness.* Beacon Press, 1987.

Truitt, Anne. *Daybook: The Journal of an Artist.* Pantheon, 1982.

Wellwood, John, ed. *Ordinary Magic: Everyday Life as a Spiritual Path.* Shambhala, 1992.

Wittman, Juliet. *Breast Cancer Journal: A Century of Petals.* Fulcrum, 1993.

About the Author

Dr. Susan Wittig Albert has been teaching writing for nearly thirty years. Her college textbooks on writing have been adopted nationwide, and she has worked with thousands of writers in classes, workshops, and seminars. She is the author of the critically acclaimed and popular China Bayles mystery series and the co-author (with her husband) of the Robin Paige Victorian mysteries. She has also written a book for women who wish to redefine their work lives: *Work of Her Own: A Woman's Guide to Success off the Career Track.*

For the past decade, Susan Albert's workshops and classes on personal narrative have offered participants guidance and encouragement in the use of the journal and the memoir as a tool for psychological and spiritual growth. If you would like to order audiotapes of the meditations in this book or inquire about scheduling a one- or two-day workshop in your community, send a stamped, self-addressed #10 envelope to the address below. If you would like to receive a sample copy of the *Story Circle Journal*, send your name and address and five dollars.

Story Circle
PO Drawer M
Bertram, TX 78605

Discover more of yourself with Inner Work Books.

The following Inner Work Books are part of a series that explores psyche and spirit through writing, visualization, ritual, and imagination.

The Artist's Way: A Spiritual Path to Higher Creativity — BY JULIA CAMERON

The Artist's Way Morning Pages Journal: A Companion Volume to The Artist's Way — BY JULIA CAMERON

At a Journal Workshop (revised edition): *Writing to Access the Power of the Unconscious and Evoke Creative Ability* — BY IRA PROGOFF, PH.D.

Fearless Creating: A Step-by-Step Guide to Starting and Completing Your Work of Art — BY ERIC MAISEL, PH.D.

Finding What You Didn't Lose: Expressing Your Truth and Creativity Through Poem-Making — BY JOHN FOX

Following Your Path: Using Myths, Symbols, and Images to Explore Your Inner Life — BY ALEXANDRA COLLINS DICKERMAN

The Inner Child Workbook: What to Do with Your Past When It Just Won't Go Away — BY CATHRYN L. TAYLOR, M.A.M.F.C.C.

A Journey Through Your Childhood: A Write-in Guide for Reliving Your Past, Clarifying Your Present, and Charting Your Future — BY CHRISTOPHER BIFFLE

A Life in the Arts: Practical Guidance and Inspiration for Creative and Performing Artists — BY ERIC MAISEL, PH.D.

The Life We Are Given: A Long-Term Program for Realizing the Potential of Body, Mind, Heart, and Soul — BY GEORGE LEONARD AND MICHAEL MURPHY

Pain and Possibility: Writing Your Way Through Personal Crisis — BY GABRIELLE LUSSER RICO

The Path of the Everyday Hero: Drawing on the Power of Myth to Meet Life's Most Important Challenges — BY LORNA CATFORD, PH.D., AND MICHAEL RAY, PH.D.

Personal Mythology: Using Ritual, Dreams, and Imagination to Discover Your Inner Story — BY DAVID FEINSTEIN, PH.D., AND STANLEY KRIPPNER, PH.D.

The Possible Human: A Course in Extending Your Physical, Mental, and Creative Abilities — BY JEAN HOUSTON

The Search for the Beloved: Journeys in Mythology and Sacred Psychology — BY JEAN HOUSTON

Smart Love: A Codependence Recovery Program Based on Relationship Addiction Support Groups — BY JODY HAYES

A Time to Heal Workbook: Stepping-stones to Recovery for Adult Children of Alcoholics — BY TIMMEN I. CERMAK, M.D., AND JACQUES RUTZKY, M.F.C.C.

True Partners: A Workbook for Building a Lasting Intimate Relationship — BY TINA B. TESSINA, PH.D., AND RILEY K. SMITH, M.A.

The Vein of Gold: A Journey to Your Creative Heart — BY JULIA CAMERON

Your Mythic Journey: Finding Meaning in Your Life Through Writing and Storytelling — BY SAM KEEN AND ANNE VALLEY-FOX

To order, call 1-800-788-6262 or send your order to:

Jeremy P. Tarcher, Inc.
Mail Order Department
The Putnam Berkley Group, Inc.
P.O. Box 12289
Newark, NJ 07101-5289

For Canadian orders:
P.O. Box 25000
Postal Station "A"
Toronto, Ontario M5W 2X8

_____	The Artist's Way	0-87477-694-5	$14.95
_____	The Artist's Way Hardcover Deluxe Edition	0-87477-821-2	$24.95
_____	The Artist's Way Morning Pages Journal	0-87477-820-4	$20.00
_____	At a Journal Workshop	0-87477-638-4	$15.95
_____	Ending the Struggle Against Yourself	0-87477-763-1	$14.95
_____	Fearless Creating	0-87477-805-0	$15.95
_____	Finding What You Didn't Lose	0-87477-909-3	$14.95
_____	Following Your Path	0-87477-687-2	$15.95
_____	The Inner Child Workbook	0-87477-635-X	$14.95
_____	A Journey Through Your Childhood	0-87477-499-3	$10.95
_____	A Life in the Arts	0-87477-766-6	$15.95
_____	The Life We Are Given	0-87477-792-5	$14.95
_____	Pain and Possibility	0-87477-571-X	$14.95
_____	The Path of the Everyday Hero	0-87477-630-9	$14.95
_____	Personal Mythology	0-87477-484-5	$12.95
_____	The Possible Human	0-87477-218-4	$14.95
_____	The Search for the Beloved	0-87477-476-4	$14.95
_____	Smart Love	0-87477-472-1	$10.95
_____	A Time to Heal Workbook	0-87477-745-3	$14.95
_____	True Partners	0-87477-727-5	$13.95
_____	The Vein of Gold	0-87477-836-0	$23.95
_____	Your Mythic Journey	0-87477-543-4	$ 9.95

Subtotal $ _____

Shipping and handling* $ _____

Sales tax (CA, NJ, NY, PA, VA) $ _____

Total amount due $ _____

Payable in U.S. funds (no cash orders accepted). $15.00 minimum for credit card orders.
*Shipping and handling: $3.50 for one book, $1.00 for each additional book, not to exceed $8.50.

Enclosed is my ☐ check ☐ money order

Please charge my ☐ Visa ☐ MasterCard ☐ American Express

Card # _____ Expiration date _____

Signature as on credit card _____

Daytime phone number _____

Name _____

Address _____

City _____ State _____ Zip _____

Please allow six weeks for delivery. Prices subject to change without notice.

Source key IWB